Longevity
by Design
The Lifestyle Wellness Plan

Living Younger, Longer: The Ultimate Guide to Health, Happiness, and Longevity

Penelope Swift

Longevity by Design

Copyright © 2024 Pocketbook Publications

Penelope Swift

First Edition

All rights reserved.

ISBN: 978-1-916989-14-6

ABOUT THE AUTHOR

Penelope Swift is a passionate advocate for holistic well-being and a lifelong explorer of natural health practices. With over two decades of experience researching and implementing wellness strategies, she has developed a comprehensive understanding of how lifestyle choices impact longevity. Drawing on her extensive travels and studies across different cultures, Penelope has observed diverse approaches to aging gracefully and maintaining vitality.

Her journey into health and longevity began as a personal quest to enhance her own life and that of her loved ones. Over the years, she has curated and refined effective techniques that blend traditional wisdom with modern insights, focusing on sustainable, realistic practices anyone can adopt.

Penelope believes that longevity is not just about extending years but enriching the quality of life. In *Longevity by Design*, she shares her practical approach to creating a health span plan that encourages readers to build habits that support physical, mental, and emotional health, empowering them to thrive at every stage of life.

DEDICATION

To my Mum and Dad, who lived long and happy.

CONTENTS

	Acknowledgments	i
1	Introduction to Living Better	1
2	Global Secrets to Longevity	21
3	Eating for Longevity	53
4	Movement Matters	79
5	Mental Wellness and Emotional Resilience	91
6	Mastering Sleep	105
7	Nutrition Beyond the Plate	125
8	Stress Less, Live Longer	145
9	The Beauty of Ageing Well	161
10	Stronger Together	175
11	Mind over Matter	189
12	The Power of Purpose	223
13	Healthspan 2.0	233
14	Designing Your Personal Wellness Plan	249

Longevity by Design

Longevity by Design

INTRODUCTION
Introduction to Living Better

Imagine a life where you not only live longer, but live better, where your extra years are vibrant, energetic, and filled with joy. Picture yourself in your 60s, 70s, or even your 80s, still hiking trails, dancing at weddings, traveling, and pursuing passions you haven't even discovered yet. This isn't just a distant dream; it's entirely possible. Longevity by design is what *The Lifestyle Wellness Plan* is all about.

We often hear about "lifespan," the total number of years we spend on this earth. But when it comes down to it, what we're really striving for is *healthspan*, the number of years we stay active, vibrant, and free from disease. While it's common to see people living well into their 80s and 90s today, these extra years are often marred by a gradual decline in quality of life, filled with the frustration of failing joints, chronic illnesses, and dependence on others. It's as though modern medicine has given us more time, but not necessarily more *life*. That's why understanding and extending our healthspan, not just our lifespan, is so crucial. It's about making those added years ones you'll *want* to live, filled with laughter, purpose, and zest.

The Lifestyle Wellness Plan is designed to guide you through every stage of your adult life, offering a roadmap to keep you living well for longer. It's not about unattainable diets or rigid exercise regimes; it's about creating a lifestyle that's realistic, enjoyable, and most importantly, sustainable. Think of it as a toolkit that evolves with you, no matter where you are on your journey. You'll find science-backed advice, practical strategies, and inspiration woven throughout these pages to help you build a personalised action plan, one small change at a time. By the end of this book, you'll have a clear, actionable blueprint tailored to your needs and aspirations, which you can continue refining as you move through each stage of life.

But let's be clear, this isn't your typical health and wellness book. It's not about adhering to faddy diets or chasing the latest fitness craze. *The Lifestyle Wellness Plan* is for real men and women living real lives, juggling responsibilities, dreams, careers, and families. It's about finding balance, making health a part of your life *today* in a way that supports your future self. Each chapter will delve into a different aspect of healthspan, from nutrition and movement to sleep, stress management, and mental wellbeing, gradually building layers of knowledge that you can put into practice. As you progress, you'll be encouraged to add a little more to your personal action plan, creating a holistic, dynamic guide that grows alongside you.

Healthspan vs. Lifespan: A Matter of Quality, Not Just Quantity
So why focus on healthspan rather than just aiming to live longer? Because it comes down to quality of life. For much of human history, healthspan and lifespan were pretty much aligned. People might have only lived to 50 or 60, but for most of that time, they were relatively healthy, strong, and capable. Now, with advances in healthcare and living standards, many people are living into their 80s and beyond. But these additional years are often marked by chronic diseases, reduced mobility, and a growing list of medications. It's like adding time to a film, but with more and more of it being spent in the "credits" rather than the main story. The *Lifestyle Wellness Plan* is here to change that, ensuring that those bonus years are *still* the prime chapters of your life.

In essence, healthspan is about living the best possible version of your life for as long as possible. It's about playing with your grandchildren in your 70s, starting a new career in your 60s, or travelling the world when you're well into your 80s. It's about being able to fully embrace every stage of life, rather than being limited by pain or illness. By focusing on your healthspan now, making small, consistent investments in your health, you're not just extending your life; you're expanding your possibilities.

The Lifestyle Wellness Plan in Action: Your Personal Blueprint for a Vibrant Life

One of the key elements that sets *The Lifestyle Wellness Plan* apart is its emphasis on action. This isn't a book that just tells you what you *should* be doing. Instead, it guides you in creating your own personalised Lifestyle Wellness Plan. Each chapter will focus on a different pillar of longevity, from nutrition and movement to sleep, stress management, mental wellbeing, and social connections. As you read, you'll be prompted to reflect on where you are right now, what's working, and what's not. Then, you'll be given simple, effective strategies to try out and gradually build upon.

Imagine starting with a foundation of balanced nutrition, not some restrictive meal plan, but a guide to understanding how food fuels your body and brain, and how to eat in a way that supports long-term health. You might start by tweaking your breakfast, adding more nutrient-dense foods to your day, or experimenting with different eating patterns that work for *you*. Then, as you move through the book, you'll build on this foundation, incorporating movement routines that are both effective and enjoyable, learning how to optimise your sleep for better energy and mood, and discovering ways to manage stress that fit seamlessly into your busy schedule.

The book will also delve into the hormonal health of both men and women, a critical component for women, particularly as they transition through perimenopause and beyond, and for men as they experience changes like testosterone decline with age. You'll learn how to support your body through these shifts naturally, using lifestyle tweaks, diet, and even mindset shifts tailored to both genders. Bbecause health is not just about physical wellbeing, you'll explore how to nurture your mental and emotional health, keep your brain sharp, and cultivate happiness and resilience throughout your life, ensuring you stay vibrant and fulfilled.

This isn't a rigid template; it's a flexible, evolving guide that you can adapt as your life changes. Think of it as creating your own health recipe, adding ingredients one by one until you've got a dish that's nourishing, satisfying, and truly delicious.

Living Younger, Longer, A Future Worth Getting Excited About
Now, I want to pause and ask you to think about something: What would your life look like if you *knew* you had another 30 vibrant, healthy years ahead of you? How would you live differently? What dreams would you pursue, and what worries would fall away?

This plan isn't just about following a set of health rules. It's about creating a future where you feel *empowered* to live fully. It's about saying yes to more experiences, not fewer; about embracing challenges and new adventures rather than retreating into caution. It's about living a life that's bold, joyful, and overflowing with vitality, no matter your age.

So, as you turn the pages of this book, remember: this is your journey. There's no rush, no need to do everything at once. Each chapter is an invitation to reflect, to experiment, and to build a little more onto your plan. By the time you've reached the end, you'll have created something uniquely yours, a healthspan strategy that's not just about living longer, but about living *younger*, for *longer*.

This is your time. Let's get started.

Defining Healthspan: What It Is and Why It Matters
So, what exactly is healthspan, and why should it matter more than lifespan? Healthspan is the period of life where we are free from chronic diseases, pain, and disabilities that significantly impair our daily activities. It's the years when we're not just alive, but *thriving*. While lifespan focuses on adding more years to your life, healthspan is about adding more *life* to your years.

Imagine your life as a long road trip. Lifespan is how many miles you get to travel, but healthspan is whether you're driving through beautiful scenery with the windows down and music playing, or crawling through traffic in a car that's falling apart. We all want our journey to be filled with adventure, comfort, and joy for as long as possible. That's what healthspan is all about, making sure the journey of life is vibrant and fulfilling, not just long.

This is the window of time when you're fully capable of enjoying everything life has to offer, whether it's playing with your children or grandchildren, pursuing your career or hobbies, travelling the world, or simply feeling good when you wake up in the morning. When healthspan ends, you might still have many years left on the clock, but those years are often defined by declining health, reduced mobility, and increasing dependence on others.

Why Healthspan Matters More Than Lifespan
As modern medicine has advanced, people are living longer than ever before. Global life expectancy has risen dramatically over the past century, with many countries now seeing average lifespans of over 80 years. But this impressive rise in lifespan hasn't been matched by a corresponding rise in healthspan. We've added years to life, but those years aren't always ones we want to live.

Imagine reaching the age of 90, but spending the last 20 years in poor health, struggling with arthritis, diabetes, or memory loss. Or picture yourself living into your 80s but unable to walk, unable to enjoy your family, or requiring constant care. While the longevity numbers look good on paper, in reality, many of us are spending more and more of our later years dealing with chronic diseases and physical decline. It's not uncommon to hear about people spending a decade or more battling conditions that drastically limit their quality of life. That's not the future we want for ourselves or our loved ones, which is why healthspan matters so much more than simply living longer.

The goal isn't just to stretch out our lives to reach an impressive number; it's to make sure we remain active, happy, and independent for as long as possible. When you focus on healthspan, you're investing in your ability to *live well*, not just live long

The Impact of Chronic Diseases on Quality of Life
Conditions like cardiovascular disease, diabetes, arthritis, and dementia are all too common as we age, and they don't just affect the person experiencing them, they also place a huge emotional and financial burden on families.

For women, the stakes are particularly high. As we tend to live longer than men, we're more likely to spend a greater proportion of our lives dealing with these chronic conditions. Consider this: women are twice as likely to suffer from Alzheimer's disease, and they also bear the brunt of arthritis and osteoporosis. As a result, many women find themselves caught in a cycle of caregiving for elderly parents or partners, while also dealing with their own health issues. It's a sobering reality, and one that makes the pursuit of a longer healthspan all the more urgent.

When chronic diseases set in, they don't just limit your physical capabilities, they can steal your joy and autonomy. Daily activities that once seemed simple, like going for a walk, cooking, or even getting dressed, can become overwhelming challenges. When physical health deteriorates, mental health often follows. Depression, anxiety, and feelings of isolation are common among those who struggle with chronic illness, leading to a diminished quality of life even if the person is still alive in the literal sense.

Global Trends in Healthspan:
Around the world, women tend to live longer than men, but they're not necessarily living healthier. This phenomenon is known as the "healthspan gap," and it's a significant issue not just for women but for men as well. While women, on average, live four to five years longer than men, they also spend more time coping with chronic illness or disability. However, the healthspan gap affects men too, as many spend their later years dealing with conditions like heart disease, diabetes, or mobility issues.

The World Health Organisation (WHO) reports that while men often have shorter lifespans, they tend to experience fewer years of chronic illness than women. For example, in the UK, the average lifespan for women is around 83 years, with a healthy life expectancy of 64 years, nearly two decades spent managing disease or disability. Men, on the other hand, have an average lifespan of 79 years, but their healthy life expectancy is closer to 63 years. In the United States, the pattern is similar. Women live on average to 81, but only 67 of those years are spent in good health, while men live to about 76, with a healthy lifespan of around 65 years. These figures paint a vivid picture: people of all genders are living longer, but those extra years aren't necessarily healthy or enjoyable.

While the healthspan gap affects both men and women, the factors influencing it can differ. Men and women experience the effects of ageing uniquely, influenced by genetics, hormones, lifestyle choices, and even societal roles. Understanding these nuances can help both genders take proactive steps to close their healthspan gap and enjoy more years in good health.

Hormonal Changes and Healthspan

For women, hormonal changes play a significant role in ageing, especially during the transition through menopause. The decline in oestrogen levels can lead to changes in bone density, cardiovascular health, and even cognitive function. Men experience their own hormonal shifts, sometimes referred to as "andropause," where levels of testosterone decrease. This decline can affect muscle mass, energy levels, and emotional well-being. While the hormonal changes may differ between men and women, the impact on overall health is clear, both genders need to pay attention to how hormones influence their long-term well-being.

Managing these changes is crucial for extending healthspan. Women, for example, can focus on maintaining bone density through weight-bearing exercises and ensuring adequate calcium and vitamin D intake. Men can benefit from strength training to preserve muscle mass, along with addressing any emotional or cognitive changes associated with lower testosterone. Hormonal health is not just a women's issue, men must also be aware of how shifting hormone levels affect their ageing process.

The Role of Diet and Nutrition in Healthspan

Nutrition is another key player in determining healthspan, and while some dietary needs are shared, there are gender-specific considerations to bear in mind. For women, maintaining adequate calcium and vitamin D levels is crucial for bone health, particularly post-menopause, when the risk of osteoporosis rises. Antioxidants and anti-inflammatory foods can help both women and men protect against cardiovascular disease, cancers, and cognitive decline.

However, men may also want to pay special attention to protein intake as they age, given the importance of maintaining muscle mass, and they should monitor heart health more closely as they are often at higher risk for cardiovascular issues.

Both men and women should focus on a balanced diet rich in whole grains, lean proteins, healthy fats, and an abundance of fruits and vegetables. The Mediterranean diet, which emphasises these food groups, has been shown to boost longevity and healthspan across genders. While nutritional needs can vary slightly between men and women, the core message is the same: a well-rounded, nutrient-dense diet is the foundation for a long, healthy life.

Physical Activity: A Healthspan Essential for Everyone
Regular exercise is one of the most important factors in extending healthspan for both men and women. Physical activity helps maintain muscle mass, supports bone density, and enhances mood and cognitive function. Unfortunately, many people, particularly in their middle years, find it difficult to prioritise exercise due to the demands of work, family, and other responsibilities. Yet even small, consistent efforts can have a significant impact on long-term health.

For women, strength training is especially important as they age, to counteract the loss of bone density and muscle mass that comes with menopause. For men, maintaining muscle mass and cardiovascular health through a combination of resistance training and aerobic exercise can reduce the risk of chronic illnesses like heart disease and type 2 diabetes. It's important to find activities you enjoy, whether it's walking, dancing, swimming, or even gardening, what matters is consistency. For those who dislike the idea of formal exercise, integrating more movement into everyday life, like taking the stairs, walking while on phone calls, or even doing household chores with vigour, can add up to significant health benefits over time.

Social and Emotional Wellbeing: Connection is Key
Strong social networks are another critical factor in extending healthspan for both men and women. Studies have shown that people with meaningful relationships and a sense of community tend to live longer and enjoy better health. However, the social landscape changes

as we age. Women are often more adept at maintaining friendships and community ties but may become more vulnerable to loneliness in later life, especially if they outlive their partners. Men, on the other hand, may struggle more with building close emotional relationships, leading to increased isolation as they age.

The importance of emotional wellbeing and social connections cannot be overstated. Regular interaction with friends and family, participation in community activities, and having a strong support network all contribute to a higher quality of life. Whether it's through joining clubs, attending classes, or simply making time for regular catch-ups with friends, these connections boost mental health and provide a sense of purpose, which can enhance both longevity and healthspan.

Addressing Mental Health and Stress Management
Chronic stress and poor mental health can significantly shorten healthspan, and this is an area that often gets overlooked. For both men and women, managing stress is crucial for maintaining overall health. Long-term stress contributes to inflammation, which is linked to nearly every age-related disease, from heart disease to Alzheimer's. Stress also weakens the immune system and can lead to unhealthy coping mechanisms, such as poor eating habits or lack of sleep.
Stress management techniques like mindfulness, yoga, and meditation are valuable tools for both men and women. Women often face unique stressors related to balancing work and family, while men may struggle with societal expectations to suppress emotional stress, leading to mental health issues later in life. By acknowledging these challenges and incorporating stress-reduction strategies into daily life, both men and women can protect their long-term health.

Bridging the Healthspan Gap
Closing the healthspan gap requires a combination of personal effort, societal change, and healthcare improvements. While women may live longer on average, they often spend more of their lives managing chronic illnesses, and men may face shorter lifespans but also endure years of poor health. Both men and women need to focus on building a Lifestyle Wellness Plan that supports not only a long life but also a life filled with vitality and good health.

From hormonal changes to nutrition, physical activity, and social connections, the strategies for extending healthspan are varied but attainable. The key is to start where you are and make gradual, sustainable changes. Whether it's through diet, exercise, stress management, or strengthening relationships, the goal is to live longer, healthier lives, together.

How to Measure Your Healthspan Potential
So, how do you know where you stand in terms of healthspan? While there's no single test that can measure your healthspan potential, there are several key indicators that can give you a good sense of your current and future wellbeing. Think of these as checkpoints on your journey, giving you a snapshot of how well your body and mind are set up to support a long, healthy life.

1. **Mobility and Strength**: Can you easily get up from a chair without using your hands? Are you able to carry your groceries or take the stairs without feeling winded? These are simple but powerful indicators of muscle strength, cardiovascular health, and overall mobility, key components of healthspan.

2. **Energy Levels**: Do you feel energised and ready to take on the day, or are you constantly battling fatigue? Persistent low energy can signal underlying health issues, from hormonal imbalances to poor nutrition or lack of sleep.

3. **Mental Sharpness**: Are you still able to learn new things, solve problems, and remember details with ease? Cognitive function is a critical aspect of healthspan, and it's something you can actively nurture through activities that challenge your brain.

4. **Mood and Emotional Wellbeing**: Do you generally feel positive, resilient, and in control of your emotions, or do you struggle with anxiety, sadness, or a sense of being overwhelmed? Mental health is deeply connected to physical health, and both need to be in balance for a full, vibrant healthspan.

5. **Chronic Conditions**: Are you managing or preventing common age-related conditions like high blood pressure, diabetes, or osteoporosis? Each of these conditions can shorten your healthspan and impact your quality of life, but they can often be prevented or managed through lifestyle choices.

6. **Social Connectedness**: Do you have a strong support network? Are you engaged with your community? Loneliness and social isolation can shorten healthspan just as much as smoking or obesity, making social health a critical factor to monitor.

By regularly assessing these areas, you can get a clearer picture of your current healthspan and identify areas for improvement. It's not about striving for perfection; it's about recognising that every small change you make today is an investment in your future self.

The New Age of Aging: Rewriting the Rules
For centuries, aging was viewed as an inevitable, unchangeable process. It was thought that, especially for women, it marked a steady decline in health, appearance, and vitality, a winding down of life's vibrancy. But we're living in a new era, one where the traditional views of aging are being challenged and rewritten. The notion that you have to become frail, less energetic, or "invisible" as you grow older is being thrown out the window. We're stepping into a time where science, wellness, and a deep understanding of the human body are converging to create a new narrative, one that's hopeful, empowering, and more exciting than ever.

Welcome to the new age of aging, where getting older doesn't mean giving up, but gearing up for some of the best years of your life. Modern research, breakthroughs in longevity science, and a deeper understanding of the unique biology of women are shifting how we approach each year beyond 30, 40, 50, and beyond. It's not just about living longer; it's about thriving at every stage, redefining what it means to be a woman as we move through life.

Common Misconceptions About Aging

It's surprising how many misconceptions about aging are still deeply embedded in our culture. Many of us have been conditioned to believe that aging is synonymous with decline. Society has painted a rather grim picture: wrinkles mean lost beauty, grey hair is something to hide, and cognitive decline is just part of the deal. But let's challenge these ideas.

The truth is, the stereotypes of aging are more about mindset than biology. The narrative that we'll inevitably deteriorate and become less capable as we grow older is being dismantled by cutting-edge research and real-world examples of people who are defying these supposed limitations every day. What if aging could be a time of renewal, growth, and even transformation?

One of the most common misconceptions is that metabolism slows dramatically, leading to inevitable weight gain. Yes, metabolism changes with age, but it's not a lost cause. The shift is gradual, and much of the slowdown is actually due to lifestyle factors rather than the aging process itself. Regular physical activity, muscle maintenance, and balanced nutrition can keep your metabolism humming along nicely for decades.

Another major myth? That your cognitive abilities will naturally decline, leading to the dreaded "senior moments" we've all been conditioned to fear. While the risk of cognitive decline does increase with age, research is showing that the brain can form new neural pathways and stay sharp well into our golden years. The key lies in nurturing cognitive health, staying socially active, and continuing to challenge the mind. It's never too late to start learning a new language, pick up a musical instrument, or take up that hobby you always thought was beyond your reach.

Then there's the idea that men, but more so, women "lose their beauty" as they age. This one is perhaps the most damaging of all. The obsession with youth has led many women to fear aging as the end of desirability and self-worth. But beauty, vitality, and radiance are not limited to a particular decade of life. In fact, many women say they feel more confident and beautiful in their 40s, 50s, and beyond than they ever did in their younger years. Beauty, as it turns out, is more closely linked to health, happiness, and self-assurance than the number of candles on your birthday cake.

Modern Research: Redefining What It Means to Age Well

Science is catching up to what many vibrant, dynamic men and women have known intuitively: aging doesn't have to mean losing your vitality. Researchers are discovering more about the biological mechanisms of aging than ever before, revealing a host of strategies to maintain and even improve our health and wellbeing as we grow older.

One of the most exciting developments in longevity research is the identification of what scientists call the "hallmarks of aging." These are nine biological processes that influence how and why we age, including things like mitochondrial function, telomere length, and cellular senescence (sometimes called "zombie cells"). By targeting these processes with lifestyle changes, nutrition, and even certain supplements, it's possible to slow down or, in some cases, even reverse aspects of aging. We will cover more of this later in the book.

This isn't just theoretical. Real-world studies are showing that regular exercise, stress management, and diets rich in antioxidants and healthy fats can significantly impact these aging hallmarks. This is science affirming what men and women have been discovering on their own, our choices today shape our future health and happiness.

Key Longevity Genes and How They Influence Aging

The story of longevity doesn't end with lifestyle; our genes also play a crucial role. Recent research has uncovered several "longevity genes" that significantly impact how both men and women age. Genes such as FOXO3, SIRT1, and the aptly named Klotho gene influence lifespan, metabolic health, and cognitive function. Understanding how these genes work and how we can interact with them through our lifestyle choices is key to enhancing our healthspan.

For both men and women, these genetic factors carry valuable insights. Take the APOE gene, for example. Variations in this gene can increase the risk of developing Alzheimer's disease, and while this condition affects both genders, women are disproportionately impacted. However, possessing a high-risk gene variant doesn't mean you're destined for poor health. Research shows that staying active, maintaining a brain-healthy diet rich in omega-3 fatty acids and antioxidants, and cultivating strong social connections can significantly mitigate the effects of these genetic risks. Similarly, for men, genetic markers associated with cardiovascular health or testosterone levels can be influenced positively by lifestyle changes like regular physical activity, balanced nutrition, and stress management.

The field of epigenetics is revealing an exciting truth: our genes are not set in stone. The way we live, what we eat, how we move, and even our stress levels, can "switch on" protective genes and "switch off" those that predispose us to disease. It's an empowering concept showing that our genetic blueprint is adaptable. With the right strategies, we can influence how our genes express themselves, ultimately adding years of health and vitality to our lives.

The Rise of Biohacking and Personalised Health Strategies

If there's one movement that's capturing the imagination of health enthusiasts everywhere, it's biohacking. This is all about using science and technology to optimise your body and mind, tweaking your biology to reach peak health and longevity. What was once seen as a fringe trend has now gone mainstream, with women of all ages experimenting with everything from intermittent fasting and high-tech wearables to nootropics (supplements for cognitive enhancement) and precision nutrition.

Biohacking is about finding out what works best for *you*. It's the ultimate personalised health strategy, whether that means tracking your sleep patterns, experimenting with supplements, or adopting certain types of exercise to see what makes you feel your best. The goal is to gather data, tune into your body's responses, and make informed decisions that enhance your health and wellbeing.

And it's not just for tech-savvy millennials. Women in their 40s, 50s, and beyond are increasingly turning to biohacking to support hormonal health, improve energy levels, and even boost longevity. It's an exciting time to be alive, with more tools and resources than ever to help you navigate the complexities of aging and thrive.

A New Chapter of Life

So, what's the takeaway? We're standing on the brink of a revolution in how we age. It's about stepping into this new era armed with knowledge, strategies, and a sense of empowerment. Aging doesn't have to be something that just happens to you, it's something you can actively shape. By understanding your body, embracing modern science, and taking a proactive role in your health, you can live better for longer.

The Healthspan Framework: First Steps

Before we start diving into the nitty-gritty of nutrition, movement, sleep, and all the other elements that will help you stay younger for longer, let's get clear on how to use this book to your advantage.

The goal of *The Lifestyle Wellness Plan* is not just to give you information, but to empower you to take that knowledge and apply it to your own life in a way that feels right for you. After all, there's no one-size-fits-all when it comes to health. Each of us is starting from a different place, with unique needs, habits, and challenges. That's why this book encourages you to create your *own* Lifestyle Wellness Plan, one that reflects who you are and who you want to become.

Step One: Assessing Where You Are Today

Before you can build a better tomorrow, you need to understand where you are today. Imagine trying to plot a route on a map without knowing your starting point, you'd quickly find yourself lost. It's the same with your health. To create an effective Lifestyle Wellness Plan, you need a solid grasp of your current state of wellbeing.

But assessing where you are doesn't mean judging yourself harshly or feeling overwhelmed by how far you have to go. It's simply about getting a clear picture, like taking a snapshot of your health at this moment. Start by asking yourself a few key questions: How do you feel physically? Do you wake up refreshed and energised, or do you often feel sluggish and drained? How's your diet? Are you eating in a way that fuels your body, or are there gaps you want to address? What's your stress level like? How often do you move your body? To make this process easier, try breaking your self-assessment into categories:

Physical Health: Let's be honest, how's the old body holding up? Are you bouncing out of bed or more like creaking your way to the kettle? Got any mystery aches and pains that seem to have appeared out of nowhere? Be real: are you carrying around a bit of "extra insulation" that you'd like to shift? Oh, and what about those joints and digestion, do they deserve some TLC?

Nutritional Habits: When it comes to your diet, are you a saint or a sinner? Is your plate full of rainbow-coloured veggies, or is the takeaway menu your closest companion? Are you getting a decent balance of protein, fats, and carbs or are you a carb monster one day and a protein saint the next? No judgement here, just take a peek at what's really going on.

Movement: How often do you *actually* move your body? … and no, lifting the TV remote doesn't count. Are you making time for those fun activities like walking, dancing, yoga, or is "moving" more of a rare event? Is there joy in your movement, or is it more like, "Ugh, fine, I'll do it because I have to"? Be honest, is your FitBit collecting more dust than steps?

Mental Wellbeing: How's the mental space doing? Are you pretty zen, or are you teetering on the edge of "If just one more thing goes wrong today…#@%! "? Got any stress-busting tricks up your sleeve, or is "eating chocolate and ignoring everything" your go-to? Are you keeping that brilliant brain of yours engaged with hobbies or activities that make you smile, or has binge-watching boxsets become the only brain workout?

Social and Environmental Health: Do your friends and family lift you up, or are there a few emotional vampires draining your energy? Do you feel more connected or a bit like you're living on a social desert island? What about your home or workspace, does it feel calm and inspiring, or is it more of a chaotic mess that even Genghis Khan would back away from? Time for a bit of a spring clean, perhaps?

Once you have a clearer sense of where you're starting, you can begin to see where you might want to go. Remember, this isn't about labelling yourself as "healthy" or "unhealthy." It's about recognising what's working well and identifying areas where you can grow.

Step Two: Setting Personalised Healthspan Goals
Now that you know where you are, it's time to think about where you want to go. Setting goals is crucial, but they need to be *your* goals, not someone else's idea of what's right for you. Maybe your aim is to have more energy, feel less stressed, or sleep better. Maybe you want to be more active, eat more mindfully, or feel more at peace. Whatever your goals, make sure they resonate with *you*.

A brilliant way to kick things off is by conjuring up a mental image of your future self. Go on, close your eyes (after reading this, obviously) and imagine yourself a few years down the line. What do you see? Are you striding confidently through your local park, smashing a yoga class, or taking on a new hobby with the enthusiasm of a teenager? Are you full of beans, running around with the kids or grandkids, or exploring far-flung corners of the world? Picture it all, how do you look, feel, and move? It's about your vibe, your energy, and how you *want* to feel as you go about your life.

Got that image? Great. Now, let's take that ideal version of you and break it down into bite-sized, achievable steps. We're not building Rome in a day here. Start by focusing on a few key areas, nutrition, movement, sleep, stress management, and mental wellbeing. We'll call these your healthspan pillars, like the sturdy foundations of your future fabulous self.

Set some goals for each of these pillars and remember: vague intentions like "I want to be healthier" won't cut it. Let's get specific. For instance, under Nutrition, maybe you want to cut back on the chocolate hobnobs (I know, it's tough) or try a few more veggie-packed meals each week. For Movement, instead of promising you'll hit the gym at 6 a.m. (let's be real, will that actually happen?), maybe aim to start with a brisk daily walk, or add a bit of strength training.

The key is to make these goals clear, achievable, and time-bound. None of that woolly "I should exercise more" nonsense bullshit! Try something like, "I'll walk 30 minutes every day" or "I'll swap my afternoon doughnut for a piece of fruit for the next three weeks." It's about setting goals you can actually measure. That way, you'll be able to see how far you've come and give yourself a well-earned pat on the back (or a celebratory smoothie, your choice).

So, take that dream of future-you and start mapping out the little steps that will get you there. You've got this! Remember, it's all about making progress, not achieving perfection. After all, life's too short not to enjoy the occasional biscuit… or three.

STOP! Before you read further, grab a pen and write anywhere in the margins of this book the commitments you are going to make to yourself. *"I would but I can't find a pen"* Really! Get out of your chair, search in that bag, come on, you know you want to.

Step Three: Tracking Your Progress

There's a saying: "What gets measured, gets managed." Keeping track of your progress is a great way to stay engaged and celebrate your wins along the way. But this doesn't have to be complicated. It's not about tracking every calorie or obsessively monitoring your steps, unless that works for you. Instead, think of tracking as a tool to help you see patterns, adjust your course, and acknowledge your achievements.

Start by choosing a tracking method that feels intuitive and enjoyable. Some people like to keep a journal, jotting down a few thoughts at the end of each day about what went well and what could be improved. If you are looking for a journal to assist, The Lifestyle Wellness Plan Journal (ISBN….) may be worth a try. Others prefer using apps to monitor their movement, sleep, or dietary habits. You might even use a simple habit tracker, a checklist where you tick off the days you complete a new habit.

If you're someone who likes visual reminders, consider creating a "healthspan map", if needed there is one in the Lifestyle Wellness Plan Journal, but it's easy to create a visual representation of your goals and progress. This could be a poster, a calendar, or even a digital chart that lets you see at a glance how far you've come. Tracking should feel supportive, not stressful. Remember, it's not about perfection. There will be days when things don't go as planned, and that's okay. It's about the overall trend and building consistency over time.

Step Four: Building Your Lifestyle Wellness Plan

Every chapter in this book is designed to add a new element to your Lifestyle Wellness Plan. As you read, you'll discover strategies for optimising your nutrition, finding movement that feels good, improving your sleep, managing stress, and nurturing your mental wellbeing. But rather than trying to overhaul everything at once, focus on building your plan gradually, one step at a time.

As you read, take notes on what resonates with you. Each chapter will offer practical exercises and reflective questions to help you pinpoint the strategies that make the most sense for your life. As you progress through the book, you'll have opportunities to build on these strategies, adding new layers to your plan until you've created something that feels cohesive and complete.

At the end of each chapter, I encourage you to pause and review. How does this new knowledge fit into your overall plan? Is there one small step you can take to put it into action? Whether it's adding a new type of food to your diet, trying out a relaxation technique, or adjusting your bedtime routine, the goal is to make *small, consistent changes*. Sorry to break this to you, but alas you're not perfect; it's about building momentum and confidence in your ability to create positive change.

Step Five: Cultivating a Health-Positive Mindset

Finally, let's talk about mindset. Creating a Lifestyle Wellness Plan is not just about changing your habits; it's about changing the way you think about health and wellness. Many of us have been conditioned to see health as a series of rules to follow, a punishment for past choices or indiscretions, or an endless struggle. But it doesn't have to be that way. What if, instead, you saw health as a joyful act of self-care, a way of investing in your future, and a celebration of what your body and mind can do?

Throughout *The Lifestyle Wellness Plan*, you'll be encouraged to cultivate a *health-positive mindset*, one that focuses on progress, not perfection; on growth, not guilt. This mindset shift is crucial because it changes the way you approach every other part of your plan. It's about embracing a mindset of curiosity and self-compassion, rather than striving for some unattainable ideal. It's about recognising that every small step counts and that setbacks are just opportunities to learn.

As you build your plan, I encourage you to let go of any lingering guilt or shame about where you are today. You're here, you're reading this book, and that means you're already investing in your health. Celebrate that! Focus on what you can do, not what you haven't done yet. The journey to better health is not a sprint, it's a long, winding path, and the most important thing is to keep moving forward and to enjoy the scenery on the way.

So, on your marks, get set….. go

CHAPTER 1
Global Secrets to Longevity

Lessons from the World's Longest-Lived Communities
Imagine living in a place where reaching 100 years old is not only possible but relatively common, where people are active, healthy, and engaged in life well into their 90s and beyond. While many parts of the world struggle with rising rates of chronic disease and declining mental health, certain unique communities have managed to beat the odds, earning a reputation as "Blue Zones", places where people consistently live longer, healthier, and happier lives.

The idea of "Blue Zones" was first popularised by Dan Buettner, who explored regions with extraordinary life expectancies to uncover common lifestyle traits that contribute to the wellbeing of their residents. These communities, dotted across the globe, showcase a life that embraces simplicity, balance, connection, and purpose. They remind us that the secrets to longevity aren't found in high-tech gadgets or miracle pills but in simple, intentional living.

In this chapter, we'll explore the essence of these Blue Zones, where they are, what makes them unique, and how they compare to the rest of the world. Understanding their habits and values can provide us with actionable insights to enrich our own lives. We may not be able to replicate every aspect of these lifestyles, but adopting some of their guiding principles can certainly help us on our journey to better health and longevity. Let's begin by taking a look at six Blue Zones around the world that hold the secrets to a life well-lived.

The World's Blue Zones: Where Longevity Thrives
The Blue Zones are small pockets of the world, each with its own cultural, dietary, and lifestyle peculiarities that contribute to longevity. These regions are often located in places where modern life's rush and stress are less dominant, allowing people to live in alignment with nature and tradition. They are dispersed across the

world and vary in geography, climate, and culture, yet they share several key characteristics that seem to foster longer and healthier lives.

1. **Okinawa, Japan** The Okinawan islands, especially the main island of Okinawa, are perhaps the most famous of the Blue Zones. Known as the "Land of the Immortals," Okinawa has one of the highest concentrations of centenarians in the world. Okinawans live by the concept of "ikigai", a sense of purpose that drives them each day, which research suggests plays a key role in maintaining their mental and physical health. Their diet, which is rich in vegetables, tofu, and sweet potatoes, is low in processed foods and animal products, which may contribute to their exceptional longevity.

2. **Sardinia, Italy** In the rugged, mountainous areas of Sardinia, especially the region of Ogliastra, men and women regularly surpass the century mark, remaining active and vibrant well into old age. Sardinians value strong familial bonds and communal living, with multiple generations often living close together or even under the same roof. They enjoy a diet centred on whole grains, locally sourced vegetables, and modest amounts of dairy and meat, often complemented by a glass of Cannonau wine rich in antioxidants. Their close-knit communities and balanced diets are key components of their impressive health and longevity.

3. **Ikaria, Greece** Ikaria, a small Greek island in the Aegean Sea, is often referred to as "the island where people forget to die." Here, the risk of diseases like heart disease, dementia, and cancer is significantly lower than in most parts of the world. Ikarians have a lifestyle that incorporates plant-based diets, regular physical activity through gardening or walking, and an emphasis on social connection. They also practice "chronically delayed time" or relaxed schedules, allowing them to live in a way that aligns naturally with their rhythms and reduces stress.

4. **Nicoya Peninsula, Costa Rica** The Nicoya Peninsula is a vibrant, tropical region in Costa Rica where people, particularly men, live exceptionally long lives. The Nicoyans enjoy a strong sense of "plan de vida", a purpose-driven life, similar to the Okinawan ikigai. Their diet is based on beans, corn, and rice, with plenty of locally grown fruits and vegetables. Nicoyans also have a profound sense of community and family support, which research suggests contributes to their high life expectancy and overall wellbeing.

5. **Loma Linda, California, USA** Loma Linda is a unique Blue Zone located within the fast-paced environment of the United States. This small community is home to a large population of Seventh-day Adventists who prioritise health, spirituality, and family. Their lifestyle is guided by principles from the Bible that encourage them to eat a plant-based diet, avoid smoking and alcohol, and regularly engage in physical activity. The community's faith-based approach promotes mental resilience and a strong social network, both of which are believed to contribute to their longevity.

6. **Hunza Valley, Pakistan** The Hunza Valley, nestled in the Himalayan region of Pakistan, is sometimes considered an unofficial Blue Zone due to its remarkable longevity and low rates of disease. The people of Hunza live in a pristine natural environment and follow a diet rich in whole grains, apricots, nuts, and fresh vegetables. They have little access to processed foods, and their lives involve natural movement through farming and household tasks. Their connection to the land, coupled with a simple, nutrient-dense diet, contributes to their high quality of life.

What Makes Blue Zones Different from the Rest of the World?
While the specifics of each Blue Zone's lifestyle vary, there are universal qualities that set these communities apart from others worldwide. As we compare them to other regions, we can see patterns in how lifestyle choices impact longevity and health.

1. **Diet and Nutrition** Blue Zones typically adhere to plant-based diets, rich in vegetables, whole grains, legumes, and natural sources of protein like fish or beans. Meat, if consumed, is enjoyed in small quantities. This contrasts with many Western diets, which are often heavy in processed foods, red meat, and refined sugars. By focusing on whole, minimally processed foods, these communities avoid the inflammatory effects of industrialised foods and maintain a more balanced nutritional profile.

2. **Purpose and Community Connection** A strong sense of purpose, whether described as ikigai in Japan or plan de vida in Costa Rica, is a powerful commonality across Blue Zones. In these communities, people of all ages feel valued and needed, which reduces stress and keeps them mentally and emotionally engaged. Additionally, family and community ties are highly valued, offering emotional support and reinforcing social bonds that enhance mental health. This focus on purpose and connection is often missing in modern societies, where individualism and high-stress environments are more common.

3. **Natural Movement and Physical Activity** Instead of formal exercise routines, people in Blue Zones incorporate physical activity naturally into their daily lives. Gardening, walking, and physical household tasks keep them fit and agile without the need for gyms. This stands in stark contrast to the sedentary lifestyles seen in many urban areas, where people often sit for prolonged periods at desks and rely on cars for transportation. In Blue Zones, movement is an inherent part of daily life, contributing to stronger muscles, better cardiovascular health, and a lower risk of disease.

4. **Stress Management and Work-Life Balance** People in Blue Zones have lower stress levels, not only because of their relaxed attitudes but also because of their structured practices for unwinding. Whether it's the daily siesta in Sardinia, regular prayers in Loma Linda, or tea ceremonies in Okinawa, these practices promote mindfulness and

relaxation, helping to buffer against chronic stress. In contrast, high levels of stress are prevalent in many parts of the world, especially in urbanised and industrialised areas, where work-life balance is often compromised.

5. **Faith, Spirituality, and Rituals** Faith and spirituality are common threads in Blue Zones. Many of these communities incorporate religious or spiritual practices into their daily lives, which provide comfort, a sense of belonging, and mental resilience. In Loma Linda, for example, Seventh-day Adventists find strength and community in their shared beliefs, while in Sardinia, religious rituals bring people together regularly. In a world where spirituality and ritual are often sidelined, these practices remind us of the value of grounding ourselves in something meaningful.

6. **Celebration, Moderation, and a Balanced Approach** Interestingly, many people in Blue Zones enjoy alcohol in moderation, particularly wine. In Sardinia and Ikaria, people consume wine as part of social gatherings, rather than in isolation or excess. Meals are often slow and intentional, creating space for social interaction and appreciation of the food. This approach to eating and drinking, marked by moderation and enjoyment, contrasts with cultures where fast food, hurried meals, and excessive alcohol consumption are common.

These Blue Zones offer a refreshing perspective on health, longevity, and quality of life. By examining their habits, diets, and outlooks, we gain insight into how lifestyle and culture shape our well-being over the long term. Alongside these insights, we will share an interview with someone from each of these regions, providing a personal glimpse into the lives of those who embody these traditions. Through their voices, we gain firsthand accounts of the daily values, choices, and philosophies that sustain their long and healthy lives. These stories serve as a bridge between their worlds and ours, helping us to see how their practices, from family gatherings to daily routines, are within reach of anyone seeking a healthier, more connected life.

While we may live far from these regions, their values and approaches offer valuable lessons we can adopt in our own lives, inspiring us to create our own "Blue Zone" at home. These interviews will show that longevity is less about following a strict regimen and more about making small, consistent lifestyle choices rooted in connection, purpose, and mindfulness. As we hear from individuals in Okinawa, Sardinia, Ikaria, Nicoya, Loma Linda, and the Hunza Valley, their stories will illuminate what living well truly means across different cultures. Their unique yet relatable perspectives remind us that a life of longevity isn't defined only by health metrics but by the depth of relationships, a sense of purpose, and an appreciation of life's simple joys.

Living well isn't just about avoiding illness or counting years, it's about embracing each day, staying connected to loved ones, and enjoying a life filled with purpose and vitality. As we dive deeper into these cultures and hear from the people themselves, we may discover that the path to longevity is simpler, and more accessible, than we might have imagined.

Okinawa, Japan: The Land of the Immortals
Nestled in the East China Sea, Okinawa is a subtropical paradise known for its lush landscapes, pristine beaches, and the calm, turquoise waters that surround its islands. This serene environment mirrors the lifestyle of its residents, who are famed for their long, healthy lives and vibrant communities. Here I interviewed 93-year-old Haruto-san (name we have changed), a sprightly and engaging resident of Ogimi Village, a community famous for its concentration of long-lived residents. Haruto-san's warmth and pride in his way of life shone through a very cheeky smile while we sat under a tree with my interpreter. Surprisingly Haruta-san was wearing a Manchester United football shirt, exactly the same as my son was wearing when I left to travel out here.

Penelope Swift: *Haruto-san, thank you for welcoming me today. I have to say, it's easy to see why you love living here in Ogimi. Could you start by telling me a bit about what life here is like?*

Haruto-san: *Ogimi is my heart. I was born here, and I'll stay here forever. It's peaceful, with green mountains, warm air, and the sea nearby. I have visited Tokyo and travelled to see my brother in America, but this is not Tokyo. Life here is simple but very good. Each morning, I go to my field with my wife, Yuki. We grow vegetables and flowers. The smell of the soil and the feel of it… I think it keeps me young! I work in the field almost every day, even now at 93. My neighbours would probably come to check on me if I didn't!* (He laughs)

Penelope: *(laughs) I love that. They'd worry if you stopped working! It sounds like staying active is very natural here, part of everyday life. Would you say exercise has been important for your health?*

Haruto-san: *We don't think of it as exercise, this is just life. I walk, I run sometimes to visit my neighbours, work in the field, carry water when it's needed. I do stretch every morning. It's important to keep my body awake, I think. When you walk with joy, it keeps the body young, I believe.*

Penelope: *That's such a beautiful way to put it. I think I'll remember that. (smiles)"Walking with joy". Now, if it's ok, I'd love to hear about your diet. What sorts of things do you enjoy eating?*

Haruto-san: *my diet… It's very much the same as when I was young. We eat many vegetables here, goya (bitter melon), sweet potatoes, carrots, cabbage. My wife cooks tofu every day, sometimes with miso or green tea leaves. We don't eat much meat, only for festival. Fish, yes, we have it sometimes. And we always say, "hara hachi bu," which means to eat until you're 80% full. It keeps the belly comfortable, you see. No need to overfill it.*

Penelope: *"Hara hachi bu", that sounds like a good rule for all of us! Now, I understand that "ikigai" is very important in Okinawa. What does ikigai mean to you?*

Haruto-san: *Yes, ikigai. Ikigai is me, it's all of us, it's why I get up in the morning. For me, it's my family, my friends, my village. It's the field I plant with my hands, knowing I'll share the food with my children and grandchildren. I feel useful, needed, you know? There's something to look forward to, even if it's just planting a new seed or helping my neighbour with a fence. It keeps my heart strong, my mind sharp. Sometimes I go to sleep thinking about those seeds I'll be planting.*

Penelope: *That's so lovely. I can see how important community is here in Ogimi. How does it feel to be part of such a close-knit place?*

Haruto-san: *We are very close. We help each other with everything. If someone is sick, the whole village will visit, bring soup, check if they're warm and comfortable. My friends, I've known some of them since we were boys, and we still talk every day, still laugh. We have gatherings, we drink tea, sometimes sing old songs. Living alone would be hard for the heart, I think. Here, nobody is alone.*

Penelope: *It sounds wonderful, Haruto-san. I can only imagine the joy that comes from those connections. Finally, if I may, what advice would you give to those of us who'd like to live a long and healthy life like yours?*

Haruto-san: *(smiles) Advice? From me?(laughs) Well, I'd say, enjoy your wife (giggles). Enjoy your food, take time with it. Find happiness in what you do each day, even if it's something simple. Don't think about what's wrong when there is so much good, just live and walk with joy, and don't worry too much. Worry makes the spirit grow old. Have friends, close friends. Living is simple, really. Just take care of each other.*

Penelope: *Thank you, Haruto-san. You make it all sound so simple and joyful. I can see why life here is so special, and it's inspiring.*

Haruto-san: *thank you. I'm happy every day, there's something beautiful to see.*

From talking to Haruto-san I took away the feeling that sometimes we pigeon-hole exercise into compartments in life, going to the gym, playing sport on a Sunday morning, and although all movement is good, perhaps we do that just because we have forgotten how to "walk with joy". Then we have "hara hachi bu," eat until you're 80% full. What we think we are discovering with modern science, has in reality been a lifestyle for many for centuries.

Haruto-san believes that worry ages the spirit and advises us to "not worry too much." His approach to life is simple, finding happiness in each day, enjoying a meal, and helping a neighbour. By letting go of worry and appreciating the present, he creates a life of peace and contentment, one that doesn't wear down his spirit. This outlook reminds us to let go of anxieties, enjoy simple pleasures, and embrace each day as it comes.

Haruto-san's "ikigai," or reason for getting up in the morning, is centered on his family, his friends, and the land he loves. He feels a deep sense of purpose in tending his garden and supporting his community, giving him something to look forward to each day. This sense of purpose keeps him mentally sharp and emotionally fulfilled. It's a reminder for us to find our own "ikigai", a purpose that brings meaning to our lives, no matter how simple.

Sardinia, Italy: Life in the Longevity-Heart of Ogliastra
The region of Ogliastra is also famed for its high concentration of centenarians. Here, the mountains rise sharply against the sky, and the air is rich with the scents of Mediterranean herbs and the salt breeze from the nearby coast. The lives of Ogliastra's residents are intertwined with the land itself; many are shepherds, farmers, and artisans who have lived here for generations. Their pace of life is gentle but purposeful, filled with hard work balanced by meaningful time spent with family and friends.

Families in Ogliastra remain tightly knit, often with three or even four generations living in close proximity. This closeness extends beyond blood relations, fostering a sense of community that brings people together in joy and sorrow alike. Meals are shared affairs together, not sitting in front of the TV, not rushed but savoured. Simple yet nourishing, the Sardinian diet includes whole grains, fresh vegetables, hearty beans, and local cheeses like pecorino, often enjoyed with a glass of Cannonau wine, a rich, dark red said to have powerful health benefits. Together, these traditions create a rhythm that promotes both physical and mental resilience, fostering a lifestyle of true longevity.

To gain insight into this remarkable lifestyle, I sat down with Signora Rosa Serra (a name we've changed for privacy) in the village of Villagrande Strisaili, a small community in Ogliastra known for its many residents who have reached a ripe old age. Although I hadn't planned to directly ask her age in case deemed not polite, when I arrived, Rosa was wearing a birthday badge saying 93! She was bustling about her kitchen, directing a young child who to be honest we didn't get to the bottom of who that was. She was like a cat on a hot tin roof. It took a good few minutes for my interpreter and me to get her to stop still long enough to pin her down and talk.

Interview with Signora Rosa Serra

Penelope Swift: *"Rosa, it's an absolute honour to meet you. Ninety-three years young I see and still running circles around everyone, I hear!"*

Rosa Serra: *(laughs heartily)* "Oh, that's what they say, but I think they're just too polite to admit I've slowed down a little!"

Penelope: *"If this is slowing down, I think the rest of us might need to speed up! Can you tell me a bit about what life is like here in Villagrande Strisaili? It seems like such a special place."*

Rosa: *"It is special. Here, we live simply, but we live well. My family has been here for many many many generations, and we are close. My son lives over there (pointing), my daughters are there and there (pointing), and my grandchildren visit every day. It's not unusual, most families here are like that, not like cities. You know, we take care of each other, now my turn for them to take care of me."*

Penelope: *"There's something beautiful in that. Do you think that closeness has helped you stay healthy all these years?"*

She looked a little confused by the question, as if I had asked a very obvious question, but then as she thought, she smiled

Rosa: *There's always someone to laugh with, someone to share your worries. My granddaughter brings me fresh bread every morning. My son helps me in the garden, and I help him with the "picioccheddu" (little ones). We are never alone here. When I go to the café, I see my friends, when we go to church I sit next to my best friend, we have been sitting together for the last 85 years."*

Penelope: *"85 years? That sounds wonderful. I imagine it must be a bit like having a big family in the whole village!"*

Rosa: *(smiling)* "Yes, yes it feels like that, my friends are my family, my neighbours are my family, everyone is our family. Everyone knows everyone. We come together for meals, for festivals, and even just for a glass of wine in the evening. That's how we keep our spirits young."

Penelope: *"Speaking of wine, I hear there's a local favourite, Cannonau, is it? I read that it's supposed to be good for the heart!"*

Rosa: *(nodding approvingly)* *"Yes, yes, Cannonau is what we drink, It's a part of life here. My husband, share a glass every evening. It's good for the heart, and it brings people together. We never drink alone; wine is something to share, to enjoy slowly. My husband says it's the only time we stop moving and talk"*

Penelope: *"And what about food? I'm curious, do you follow a specific diet, or is it just the way of life here?"*

Rosa: "No diet, we eat like kings! We eat what we grow, what's around us. Lots of vegetables, beans, and the bread we bake ourselves. Pecorino cheese, a little bit of meat when we have it, usually from a family animal, an animal who we have thanked for being a part of us, not the supermarket! Food here is real; it's part of the land."

Penelope: *"And how about sweets? Are there any Sardinian treats you enjoy?"*

Rosa: *(laughing)* "Oh, I do have a sweet tooth! I love honey, or ricotta with a little sugar. My mother used to make a pastry called seadas, a fried dough with cheese and honey. But we don't eat too much. A little taste, (the little girl looks at Rosa, who adds)… but often."

Penelope: *"I think that's a lesson we could all learn, just a taste is enough. Now, Rosa, you're quite active for someone of any age, let alone ninety-three! What's your secret?"*

Rosa: "I've never had a car, I don't like cars, so I walk. I work in the garden every day. I take care of my chickens, I cook, I clean, lazy people grow old."

Penelope: "No gym membership, then?" (chuckling)

Rosa: (laughing heartily) "No, no gym! Have you not seen the hills (she says waving outside at the towering mountains)

Penelope: "Rosa, I think that might be another secret, living in harmony with your environment. Do you think that connection to the land has influenced your health?"

Rosa: "The land gives us everything, our food, our strength, our spirit. When I was young, we spent our days in the fields, my father herding sheep, my mother planting vegetables. I think it's because we are so close to the earth, we learn to respect it and take care of it. When you live like this, you don't need much else."

Penelope: "That's so beautifully put. Rosa, thank you so much for sharing your story. It's truly inspiring, and I can see how much love and pride you have for this place and your way of life."

Rosa: (smiling warmly) "Thank you, Penelope. I am proud, yes. Sa vida est sencilla ma prena. Life here may be simple, but it is full. Fattos de sa familia, no si pesant' in sa bascula. (the weight of family doesn't weigh on the scales.). When you have those things, you have everything."

Penelope: "I think that's the perfect takeaway. You've given us all something to aspire to, Rosa, a life that's rich in the things that truly matter."

Rosa: "Thank you, dear. I hope you come back and visit again, maybe stay a little longer next time."

Penelope: "Oh, I'd love that! And maybe you can teach me how to make that seadas pastry."

Rosa: (laughs) "Custaì, mi faeddat piacere"

Sitting with Rosa in her kitchen in the heart of Villagrande Strisaili, I felt as if I were uncovering not just secrets to longevity but a completely different way of approaching life. Rosa lives in harmony with the land, eating only what she grows or sources nearby, and savours life's small indulgences with moderation and gratitude. I learned that balance is woven into her way of life, a glass of Cannonau shared with loved ones, a taste of honey or seadas, but never in excess.

Family is everything to Rosa. It struck me how naturally interconnected her life is with those around her, her son, her grandchildren, her lifelong friends. She laughed at the idea of being "alone" because, for her, it's unimaginable. As you will read later in the book connection with others is one of the strongest drivers for a healthy old age. Loneliness for pack animals like humans is one of the worst experiences. To have a life where loneliness is unimaginable like Rosa probably stuck with me the most. That confidence.

More-so everyone here is family, and they're there for one another through thick and thin. Rosa showed me that true wealth isn't about material possessions; it's in the bonds we build, the love we share, and the joy of being surrounded by those who care for us.

Rosa's world isn't complicated, but it's incredibly rich….. As I read this back, it's exactly that, she felt like the richest woman on earth, whilst she cares for her chickens.

Her simple words, *"Sa vida est sencilla ma prena"*, life is simple, but it is full, left a profound impression on me. Rosa's life taught me that longevity is less about what you have and more about how deeply you connect with what's around you. She showed me that when life is rooted in love, family, and a grateful connection to the land, **you already have everything you need** for a life well-lived.

Ikaria, Greece - The island where people forget to die
With an environment marked by rocky hillsides, olive groves, and sun-dappled coastline, the island offers its residents a lifestyle deeply in tune with nature. The people of Ikaria lead lives rich in tradition and simplicity, relying on a largely plant-based diet, daily physical activities like gardening and walking, and a relaxed approach to time,

often referred to as "chronically delayed time." Here, people live by the rhythms of the day, placing high value on community, friendship, and meaningful connection.

Today, we have the pleasure of speaking with *Yiannis*, a 92-year-old Ikarian from the village of Raches. Yiannis is a lively figure, his sun-kissed skin and warm smile reflecting his zest for life. He's a regular in his garden, a beloved storyteller in the local kafeneio (coffeehouse), and a firm believer that the island's way of life is key to his long and healthy years. As I sit down with Yiannis (92) in the shade of his olive tree, I'm immediately charmed by his humour and warmth. This is not just an interview; it's a glimpse into a way of life that has stood the test of time.

Penelope Swift: *[smiling] Yiannis, it's a pleasure to meet you! Your son walked with us up to the village. He said he was 70 last week. I can't believe you all look so young. (his eyes were so bright - clear white and hazel which kind of reminded me of my Golden Retriever puppy) What's the secret?*

Yiannis: *[grinning] Ah, Penny, if I knew the secret, I'd be a rich man! But I can tell you this (tapping his wrist where a watch was missing): here in Ikaria, we don't live by the clock. We wake up with the sun and go to bed when we're tired. We eat when we're hungry, and we drink wine when we're happy, which is often! (he gives a naughty smile)*

Penelope: *[laughing] That sounds like the best philosophy! I know people in other parts of the world who live by alarms and schedules, and they're exhausted. Is this "Ikarian time" something you were born with, or did you grow into it?*

Yiannis: *Oh, it's in our blood, I think. When I was young, my grandfather would say, "Why rush? The fish will still be in the sea, the olives will still grow, and the wine will wait for you." We live slowly here. We believe that stress makes you old, so we avoid it! We don't measure life by the hours; we measure it by the laughter, the meals, the stories.*

Penelope: *Speaking of meals, I have to ask about your diet. The Ikarian diet is mainly plant-based I'm told. What does a typical day of meals look like for you?*

Yiannis: *In the morning, I might have some bread with olive oil, It is important that you put the oil on the plate and dip the bread, not spreading like butter. maybe a bit of honey from our own bees. Lunch is vegetables, garden greens, beans, sometimes a little fish. Of course, dinner is light. We don't eat big meals late; it doesn't sit well. Always lots of greens, fresh herbs, and maybe a glass of wine, maybe even two (with a wink).*

Penelope: *I've heard that the wine is often homemade. Is that right?*

Yiannis: *[nodding proudly] Yes! Nikos who you met, and Stavros, my sons and I make it ourselves, just as my father and grandfather did. Κρασί και καλή παρέα είναι το μυστικό της ευτυχίας A glass here and there, shared with family and friends, keeps you warm in the heart. It's not about drinking a lot; it's about enjoying the taste, the company. We say, Εβίβα! Στην υγειά μας! "Good wine, good health!"*

Penelope: *I love that! Now, tell me about your daily activities. I noticed your beautiful garden when I arrived, do you spend much time there?*

Yiannis: Oh yes, every morning, I check on the vegetables, pick the weeds, and water the plants. I walk to the village every day to see friends, maybe play a game of dominoes or just have a chat at the kafeneio.

Penelope: So, no fancy gym memberships or exercise routines?

Yiannis: *[laughing heartily] Do you dance Penny? We dance at festivals, and even now, I still join in. There's no need for machines when you dance.*

Penelope: *Speaking of the festivals, the community here seems incredibly close. How important is that to you?*

Yiannis: *It's everything. If their shed falls down, we all rebuild it. If someone is sad, we sit with them. When there is joy, we dance. I think being together is why we live so long. We share everything, good and bad.*

Penelope: That sense of connection must bring you such peace, and, if I may ask, what keeps you going? What brings you joy?

Yiannis: *[pauses thoughtfully]* *Every day is a gift, Penny. I am happy to wake up, to see the sun, to feel the earth. I suppose, knowing that I have my family, my friends, my land. I'm still needed, still useful, still smart (tapping his head). I help my family with the garden, I teach my grandchildren about the old ways. That keeps me young.*

Penelope: *[smiling] What advice would you give to people who don't live in Ikaria but want to live like an Ikarian?*

Yiannis: *Ah, that's easy. Slow down! Enjoy the food on your plate, enjoy the faces of the people you love, and don't be in such a hurry. Eat real food, from the earth if you can. Dance. Always find time for friends, for laughter. Η ζωή δεν μετριέται σε χρόνια, αλλά σε στιγμές Life isn't about the years; it's about the moments.*

Penelope: *Yiannis, thank you. This has been such a gift. I have to say, I can see why they say "Ikaria is the island where people forget to die." You make living sound so… simple, so joyful, you don't seem to let even the propsect of dying bother you.*

Yiannis: *[smiling warmly]* We have everything we need here. As long as the olives grow, as long as there is laughter, Yiannis will keep going.

Yiannis has no use for clocks or rigid schedules; in Ikaria, people live by the natural rhythms of the sun and their own needs. This concept of "Ikarian time" is a gentle reminder that life is richer when we focus less on the clock and more on the joy of each moment. As Yiannis said, "We don't measure life by the hours; we measure it by the laughter, the meals, the stories." This outlook on time nurtures calm, reduces stress, and allows for a life fully lived.

Yiannis enjoys a diet that's largely plant-based, balanced, and never rushed. His meals are filled with love and tradition, like the ritual of dipping bread in olive oil or enjoying honey from his own bees. By eating simply and seasonally, and avoiding large meals late at night, Yiannis reminds us of the power of eating real, unprocessed food in moderation.

When someone is down, the whole village offers support; when there is joy, they all celebrate together. "If someone is sad, we sit with them. When there is joy, we dance," he says, reminding us of the importance of supporting each other and building close-knit communities. This deep sense of connection creates resilience and gives life meaning.

At 92, Yiannis still feels useful, needed, and valued. He takes pride in teaching his grandchildren about the old ways and in being a part of his family's daily life. His sense of purpose keeps him engaged, happy, and, as he put it, "still smart." Knowing that we have something meaningful to contribute, no matter our age, enriches life and keeps us young at heart.

Perhaps the most profound lesson Yiannis offers is that "Life isn't about the years; it's about the moments." His life is rich with laughter, stories, and simple pleasures, and he measures it in terms of experiences, not in age or achievements. His words remind us that true wealth is found in the moments we cherish, in the love we give and receive, and in the joy we create along the way. It's a humbling perspective that invites us to shift our focus from quantity to quality.

Nicoya Peninsula, Costa Rica: A Land of Purposeful Longevity
The Nicoya Peninsula, on the Pacific coast of Costa Rica, is a lush, tropical region where time seems to stretch just a little longer than usual. Known for its natural beauty, Nicoya boasts golden beaches, dense rainforests, and rolling hills dotted with family farms. The climate is warm year-round, with gentle coastal breezes and a seasonal rhythm that brings the land to life with tropical fruits, vegetables, and rich, volcanic soil ideal for growing food. This fertile environment provides a constant supply of fresh produce, including vibrant fruits and the staples of the Nicoyan diet: beans, corn, and rice. It's a place where people live in close connection with nature, nurturing both the land and each other.

The people of Nicoya enjoy what they call a "plan de vida", a deeply ingrained sense of purpose that shapes their lives. It's about having goals, staying involved in family and community, and rising each day with gratitude and direction. Many Nicoyans live well into their 90s and beyond, and the sight of an elderly person working in the garden or strolling down a path with friends is a familiar one. For them, life is rich, meaningful, and filled with community.

Today, I had the privilege of sitting down with 92-year-old don Roberto in his village of Hojancha, a skilled carpenter and labourer, a man who embodies the Nicoyan approach to long, healthy living. His face creases easily into a warm smile as he greets me, his eyes twinkling with a mix of pride and mischief.

Interview with don Roberto

Penelope Swift: *Thank you for making time to talk with me today, don Roberto. It's a true pleasure to meet you. How are you today?*

don Roberto: *Oh, I'm very well, thank you, Ms. Penelope. The birds are singing, the sun is shining... What more could a man ask for? Every day is a good day, you know. I wake up, drink my coffee, and greet the morning.*

Penelope: *I love that. You make it sound so simple! I understand you've lived here in Hojancha your entire life?*

don Roberto: *Yes, born and raised. This village, these hills, they're a part of me. There isn't a house here that either my father, my sons or I haven't worked on, (Carpenters) My family has been here for generations. My father and grandfather, they lived long lives too. Maybe there's something in the air here... or in the water! (He laughs)*

Penelope: *You could be onto something! Tell me, don Roberto, what is a typical day like for you? What keeps you busy?*

don Roberto: *Well, I start with my coffee, of course. Then, I spend a little time in my garden. I grow beans, yucca, and a few papaya trees. There's always work to do with the plants, they are like my wife, they don't let me sit down for too long! (He chuckles.) I like to walk, too. I visit my neighbours or help out when there's work to be done. Sometimes, I'll walk down to the river and sit for a while. There's something about that sound of water, you know? It makes you feel alive.*

Penelope: *That sounds wonderful. So, it sounds like you stay very active?*

don Roberto: *Yes, yes, always. In Nicoya, we don't stop because we're getting older, we just keep going. "En Nicoya, decimos que cuando bajas por una pendiente pronunciada, puedes detenerte un momento, pero al empezar de nuevo, tus pies se mueven rápido por sí solos. La vida es así también: cuando comienzas con un propósito, hay una inercia que te lleva hacia adelante." "In Nicoya, we say that when you're walking down a steep hill, you can pause for a moment, but once you start again, your feet pick up speed on their own. Life is like that too, when you set out with purpose, there's a momentum that carries you forward." There's always something to do, and I have my family nearby. My children, grandchildren… they visit often. When they're here, I feel younger, like I'm part of everything that's happening, even now.*

Penelope: *That's beautiful, don Roberto. I've read that having family close is so important for people here. You seem to have such a strong connection to your family and community.*

don Roberto: *Oh, absolutely. Family is everything here. We look after each other, help each other. We laugh a lot, Ms. Penelope! Laughter is good medicine, I truly believe that. When you're surrounded by people who love you, it keeps your heart strong.*

Penelope: *And what about your diet? I understand that Nicoyans have a very unique way of eating.*

don Roberto: *We eat what the land gives us. Mostly beans, corn, rice, fresh vegetables, and fruits. My favourite is gallo pinto, it's simple, rice and beans cooked together. We eat that for breakfast with a bit of egg or cheese. It's a good start to the day, keeps you going for hours. I don't eat much meat, only a little bit now and then. Here, we don't eat a lot, but we eat well.*

Penelope: *It sounds like a very simple, but nourishing way to eat. Do you think that diet is one of the reasons why people here live so long?*

don Roberto: *(He nods thoughtfully.) Yes, but it's more than that. It's eating good food, grown here on our land, and not too much. We never eat until we're too full. We call it "eating with respect" respect for the food, for your body. I think that makes a big difference.*

Penelope: *That's such a wonderful way to look at it. I can see there's a lot of wisdom in that approach. I'm curious, don Roberto, you seem so content and happy. What do you think is the secret to a good, long life?*

don Roberto: *The secret? (He chuckles and leans in a bit.) Well, Ms. Penelope, I'll tell you what my father told me: live with joy. Don't get too serious about things, and don't worry too much. Laugh every day, work with your hands, yes God gave us hands, work with your hands. When you live like that, life doesn't feel so heavy.*

Penelope: *That's wonderful advice. You certainly seem to live by it, don Roberto, and may I ask, what is your purpose now? What keeps you going?*

don Roberto: *My purpose now… Well, it's my family, my friends, this land. I am teaching my great grandchildren the skills of being a carpenter while their dad is out being a carpenter, it won't be long until he takes them with him, and then they have to be useful. I enjoy teaching them and if they remember what I taught them, then I'll still be here, even when I'm gone.*

Penelope: *(Smiling) I think they're very lucky to have you as a teacher, don Roberto. Thank you so much for sharing this with me today. Your life is truly inspiring, and I'm sure many people will learn from your wisdom.*

don Roberto: *Thank you, Ms. Penelope. I'm glad you came all this way to talk to an old man like me. (He laughs) let life be good to you.*

Don Roberto's day begins with a simple coffee and a moment of gratitude for the sun, birds, and beauty of the day. He shows us that starting each morning with appreciation can set a positive tone and help us find joy in the ordinary. Life doesn't need to be complicated; appreciating small blessings brings happiness.

Even at 92, don Roberto is active, tending to his garden, walking to visit friends, and working with his hands. For him, age is not a reason to stop but to keep going. Whether it's planting beans, teaching carpentry to his grandchildren, or spending time outdoors, Roberto finds purpose in staying engaged with life's simple, meaningful activities.

Roberto's diet is simple yet nourishing, focusing on locally grown beans, rice, corn, and vegetables. He speaks of "eating with respect", never too much, and with appreciation for the food and what it does for the body. This respectful, mindful approach to food teaches us the value of nourishing ourselves in moderation and with gratitude.

Roberto has a purpose at every stage, and now it's teaching his great grandchildren the skills of carpentry. He believes that as long as they remember what he taught them, he will live on through them. His purpose isn't only about self-fulfillment; it's about giving back and leaving a legacy, reminding us of the importance of contributing to future generations.

"Live with joy. Don't get too serious about things," he says, with a chuckle. For Roberto, life's challenges are best met with a light heart and a joyful spirit. His laughter and positive outlook show us that the way we approach life can have a profound impact on our wellbeing, reminding us not to let life's burdens weigh us down too much.

Don Roberto finds meaning in working with his hands, whether it's in his garden or building as a carpenter. He believes there's a special connection between hands and the soul, given to us to create and nurture. His example shows us that meaningful work, especially physical and creative work, keeps the body and spirit alive.

One of his favourite sayings is, "When you're walking down a steep hill, you can stop, but the moment you start again, your feet move quickly on their own." This wisdom reflects how he sees life: we can pause for rest, but life has a momentum that carries us forward, especially when we walk with purpose.

For me having interviewed many people, one thing I know I will have to research much. Much more, is how so many people who live long with a clear mind and healthy body, worked for the most part of their lives with their hands. Not teachers, accountants or computer scientists who you think might be exercising their mind – hands!

Loma Linda, California, USA

Loma Linda is an oasis of health and longevity in a fast-paced, high-stress world. Despite being surrounded by the rapid rhythm of American life, Loma Linda has cultivated a unique environment where people regularly live into their nineties and beyond. This small city is home to a large population of Seventh-day Adventists, a group whose faith-based lifestyle includes a commitment to health, spirituality, and family. Adventists believe that the body is a temple, and they strive to honour it through plant-based diets, regular exercise, and a commitment to community service. Smoking and alcohol are avoided, and daily life includes prayer, reflection, and support from a tight-knit community.

One resident who embodies these principles is 96-year-old Ruth Thompson (a pseudonym for privacy), who lives in the charming village of Bryn Mawr, a close-knit neighbourhood within Loma Linda. Ruth is spry, full of humour, and keen to share her experiences of long and healthy living.

Penelope Swift: *"Ruth, it's a pleasure to be here with you today. I can see you're as bright-eyed as ever! What's your secret?"* (Penelope laughs, and Ruth chuckles along.)

Ruth: *"Oh, I don't know about any secret, dear. I just live my life with joy and gratitude each day. I think it's all about faith, family, and good food. It's hard to slow down with great grandchildren running about!"* (She grins, her eyes sparkling.)

Penelope: *"You're 96, is that right? And still running around with great grandchildren! That's remarkable. What's a typical day like for you?"*

Ruth: *"Well, I'm up by 6 a.m. most mornings. I like to start with some quiet prayer and reflection, just thanking God for another day. Then, after breakfast, usually oatmeal with some fresh fruit, I head out for a walk. It's a peaceful time of day, and there's usually a few of us from Bryn Mawr out there, catching up or sharing a laugh. In the afternoons, I'll work in my garden or do some light housework. I like to keep busy."*

Penelope: *"It sounds like you have a lovely balance. I know that in Loma Linda, a plant-based diet is a big part of life. What does your diet look like?"*

Ruth: *"Yes, it's true, most of us here follow a vegetarian diet. I've been eating this way my whole, no that's not true, at least most of my life, lots of vegetables, whole grains, beans, and nuts. We grow a lot of our own food here, so it's fresh and good for the soul."* (She pauses, thoughtful.) *"I do love a good nut loaf, and there's always a big salad on the table. Eating simply hasn't let me down yet."*

Penelope: *"That sounds delicious, Ruth! And what about exercise? I know you mentioned your walks, but do you do anything else to stay active?"*

Ruth: *"Oh, yes, I believe in keeping active. I don't do anything too strenuous, just what feels good. I love to garden, and that keeps me bending and stretching. I walk everywhere around the neighbourhood. Exercise isn't something we 'have to do' here; it's just part of life. Staying active has always come naturally."*

Penelope: *"It seems like there's a lot of joy in these daily routines. Do you think your faith has played a big role in your health and happiness?"*

Ruth: *"Absolutely. My faith is the foundation of everything. It reminds me to live with purpose and peace. We have a strong church community here in Bryn Mawr, and that's such a blessing. I know I'm never alone, and we're always looking out for each other."* (She smiles gently.) *"Our faith teaches us to be kind to ourselves and others. That's good medicine for the heart."*

Penelope: *"You have such a lovely outlook, Ruth. Now, do you ever have an indulgence? A treat?"*

Ruth: *"Oh, I do love a slice of homemade pie now and then! don't deprive ourselves, but we keep everything balanced. A slice of pie now and then is good for the spirit."* (She laughs, with a wink.)

Penelope: *"Favourite pie?"*

Ruth: *"Cherry and Orange."*

Penelope: *"Delicious, must try that! So, what would you say is the most important lesson you've learned over the years that is a clue to your long life?"*

Ruth: *"Life is precious, Penelope. I've lost friends and loved ones along the way, as everyone does, but I've learned to be thankful for every day I have and had with them. I try to make each day count. Love your family, keep moving, eat well, and have faith. It's simple, really."*

Penelope: *"Thank you, Ruth. You've certainly given me a lot to think about. It's clear that Loma Linda has something truly special here, and people like you are a testament to the power of living with joy, purpose, and simplicity."*

Ruth: *"Oh, it's been my pleasure, dear. I hope people can take a bit of Loma Linda's spirit into their own lives. Life doesn't have to be complicated to be beautiful."*

Reflecting on my time with Ruth, I'm left feeling both inspired and humbled. Here is a woman who, at 96, radiates vitality, joy, and a groundedness that's rare in today's world. Sitting across from her, I felt as though I was speaking to a friend who had mastered the art of living well, not through strict rules or complicated plans, but through simple, deeply held values. Ruth's secret isn't really a secret at all; it's a life infused with purpose, gratitude, and care for both herself and those around her.

From the start, Ruth made it clear that faith is her foundation. She spoke with such warmth about her morning prayers and her sense of peace, which she credits with giving her strength and focus. Her faith guides her through every day, and I could see how it brought her a kind of inner calm and happiness that's rare. She's connected not only to her beliefs but to her community, a network of friends and family in Bryn Mawr who look out for each other and share in life's simple joys. I think this sense of belonging is something we all long for, and it's clear that for Ruth, it's been key to her longevity. I noticed a similar theme in other interviews, security, the friendship, the knowing that they're never alone, and her faith being always with her, will for her, ensure she never feels alone.

Ruth's approach to eating is refreshingly straightforward and joyful. She's followed a plant-based diet for most of her life, (she did admit to once trying a burger from McDonalds, but if that's her worst sin then she's got a bit of catching up on me)) with a colourful array of vegetables, whole grains, beans, and nuts making up the majority of her meals. "Good food is good for the soul," she said, with a smile that warmed the room. Her diet isn't something she thinks about in terms of strict health rules; rather, it's a way of eating that brings her pleasure and energy without sacrificing balance. Yes, she loves a slice of homemade pie now and then, and the way she talks about it shows her philosophy perfectly: indulgences aren't off-limits; they're just savoured and balanced with healthy choices. It's the kind of wisdom that's so easy to overlook in our rush to find the latest "miracle diet," yet Ruth's life is proof that simplicity and balance can be powerful tools for health.

I was also struck by how naturally Ruth keeps moving. She gardens, she walks, she keeps busy in her home, and none of it feels like a chore. "Exercise isn't something we 'have to do' here; it's just part of life," she told me. Watching her laugh about bending and stretching in the garden, I realised she's found ways to stay active that feel effortless and enjoyable, a true testament to a life where movement is integrated into daily routines rather than scheduled as an obligation. This too reminded me of other interviews in that staying active doesn't have to be about gym memberships or strict routines; it's about moving with joy and ease.

Perhaps what touched me most, though, was Ruth's genuine sense of gratitude and appreciation for life. She described each day as "precious," a word that seemed to sum up everything she values. She's lost friends and loved ones over the years, but she speaks about them with a gentle, loving fondness. Instead of focusing on what she's lost, she is thankful for the days she had with them. Ruth's outlook reminds me that longevity isn't just about counting years; it's about making each day count. Her life is a beautiful example of living with purpose and joy, and it's clear that this is what has kept her going strong all these years.

I walked away from our conversation with a lot of thoughts swirling in my head, as I must admit that I'm not a person of faith, of any faith. Ruth's way of living is simple, yes, but it's also profoundly rich. It's a life rooted in her faith, filled with family, grounded in healthy choices, and balanced by moments of indulgence. She embodies the heart of what it means to live well, and I left feeling inspired to embrace these principles in my own life. Ruth's words echo in my mind even now: "Life doesn't have to be complicated to be beautiful." I believe her.

Hunza Valley, Pakistan

The Hunza Valley, tucked away in the breathtaking Himalayan region of northern Pakistan, is known not just for its natural beauty but for the remarkable health and longevity of its people. The valley is surrounded by towering peaks, lush green terraces, and glacial rivers, creating a pristine environment that nourishes both body and soul. Life here is deeply connected to the land, and most residents work with nature in ways that keep them moving daily. Farming, tending to animals, and managing households all provide a natural rhythm of physical activity that keeps the Hunza people fit well into old age.

Their diet is simple but highly nutritious, based on what they grow: whole grains, apricots, nuts, fresh vegetables, and occasional dairy. Due to limited access to processed foods, meals are homegrown and home-cooked, made from recipes passed down through generations. This lifestyle and environment contribute to a population that enjoys a long active life with little incidence of chronic disease.

To gain deeper insight into this unique lifestyle, I had the pleasure of speaking with Karim, a proud 94-year-old resident of Karimabad, a charming village in the heart of the Hunza Valley. His eyes are bright, his smile warm, and his handshake is as strong as that of someone half his age. Karim's joy and pride in his community and way of life are evident in every story he shares.

Penelope: *Karim, thank you so much for inviting me to speak with you. You look as though you're in the prime of life, not pushing a hundred! What's the secret here in Hunza?*

Karim: *(laughs) Ah, thank you. There's no secret, really. Life here is simple. We eat what we grow, we move with the land, and we take our time. I think it's the simplicity that keeps us young. But yes, maybe our apricots help, too! We have apricots every day, dried in winter, fresh in summer.*

Penelope: *Apricots, noted! I've seen them drying on rooftops all over. They're a favourite, then?*

Karim: *Oh, yes! We call them "Hunza gold." They are a gift from the mountains, full of goodness. We dry them in the sun, eat them as they are, or add them to our bread and stews. We also make oil from the kernel, which is good for the skin, you know.*

Penelope: *You look as though you know quite a bit about staying healthy. What does a typical day look like for you?*

Karim: *Well, I wake up early, with the sun. First, some tea and bread. Then, I'm outside, working in the fields. I grow wheat, apricots, potatoes, and some vegetables. If I don't work, my body feels stiff, so I like to keep busy. After some hours, I come home for lunch, usually a bowl of lentils or vegetable soup, and more bread.*

Penelope: *And all of this keeps you so active?*

Karim: *"Aram bay ostar agásh chu kharbay biush." If you sit too much, you get old quickly, yes? My wife, Noor, is also 92, and she's still up early making our meals and weaving baskets. We don't think much about age; we think about what needs to be done that day.*

Penelope: *It sounds like a beautiful way of life, and there's so much joy here. I see smiles everywhere I go. What is it about Hunza that makes people so happy?*

Karim: *That is easy. My children, grandchildren, they live nearby, and we share our meals, our stories. When I need help, I call on my family, and when they need me, I am there. This connection keeps the heart young.*

Penelope: *You make it sound so lovely, Karim. I think many people would love to have that closeness. Does your faith also play a part in your happiness?*

Karim: *Yes, of course. We believe in living peacefully, with respect for each other and the land. Every day, I am thankful for what we have here, the mountains, the fresh air, the water from the glacier. Life here is not always easy, but we have all we need, and we remember to be grateful.*

Penelope: *It's inspiring. How do you take care of your health if you're unwell? Any medicines or doctors?*

Karim: *We have some herbs here that our mothers taught us to use. Wild mint, black cumin, garlic, these keep us strong. We rest when we need to. But, truly, we do not have much illness. Maybe the air and our way of life protect us. I have never needed much medicine.*

Penelope: *It sounds like you've mastered the art of living, Karim. Do you have any advice for those of us who live in fast-paced cities?*

Karim: *(smiles) Slow down! Take time to eat, time to move, time to talk to your neighbours. The world outside Hunza feels too fast, like people are running but don't know where they are going. Here, we know where we are. We are part of the land, part of each other's lives. This is what gives peace.*

Penelope: *Karim, I couldn't agree more. Thank you for sharing your wisdom. I can't wait to tell others about the secrets of the Hunza people, and especially about those apricots!*

Karim: *(laughs) Yes, remember the apricots! And enjoy each day. This is the Hunza way.*

For Karim, life in Hunza is beautifully straightforward. There's no secret formula, just a commitment to living naturally and working with the land. They eat what they grow and move according to the needs of the day. There's something refreshing in this simplicity; no rush, no urgency, just a deep respect for the natural rhythm of life. Karim's daily routine, waking with the sun, working in the fields, sharing simple meals, reminds us that sometimes the most nourishing way of life is also the simplest.

I couldn't help but wonder if apricots are magical after hearing Karim talk about them. Known locally as "Hunza gold," these vibrant fruits are a staple in their diet. Fresh in summer, dried in winter, and even pressed into oils, apricots are deeply cherished in Hunza. Karim credits them with keeping him strong and healthy, and he may be onto something. Apricots are packed with antioxidants, fibre, and nutrients. And while we might not have Hunza apricots, his joy in these simple foods reminds us to cherish local, seasonal fruits and incorporate nature's gifts into our daily diets.

Karim's saying, "Aram bay ostar agásh chu kharbay biush," speaks to a core Hunza belief: movement is essential to life. "If you sit too much, you get old quickly." In Hunza, movement isn't a chore or an obligation, it's woven into the fabric of their daily lives. Karim and his wife, Noor, still move, cook, weave, and tend to their fields. This idea that constant, gentle activity keeps the body youthful challenges the modern notion that we need formal exercise to stay fit. Instead, Hunza teaches us that our bodies thrive on natural, consistent movement.

When I asked Karim what made life in Hunza so joyful, his answer was immediate: family. Living close to his children and grandchildren, sharing meals and stories, and having a deep sense of connection brings Karim happiness and keeps his heart young. In a world where isolation and loneliness are increasingly common, the Hunza way serves as a reminder that our well-being is deeply tied to the people around us. Family, friends, and community are the threads that keep life meaningful and vibrant.

Karim's faith, similarly to Ruth's from California, is an integral part of his daily life, bringing peace and grounding him in a sense of purpose. "Every day, I am thankful," he told me. In Hunza, they see life as a gift, with the mountains, fresh air, and glacier water as blessings to be respected. This daily gratitude, a humble appreciation of what they have, creates a resilient, peaceful outlook on life. Karim's words reminded me that gratitude doesn't require grand gestures; it can be as simple as appreciating the natural world around us.

My personal take-away was however Karim's message to those of us in the fast-paced world beyond Hunza: **slow down**. "The world outside Hunza feels too fast, like people are running but don't know where they are going." In Hunza, people know where they are because they are deeply rooted in their land and community. Karim's advice was to take time to eat, time to move, and time to talk to your neighbours. **This notion of living in the present, rather than rushing through life, feels almost revolutionary in our busy world.**

My Takeaway
Reflecting on the beautiful stories and wisdom shared by the remarkable people I met in these long-lived communities, there's an undeniable thread weaving their lives together, despite differences in culture, geography, and lifestyle, there are common themes that contribute to their longevity. What struck me most was how these communities embrace simplicity, purpose, community, and a gentle, joyful approach to life.
Here are the themes that resonated across Okinawa, Sardinia, Ikaria, Nicoya, Loma Linda, and Hunza Valley.

Purposeful Living: A Reason to Get Up Each Morning
Each person I spoke with had a deep sense of purpose that brought structure and meaning to their daily life. In Okinawa, they call it *ikigai*; in Nicoya, it's known as *plan de vida*. For people like Haruto-san in Okinawa, it's the satisfaction of working in his field and feeding his family; for don Roberto in Nicoya, it's teaching his great grandchildren carpentry and caring for his community. This sense of purpose gives their lives direction, keeping them active, engaged, and mentally resilient. It's a reminder that we all need something meaningful to look forward to, whether it's spending time with loved ones, nurturing a skill, or contributing to our communities.

Simplicity in Movement: Life as Natural Exercise
In each of these communities, physical activity isn't about going to the gym or following a strict regimen. Instead, movement is woven into daily life, arising naturally from farming, gardening, walking, and even dancing. In Hunza, Karim and his wife stay active by tending to their fields, carrying water, and weaving, while in Sardinia, Signora

Rosa climbs hills and tends to her garden and chickens. This approach contrasts with our compartmentalized view of exercise, reminding us that our bodies thrive on natural, gentle movement. As Karim said, "If you sit too much, you get old quickly", words that capture the essence of movement as a way to maintain youthfulness and vitality.

Eating Mindfully and Moderately: Food as Nourishment, Not Overindulgence
One of the most common themes was a simple yet nourishing approach to food. None of the people I met followed restrictive diets; instead, they ate a variety of whole, seasonal foods grown locally, often from their own land. In Okinawa, Haruto-san spoke of "*hara hachi bu*", the practice of eating until you're 80% full. This mindful approach to eating was echoed across all regions. Meals are also communal and slow, an opportunity to connect with family and friends. Whether it's apricots in Hunza, Cannonau wine in Sardinia, or beans and corn in Nicoya, these communities remind us that food can be a source of health and joy without the excess.

Community and Connection: A Pillar of Emotional Health
One of the most beautiful similarities across the communities was the strength of their social bonds. In Villagrande Strisaili, Rosa's family lives nearby, bringing fresh bread and sharing meals, while in Ikaria, Yiannis talks of neighbours who join him daily for coffee and conversation. Each community has a support network, friends, family, and neighbours who help in times of need and celebrate together in times of joy. The power of community is more than just companionship; it provides emotional security, purpose, and a buffer against loneliness. These connections keep them grounded, happy, and less stressed, reinforcing how crucial social interaction is to our mental and physical health.

Faith, Gratitude, and a Peaceful Outlook on Life
For many, faith plays a central role in their lives. Ruth in Loma Linda begins her day with quiet prayer, and Karim in Hunza gives thanks daily for his family and the beauty of his surroundings. This sense of gratitude and respect for life's blessings brings them peace, creating a resilient and positive mindset. Many people, like Yiannis

from Ikaria, spoke of not letting stress become a burden. His advice was to "slow down and enjoy the faces of the people you love." Across these regions, faith, gratitude, and peace are interwoven, reminding us that a content mind supports a healthy body.

Joy in Everyday Life: Celebrating Small Moments

Perhaps what struck me most was the joy each person found in everyday moments. From Haruto-san's joy in planting seeds to Rosa's laughter with her grandchildren and Yiannis' stories shared over a glass of wine, these moments create a life filled with happiness, connection, and meaning. None of these people are in a hurry; instead, they savour each day and take time to notice the small pleasures, a shared meal, a good conversation, a sunset over the hills. This approach is in stark contrast to our often-rushed lives, where we overlook the beauty of the present in pursuit of future goals.

The simplest message

Live in the present, enjoy it, break bread with those you love, live a life full of laughter, wine and pie, be thankful for those in your life and the land we live on. Respect the animals and the land and above all - have purpose. This may oversimplify it but: being happy equals a longer, healthier life. Everyone I interviewed thought they were rich. So many people with large houses or cars or bank balances will never feel rich or content. To be happy you need to find the riches in what you have.

CHAPTER 2
Eating for Longevity

Let's be honest, food is one of life's greatest pleasures. It's not just fuel; it's the centrepiece of so many of our most cherished moments. Think about it: a Sunday roast with your family, sharing dessert over a good gossip with friends, or that one comforting meal you always crave when you're feeling under the weather. Food is entwined with our memories, our culture, and our wellbeing. But what if I told you that your daily choices in the kitchen could do more than just satisfy your taste buds, they could actually shape how well you age?

Yes, what you put on your plate can be one of the most powerful tools for living a long, vibrant, and healthy life. Food is medicine, nourishment, and a secret weapon in the fight against the march of time. But here's the thing: you don't have to resign yourself to a lifetime of bland salads or give up all your favourite foods, it is about enjoying a variety of delicious, nutrient-packed foods that are scientifically proven to support your health, now and in the decades to come.

The Role of Nutrition in Aging: What You Eat Can Change Everything

We've all heard the saying, "You are what you eat," but when it comes to aging, that phrase takes on a whole new level of importance. Your diet isn't just about how you look in your jeans or whether you can button your favourite blouse comfortably. It's about how well your cells function, how resilient your body is to disease, and even how long you live. Studies show that diet alone accounts for a massive part of your health outcomes, perhaps even more than genetics. So, while you can't change your DNA, you can certainly alter how those genes express themselves, simply by changing what's on your plate.

The food you eat acts like a set of instructions for your body, affecting everything from inflammation and immune function to brain health and energy levels. Nutrient-rich foods provide the building blocks your cells need to repair, regenerate, and function optimally. Meanwhile, highly processed foods filled with sugars, trans fats, and artificial ingredients can do the opposite, triggering inflammation, oxidative stress, and metabolic issues that accelerate aging. In short, food can be your best ally, or your worst enemy, in the quest for a longer healthspan.

But here's the good news: the key to using food as medicine isn't about following a restrictive diet or counting every calorie. It's about making informed, nourishing choices that align with your body's needs. The goal is to adopt dietary patterns that support longevity and healthspan by prioritising nutrient-dense, anti-inflammatory, and balanced meals.

Key Dietary Patterns for Women's Healthspan: What to Eat and Why

Let's dive into some of the most effective dietary patterns for boosting healthspan. These aren't just trendy "diets of the month"; they're backed by robust scientific research and are particularly beneficial for women. As we age, hormonal shifts, bone density changes, and increased risk of chronic disease become part of the picture, making it crucial to adapt our nutrition accordingly. The following patterns provide the essential nutrients, antioxidants, and balance needed to thrive at any stage of life.

1. The Mediterranean Culinary Lifestyle: A Delicious Path to Longevity

When it comes to healthspan, the Mediterranean diet is the gold standard. It's not about cutting out food groups or obsessing over portions; it's about savouring real, wholesome food that's bursting with flavour. Think of it as a celebration of life on a plate. This way of eating is rich in fruits, vegetables, whole grains, lean proteins (like fish and poultry), and healthy fats (hello, olive oil and nuts!).

The beauty of the Mediterranean diet is that it's inherently anti-inflammatory and packed with antioxidants, which help protect your cells from damage and reduce the risk of heart disease, cognitive decline, and even some cancers. But let's not overlook the fact that it's also downright delicious, who wouldn't want to dig into a fresh Greek salad or a perfectly grilled piece of fish drizzled with lemon and herbs?

2. The Plant-Based Approach: Powering Up with Plants

No, you don't have to give up your Sunday roast to reap the benefits of a plant-based diet, but incorporating more plant-based meals into your week can have a dramatic impact on your health. Plant-based eating isn't just for vegans; it's for anyone looking to increase their intake of vegetables, fruits, legumes, and whole grains. These foods are high in fibre, vitamins, and minerals, which support digestive health, help regulate hormones and provide essential nutrients for aging gracefully.

Studies show that women who eat more plant-based diets tend to have lower rates of hypertension, obesity, and heart disease. Plus, the fibre found in these foods helps maintain a healthy gut microbiome, something that's increasingly linked to everything from mood and metabolism to immunity and, yes, longevity.

3. The Anti-Inflammatory Eating Habit: Keeping Your Body Cool, Calm, and Collected

Inflammation is like a fire smouldering in your body. When it's short-term, it's helpful, think of it as your body's natural defence system kicking in to fight off illness or injury. But when it's chronic, inflammation becomes one of the biggest drivers of aging and disease. The anti-inflammatory lifestyle is all about extinguishing that flame, focusing on foods that reduce inflammation and keeping out the ones that fan the flames.

This means lots of colourful fruits and vegetables, omega-3-rich foods like salmon and flaxseeds, and anti-inflammatory spices such as turmeric and ginger. It's about balancing your meals with whole grains, lean proteins, and healthy fats, while cutting back on processed foods, refined sugars, and excessive alcohol. An anti-inflammatory diet won't just help you feel better in the short term; it'll pay dividends for your health in the long run.

Anti-Inflammatory Foods to Prioritise: Nature's Best Remedies

So, what exactly should you be filling your plate with? Here's a quick peek at some of the most powerful anti-inflammatory foods you can add to your diet:

- **Berries**: Blueberries, strawberries, and raspberries are bursting with antioxidants called anthocyanins, which help combat oxidative stress.
- **Leafy Greens**: Spinach, kale, and Swiss chard are packed with vitamins, minerals, and anti-inflammatory compounds.
- **Fatty Fish**: Salmon, sardines, and mackerel are rich in omega-3 fatty acids, known to lower inflammation and support heart health.
- **Nuts and Seeds**: Almonds, walnuts, chia seeds, and flaxseeds are high in healthy fats and fibre, promoting overall wellbeing.
- **Turmeric**: The golden spice has potent anti-inflammatory properties, thanks to its active compound, curcumin.
- **Green Tea**: Swap your usual cuppa for a soothing green tea, it's packed with polyphenols that fight inflammation and support brain health.

Superfoods That Boost Longevity: Your Secret Weapons

The term "superfoods" might seem a bit trendy, but these nutritional powerhouses really do pack a punch when it comes to boosting longevity. Superfoods are packed with nutrients, antioxidants, and other compounds that go above and beyond basic nourishment. Incorporating them into your diet can help reduce the risk of chronic diseases, improve brain function, and keep your energy levels steady.

Blueberries: Often hailed as the king of superfoods, these tiny berries are filled with antioxidants that support brain health, reduce oxidative stress, and may even improve memory.
Dark Chocolate: Yes, you read that right, dark chocolate (in moderation) is loaded with flavonoids that can improve heart health and lower blood pressure.
Cruciferous Vegetables: That's Broccoli, cauliflower, and Brussels sprouts to you and me, rich in sulforaphane, a compound that helps detoxify the body and protect against cancer.
Garlic: With its potent anti-inflammatory and immune-boosting properties, garlic is a must-have in your healthspan arsenal.

Olive Oil: A staple of the Mediterranean diet, extra virgin olive oil is packed with healthy monounsaturated fats and polyphenols that support heart and brain health.
Matcha: This finely ground green tea powder is a concentrated source of antioxidants and has been shown to boost metabolism and protect against chronic disease.

Balancing your macronutrients, carbohydrates, proteins, and fats, is crucial for maintaining energy, supporting muscle function, and keeping your metabolism ticking along nicely. While it's easy to get bogged down in the numbers, the key is to focus on quality over quantity. Here's a quick breakdown of how to balance your macros:

- **Carbohydrates:** Opt for complex carbs like sweet potatoes, quinoa, and whole grains, which release energy slowly and keep blood sugar levels steady.
- **Proteins:** Include lean sources such as chicken, turkey, tofu, and beans to support muscle maintenance and repair.
- **Fats:** Prioritise healthy fats like avocados, olive oil, and nuts, which are essential for brain health and hormone production.

The goal is to create a balance that works for *you*. Some women feel best with higher protein, others prefer more plant-based fats. There's no one-size-fits-all formula, but by focusing on whole, unprocessed foods and listening to your body, you can find the sweet spot that keeps you feeling energised and satisfied.

The Benefits of Intermittent Fasting and Calorie Restriction: Eating Less, Living More

If there's one thing that's gaining a lot of attention in the world of nutrition and longevity, it's the concept of intermittent fasting (IF) and calorie restriction. Now, before you roll your eyes and think this is just another fad diet, let's clarify: intermittent fasting and calorie restriction are not about starving yourself. They're about giving your body a chance to rest, reset, and repair itself, unlocking health benefits that go way beyond weight management.

Intermittent fasting involves cycling between periods of eating and fasting. There are many different styles, from the popular 16:8 method (16 hours of fasting, 8 hours of eating) to alternate-day fasting, where you reduce your intake every other day. Meanwhile, calorie restriction is about reducing your overall calorie intake by 20-30% without skimping on essential nutrients. So, you're eating less, but what you're eating is packed with everything your body needs.

But why do this? Well, when you give your body a break from constant eating, something magical happens. During the fasting period, your body switches gears and goes into repair mode. It triggers a process called *autophagy*, which literally means "self-eating." This isn't as gruesome as it sounds; in fact, it's a good thing! During autophagy, your body clears out damaged cells and proteins, making room for new, healthy ones. Think of it like tidying up your room, clearing out the clutter, and organising everything so it functions better.

What's more, both intermittent fasting and calorie restriction have been linked to lower risks of chronic diseases like diabetes and heart disease. They can improve insulin sensitivity, reduce inflammation, and even activate longevity genes like SIRT1, which play a role in DNA repair and cellular health. In other words, these practices can help slow down the aging process at the cellular level.

But don't worry, this doesn't mean you have to skip breakfast every day or go hungry. The beauty of these approaches is that you can tailor them to suit your lifestyle and goals. Perhaps start by fasting for 12 hours overnight (from 8 p.m. to 8 a.m.) and see how you feel. As you get more comfortable, you can extend your fasting window or try a full day of calorie reduction once a week. The key is to find a rhythm that works for *you*, one that feels sustainable and doesn't interfere with your enjoyment of food.

It's Not Just What You Eat, But How You Eat: The Art of Mindful Eating

Now, let's talk about a concept that's as important as the food itself: *how* you eat. If you're wolfing down your lunch while answering emails or barely tasting your dinner because you're catching up on your favourite show, you're not alone. But here's the thing, how you eat can be just as influential as what you eat when it comes to healthspan.

Mindful eating is all about being present and savouring your food. It's about engaging all your senses, taking the time to appreciate the colours, textures, and flavours. Why does this matter? For one, it helps you tune into your body's hunger and fullness cues, making it easier to eat just the right amount. It also reduces stress, which is a sneaky contributor to inflammation and weight gain. And, most importantly, it makes eating a joyful, pleasurable experience, a ritual that nourishes your mind as well as your body.

Try setting aside distractions at mealtimes. Eat slowly and take a moment to breathe between bites. Notice how your food makes you feel, energised, satisfied, or perhaps sluggish? This simple practice can transform your relationship with food, making healthy eating feel less like a chore and more like self-care.

The Power of Hydration: Don't Forget to Drink Up
While food tends to steal the spotlight, let's not forget about one of the most fundamental aspects of the Healthspan Diet: *hydration*. Water is essential for every function in your body, from digestion and circulation to temperature regulation and detoxification. Yet so many of us wander around in a state of mild dehydration, which can leave us feeling tired, foggy-headed, and more prone to overeating.

Aim to drink at least 6-8 glasses of water a day, more if you're active. If plain water isn't your thing, jazz it up with a slice of lemon, cucumber, or a sprig of mint. Herbal teas are another great option, offering hydration with a hint of flavour. And don't forget that plenty of fruits and vegetables, like watermelon, cucumber, and oranges, are naturally hydrating, giving you a double whammy of nutrients and water.

The bottom line? Hydration isn't just about avoiding thirst. It's about keeping your cells functioning optimally, supporting detoxification, and even improving your mood and energy levels. So, make it a habit to keep that water bottle close and sip regularly throughout the day.

Breaking the Rules: Guilt-Free Indulgences and Finding Balance

Let's be real for a second: life is too short to never have a slice of cake or a glass of wine. The Healthspan culinary lifestyle is not about denying yourself the pleasures of good food but rather finding a balance that supports your health without sacrificing joy. The key is to keep indulgences as just that, occasional treats that you truly savour, rather than daily habits that derail your health goals.

When you do decide to indulge, do it mindfully. Choose the best quality you can afford, a really good dark chocolate bar instead of a cheap candy, or a beautiful glass of red wine instead of a sugary cocktail. Enjoy every bite or sip and then move on without guilt or regret. This approach allows you to satisfy cravings while staying on track with your Lifestyle Wellness Plan.

Remember, food is about pleasure and nourishment. It's a means to support your body, yes, but it's also a source of joy, creativity, and connection. So, embrace the Healthspan lifestyle not as a set of rules, but as a flexible, joyful way of eating that celebrates what your body can do and how it feels when it's fuelled well.

Putting It All Together: Building Your Healthspan Plate

It doesn't have to be complicated. Think of it like building a vibrant, nutrient-packed plate that leaves you feeling satisfied and energised. Start with a foundation of colourful vegetables (think greens, reds, purples, and oranges), add a quality protein source (like beans, fish, or lean meats), sprinkle in some healthy fats (avocado, olive oil, or nuts), and round it out with a serving of complex carbs (such as quinoa or sweet potatoes).

Feel free to mix and match based on your preferences and needs. The goal is to keep your plate balanced, nourishing, and most importantly, enjoyable. There's no need to follow a rigid meal plan; just aim for variety, freshness, and a rainbow of colours.

By making small, consistent changes to your diet, you can transform your healthspan one meal at a time. Each meal is an opportunity to support your body, protect your cells, and boost your vitality. And remember, this isn't just about what you eat today, it's about building habits that will serve you well for years to come, making your later decades as vibrant and joyful as your younger ones.

Your Lifestyle Wellness Plan
As you progress through this chapter, take a moment to think about where you are with your nutrition. Are there simple swaps you could make to increase your intake of anti-inflammatory foods? Could you try adding an extra serving of vegetables to your dinner or swapping out refined grains for whole ones? Could you experiment with a few days of intermittent fasting to see how your body responds?

This is a journey, not a destination. It's about making gradual changes that add up over time, so don't feel pressured to overhaul your entire way of eating overnight. Instead, pick one or two ideas from this chapter and start incorporating them into your routine. Once they become habits, add a few more.

Nutrition Myths Busted: Separating Fact from Fiction
You've probably heard it all when it comes to nutrition advice "carbs are the enemy," "fats make you fat," or "you need to eat like a caveman to be healthy." But let's face it, the world of nutrition is full of more myths than an ancient Greek epic. It's no wonder so many of us are left feeling confused and overwhelmed by all the conflicting information. One day, we're told to eat more eggs for protein; the next day, eggs are suddenly as bad as smoking! With so much noise, how do we figure out what's actually true?

Well, you've come to the right place. In this section, we're going to take a sledgehammer to some of the biggest dietary myths out there. We'll talk about carbs, fats, proteins, supplements, and how to sift through the latest health headlines without wanting to throw your avocado toast at the TV. Whether you're a health enthusiast or someone who just wants to eat without guilt and confusion, this is where we get real, dispel the nonsense, and help you build a nutrition plan that's sustainable, realistic, and backed by science. So, grab a cuppa and let's dive in!

Myth 1: Carbs Are the Enemy ~ Avoid Them at All Costs!

Let's start with one of the most pervasive myths out there: "Carbs make you fat." This myth has been doing the rounds for decades, leaving many of us feeling guilty for even looking at a slice of bread. But here's the truth, carbs are not the enemy! In fact, they're a crucial part of a balanced diet, providing us with energy and essential nutrients.

The problem isn't carbs per se, but the *type* of carbs. There's a world of difference between a bowl of quinoa and a doughnut. Whole grains, fruits, vegetables, and legumes are full of fibre, vitamins, and minerals. These "good carbs" are digested slowly, keeping you fuller for longer and preventing those mid-afternoon slumps. On the other hand, refined carbs, like white bread, sugary cereals, and pastries, are stripped of their nutrients and can cause blood sugar spikes that leave you craving more.

So, the next time someone tells you to ditch all carbs, remember that the key is choosing the *right* ones. Carbs are not the enemy; they're just misunderstood. Think of them as the nice-but-shy kid at school, if you give them a chance, you might discover they're actually pretty great.

Myth 2: All Fats Are Bad ~ They'll Clog Your Arteries!

Ah, the '80s and '90s, a time when fat was Public Enemy Number One. From low-fat yoghurts to fat-free biscuits (packed with sugar, mind you), everything was designed to cut the fat out of our diets. But now we know that not all fats are created equal. In fact, some fats are downright essential for good health.

The fats you want to avoid are the trans fats found in processed foods like margarine, fast food, and packaged snacks. These have been linked to heart disease and inflammation. But healthy fats, like the ones found in olive oil, avocados, nuts, seeds, and oily fish, are crucial for brain health, hormone production, and even maintaining a healthy weight. They're the good guys, the superheroes of the fat world.

One of the most frustrating myths is the idea that eating fat makes you fat. Here's the deal: fat is more calorie-dense than carbs and protein, so it's easy to overeat. But it's also incredibly satiating, which means it can help prevent overeating and mindless snacking. Instead of fearing fat, try incorporating more healthy fats into your diet and see how much more satisfied you feel.

So, say goodbye to the "fat phobia" of the past, and embrace fats in all their creamy, nutty, delicious glory—just be smart about which ones you choose.

Myth 3: Protein Is King ~ The More, the Better!
Thanks to the rise of high-protein diets, it seems like we're all a bit obsessed with this macronutrient. From protein shakes to protein bars and even protein-enriched cereal, it's become a bit of a craze. But is more protein really better?

While protein is crucial for building and repairing tissues, supporting immune function, and maintaining muscle mass, most people are already getting enough. Unless you're a professional bodybuilder or training for a marathon, you don't need to be guzzling protein shakes with every meal. Overloading on protein can even backfire, putting strain on your kidneys and crowding out other essential nutrients.

Instead of obsessing over protein, focus on getting a balance of all three macronutrients, carbs, fats, and proteins, at each meal. Include a variety of protein sources like beans, nuts, seeds, eggs, and lean meats. But there's no need to wolf down that extra chicken breast if you're already full. More isn't always better; balance is key.

Myth 4: Supplements Are a Shortcut to Health ~ Pills Over Food!
Walk down any health store aisle, and it's easy to be seduced by the shiny bottles promising to "boost immunity," "burn fat," or "increase energy." But here's a little secret, supplements are just that, supplements. They're meant to *supplement* a healthy diet, not replace it.

The truth is most people don't need a whole arsenal of pills. If you're eating a varied, balanced diet, you're likely getting the vitamins and minerals you need. The exception is if you have specific deficiencies or dietary restrictions, like vitamin D if you're not getting enough sun, or B12 if you're vegetarian. But for most of us, popping a multivitamin isn't going to turn us into superwomen overnight.

Instead of spending your money on a cabinet full of pills, invest in high-quality, nutrient-dense foods. Colourful vegetables, fresh fruits, whole grains, and lean proteins will give you far more bang for your buck. And if you're unsure, get a blood test and talk to your doctor before loading up on unnecessary supplements. Remember, there's no magic pill that replaces a healthy lifestyle.

Myth 5: Fad Diets Are the Answer ~The More Extreme, the Better!

The keto diet, juice cleanses, cabbage soup diet, grapefruit diet, the list of extreme diets promising rapid weight loss is endless. And while these diets might help you shed a few pounds in the short term, they're not sustainable, and they can do more harm than good in the long run. They won't help you live longer and healthier!

Fad diets usually work by slashing calories, cutting out major food groups, or creating a massive deficit. But they often leave you feeling deprived, grumpy, and constantly hungry. And here's the kicker: once you go back to eating normally, you gain the weight back, and sometimes even more.

Instead of jumping on the latest diet bandwagon, focus on building healthy, enjoyable eating habits that you can stick with for life. The best diet is the one you don't even realise you're on, because it's just a natural part of how you eat. Balance, variety, and moderation are the keys to long-term success.

Myth 6: You Have to Eat Small, Frequent Meals to Boost Metabolism

For years, we were told that eating five or six small meals a day would "keep the metabolism firing" and prevent weight gain. But recent research suggests that meal timing is far less important than *what* you're eating. There's no magic number of meals; it's all about finding what works for your body and lifestyle.

Some people thrive on three square meals a day, while others prefer grazing. The key is listening to your body and eating when you're genuinely hungry. This isn't rocket science. If you're always snacking because you think it'll help burn more calories, but you end up eating more throughout the day, then it's not serving you.

Myth 7: Intermittent Fasting Is Just Another Diet Fad

Let's clear this up, intermittent fasting (IF) is not a diet; it's an eating *pattern*. It doesn't dictate *what* you eat, but *when* you eat. And while it's been hyped up lately, it's not a new concept. Our ancestors naturally fasted when food was scarce, and many religious practices incorporate fasting.

The benefits of intermittent fasting go beyond weight management. It has been linked to improved insulin sensitivity, enhanced brain health, and even a longer lifespan. But it's not a magic bullet, and it's not for everyone. If you're the kind of person who gets "hangry" by lunchtime, skipping breakfast probably isn't going to make you a happy bunny. The key is experimenting to see if it suits your lifestyle.

Myth 8: Calorie Restriction ~ The Fountain of Youth?

Calorie restriction (CR) has been studied for decades as a potential way to extend lifespan and delay ageing. It works by creating a slight energy deficit, which triggers a survival response in the body. But while it might help some people live longer, it's not without risks. Over-restricting can lead to malnutrition, weakened bones, and a host of other issues.

Instead of focusing on cutting calories, aim for *nutrient density*, or packing as many vitamins, minerals, and antioxidants into your meals as possible. This way, you're nourishing your body and supporting your long-term health without feeling deprived.

Building a Sustainable, Long-Term Eating Plan

Building a sustainable, long-term eating plan means focusing on creating a positive relationship with food, one where you're nourishing yourself, enjoying your meals, and feeling energised rather than restricted or guilty. So, how do you create this plan? It starts by making small, gradual changes that you can stick to, not overhauling your entire diet overnight.

First, think about your meals as a balancing act. Aim for a variety of colourful vegetables, lean proteins, whole grains, and healthy fats on your plate. The more colours and textures, the better! This isn't just to make your meals look pretty on Instagram (though that's a bonus), mostly different colours mean a wider range of nutrients, each with its own unique benefits. Eating the rainbow is not just a whimsical phrase; it's sound nutritional advice.

Next, focus on tuning into your hunger and fullness cues. This might sound simple, but many of us have lost touch with these signals, thanks to years of dieting or eating mindlessly while watching TV. Start paying attention to how you feel before, during, and after meals. Are you eating because you're hungry or just because it's a certain time? Are you still eating even when you feel full, out of habit or for emotional reasons? By becoming more mindful of your eating patterns, you can start to develop a healthier, more intuitive approach to food.

Also, give yourself permission to enjoy food! For many women, food has become a source of stress and anxiety. But remember, food is not just fuel, it's meant to be enjoyed. It's a source of pleasure, a way to connect with others, and a form of self-care. Don't demonise certain foods or think of them as "bad" or "off-limits." When you take away the stigma, you're less likely to overindulge when you do have them.

One of the best ways to build a sustainable eating plan is to focus on adding more good things rather than taking things away. Think about what you can add to your diet to support your health, more veggies, more fibre, more water rather than obsessing over cutting out certain foods. This approach shifts the mindset from one of deprivation to one of abundance, making it easier to stick with long-term.

Navigating the World of Nutrition Advice: What to Believe?
By now, you might be thinking, "All of this sounds great, but how do I know who to trust?" It's a valid question. The internet is flooded with self-proclaimed "nutrition gurus" touting miracle diets and instant fixes. One minute, you're told that dairy is a must-have for bone health; the next, you're warned that it's a major cause of inflammation. So, how do you sift through the noise?

First, consider the source. Be wary of anyone who uses extreme language or promises miraculous results ("Eat this one food and burn fat fast!"). Health and nutrition are complex, and real experts will acknowledge that there's rarely a one-size-fits-all answer.

Secondly, beware of nutrition advice that's heavily tied to selling a product. If someone's trying to convince you that their expensive shake or supplement is the missing piece of your health puzzle, take it with a pinch of salt. While some supplements can be helpful, they should complement, not replace, a healthy diet.

Lastly, listen to your body. You are the expert on how you feel. If a particular diet or way of eating makes you feel sluggish, deprived, or unwell, then it's probably not right for you, no matter what the latest study or influencer says. Nutrition science is always evolving, and what works for one person may not work for another. Learning to trust yourself is just as important as understanding the science.

The Dangers of Diet Culture: Why Fad Diets Can Do More Harm Than Good

We've all been there, yes me too, seduced by the promise of a quick fix. The juice cleanse that will "detoxify" your body, the meal plan that promises to help you drop a dress size in a week, the magic pill that'll melt away fat without any effort. But here's the thing—if these diets sound too good to be true, it's because they are.

Fad diets are often based on pseudoscience or oversimplified truths. They might help you lose weight quickly, but they rarely lead to sustainable results. More importantly, they can be harmful. Extreme calorie restriction can slow down your metabolism, making it harder to keep weight off in the long run. Cutting out entire food groups can lead to nutrient deficiencies. And yo-yo dieting, the cycle of losing and regaining weight, can wreak havoc on your body and your mental health.

The problem with fad diets is that they're built on the idea that weight loss equals health, which is simply not true. Health is about much more than what you weigh; it's about how you feel, how your body functions, and your overall well-being. That's why this book is all about healthspan, living a longer, healthier, more vibrant life, not just squeezing into a smaller pair of jeans.

So, the next time you see a diet that promises to "melt away belly fat in 7 days," ask yourself: is this really sustainable? Will I be able to live like this forever? If the answer is no, then it's time to look for something more balanced and realistic. The only plan worth sticking to is one that you can imagine following for the rest of your life, not just for a few weeks.

The Science of Intermittent Fasting and Calorie Restriction: What's the Deal?

Intermittent fasting and calorie restriction have been getting a lot of buzz lately, and for good reason. Unlike typical fad diets, these approaches have some solid science backing them up. Intermittent fasting involves cycling between periods of eating and fasting, such as the popular 16:8 method, where you fast for 16 hours and eat within an 8-hour window. The benefits? It can improve insulin sensitivity, reduce inflammation, and even promote cellular repair through a process called autophagy.

But here's the catch, it's not for everyone. If you're someone who struggles with disordered eating or a history of restrictive dieting, fasting might not be a healthy choice. The key is to listen to your body and approach it with a sense of flexibility. If it suits your lifestyle and helps you feel good, great! If not, there's no need to force it.

Calorie restriction, on the other hand, involves eating slightly fewer calories than your body needs, which has been shown to extend lifespan in various animals. But it's not about starving yourself; it's about choosing nutrient-dense, low-calorie foods that provide everything your body needs without excess. It's a concept known as "nutrient density" over "caloric abundance."

Building Your Lifestyle Wellness Plan: How to Eat for Longevity and Joy

So, what's the takeaway from all of this? The perfect diet doesn't exist. There's no one magical way of eating that will work for everyone. Instead, it's about finding what works for *you*. Building a long-term eating plan is about balance, enjoyment, and sustainability. It's about nourishing your body, mind, and spirit in a way that enhances your life, rather than detracting from it.

Start small. Maybe you add an extra serving of vegetables to your dinner, swap out sugary snacks for whole fruit, or experiment with a new way of cooking. Whatever it is, make it enjoyable, make it personal, and make it sustainable. Your Lifestyle Wellness Plan isn't a diet, it's a lifestyle. One where you're empowered to make choices that make you feel your best, for life.

At the end of the day, what you eat should help you feel energised, vibrant, and happy. It should support your goals, not restrict you from living your life. So, here's to letting go of the myths and embracing a new approach to nutrition—one that's focused on living younger, longer, and with more joy. Cheers to that!

The Hormone Connection: Eating for Hormonal Balance
Let's talk about hormones. Those little chemical messengers we often blame for our bad moods, chocolate cravings, and why a seemingly simple day can suddenly spiral into an emotional rollercoaster. But hormones are so much more than the culprits behind the occasional tears at a TV advert or that sudden craving for something salty. They're the body's conductors, orchestrating everything from energy levels and metabolism to sleep, mood, and, of course, reproductive health. The truth is, keeping our hormones in balance is crucial for overall wellbeing. And what's one of the best ways to ensure these chemical messengers stay on good terms with us? Through what we eat.

If you've ever wondered why some days you feel invincible while on others you can barely drag yourself out of bed, hormones might be at play. And they're sensitive little things, easily influenced by stress, sleep (or lack of it), and perhaps most importantly, our diet. The good news is, eating for hormonal health doesn't mean completely overhauling your pantry or following an obscure, joyless eating regime. With a few savvy swaps and a little understanding, you can fuel your body in a way that supports hormonal harmony, helping you to feel energised, balanced, and more *you*.

Understanding the Link Between Diet and Hormones

First things first, what exactly is the connection between food and hormones? In short, everything you eat influences the production and function of your hormones. Our bodies are finely tuned machines, and just as putting the wrong fuel in a car will cause it to splutter and stall, the wrong diet can throw your hormones out of whack.

Different foods affect your body's hormonal balance in different ways. For example, refined sugars and simple carbs (like white bread and pastries) can spike insulin levels, a hormone that helps control blood sugar. When insulin levels are high over time, the body can become less sensitive to it, leading to something called insulin resistance, a key factor in hormonal imbalances and conditions like polycystic ovary syndrome (PCOS).

And it's not just insulin. Oestrogen, cortisol, thyroid hormones, and many others are all influenced by what you eat. For women, this relationship becomes even more significant during times of hormonal transition—like menopause or perimenopause, when the natural ebb and flow of hormone levels can lead to symptoms like hot flushes, mood swings, and weight gain. Understanding how food affects your hormones can be a game-changer in managing these transitions.

Foods That Support Hormonal Health

If there's one takeaway here, it's that a hormone-friendly diet isn't complicated. It's all about choosing whole, nutrient-rich foods that support your body's natural processes and steering clear of those that mess with them. So, what should be on your plate?

Healthy Fats: Hormones are made from fats, so you need good-quality fats to keep them happy. Think avocados, nuts, seeds, and olive oil. Omega-3 fatty acids (found in oily fish like salmon, sardines, and mackerel, as well as chia seeds and flaxseeds) are particularly important because they help reduce inflammation, a major disruptor of hormonal balance.

Protein Power: Proteins are essential for hormone production and the enzymes that help hormones do their job. Include lean meats, eggs, tofu, beans, and legumes in your diet. Also, don't shy away from plant-based proteins like lentils and chickpeas, which offer the added benefit of being rich in fibre, a crucial nutrient for regulating blood sugar and, by extension, insulin levels.

Complex Carbohydrates: Not all carbs are the enemy. Whole grains, sweet potatoes, and fibrous vegetables like broccoli and carrots are your friends. These help stabilise blood sugar levels and keep insulin in check, which is particularly important for women dealing with PCOS or insulin resistance.

Leafy Greens: Kale, spinach, and Swiss chard are not just salad fluff. They're packed with magnesium; a mineral that helps regulate cortisol (the body's main stress hormone) and aids in oestrogen detoxification. They're also high in folate, which is essential for hormone production and mood regulation.

Cruciferous Vegetables: Broccoli, Brussels sprouts, cauliflower, these are hormone superfoods. They contain a compound called indole-3-carbinol, which helps metabolise oestrogen in the body, potentially reducing the risk of oestrogen-related conditions like fibroids and breast cancer.

Colourful Fruits and Veggies: Eat the rainbow! Different coloured fruits and vegetables provide a range of antioxidants, vitamins, and minerals that support overall hormonal health. Berries, for example, are packed with antioxidants that reduce oxidative stress—a factor that can disrupt hormones.

Fermented Foods: Your gut health is closely linked to hormone health, as your gut bacteria play a role in the regulation of hormones like oestrogen. Incorporating foods like yoghurt, sauerkraut (yuk!), kimchi, and kombucha can help keep your gut flora balanced and your hormones happy.

Managing Menopause Through Nutrition

When it comes to menopause, many women feel like they're fighting a losing battle against their own bodies. But diet can be a powerful ally during this stage of life. Certain foods can help manage common symptoms like hot flushes, weight gain, and mood changes.

For instance, phytoestrogens (more on those shortly) found in soy products, flaxseeds, and chickpeas can act like a milder form of oestrogen in the body, helping to ease symptoms caused by declining oestrogen levels. Additionally, calcium-rich foods (like dairy, leafy greens, and almonds) are crucial for bone health as oestrogen declines.

It's also worth focusing on foods that support liver function, as your liver plays a key role in metabolising hormones. Beets, leafy greens, and lemon water can help your liver detoxify more effectively, reducing the intensity of menopause symptoms.

How to Avoid Foods That Disrupt Your Hormones
Just as certain foods support hormonal balance, others can wreak havoc. For example:

Sugar: Sugar causes insulin to spike, and over time, chronically elevated insulin can lead to weight gain and insulin resistance, which in turn disrupts other hormones. Think of sugar as the ultimate hormonal hijacker.

Processed Foods: These are often loaded with unhealthy fats, additives, and chemicals that can mimic hormones in the body and interfere with their natural function. Trans fats, found in many fried and packaged foods, are particularly harmful and have been linked to an increased risk of hormone-related disorders.

Alcohol: Your liver is responsible for breaking down oestrogen, but alcohol adds extra stress, making it harder for your body to maintain balance. Regular alcohol consumption can raise oestrogen levels, contributing to weight gain and an increased risk of some cancers.

Caffeine: While a morning cup of coffee is a staple for many, too much caffeine can mess with cortisol levels, disrupting your sleep and leaving you feeling wired but tired. If you're struggling with anxiety or insomnia, consider cutting back.

The Role of Phytoestrogens in Women's Health
Phytoestrogens are plant-based compounds that resemble oestrogen and can have a balancing effect on hormone levels. Found in foods

like soy, flaxseeds, and lentils, phytoestrogens can attach to oestrogen receptors in the body, potentially helping to balance hormone levels during menopause.

But what about the worry that phytoestrogens can *increase* the risk of oestrogen-sensitive cancers? The research is mixed, but most studies suggest that, when consumed in moderate amounts, these foods are safe and may even have protective effects. It's all about moderation and choosing whole food sources rather than processed soy products.

The Role of Zinc and Magnesium in Men's Health
For men, zinc and magnesium are two key minerals that play an essential role in supporting healthy testosterone levels. These minerals are found in foods like pumpkin seeds, spinach, and almonds. Zinc, in particular, is critical for testosterone production and regulation, while magnesium supports muscle function and overall hormonal balance.

But what about the concern that taking too much zinc or magnesium might disrupt hormone levels or cause other health issues? The research shows that moderate consumption through whole food sources is generally safe and beneficial. Supplements should be used with caution and ideally under medical supervision, as excessive intake could lead to imbalances or unwanted side effects. It's all about maintaining balance and choosing nutrient-rich foods over relying heavily on supplements.

Creating a Hormone-Friendly Meal Plan
Designing a hormone-friendly meal plan doesn't have to be a chore. Start by focusing on balance, include healthy fats, lean proteins, and complex carbs in each meal, and aim for a variety of colours on your plate. For breakfast, think scrambled eggs with spinach and avocado. For lunch, perhaps a quinoa salad with grilled salmon and a sprinkling of seeds. Dinner could be a nourishing stew filled with beans, root vegetables, and greens.

For snacks, try hormone-supporting foods like a handful of nuts, a piece of dark chocolate (rich in magnesium), a cup of green tea (which contains compounds that support healthy hormone metabolism).

And remember to stay hydrated! Water is crucial for overall health and plays a significant role in the detoxification processes that help your body maintain hormonal balance.

The Benefits of Intermittent Fasting and Calorie Restriction
Intermittent fasting has gained popularity in recent years, and for good reason. Studies suggest that intermittent fasting can improve insulin sensitivity, reduce inflammation, and even support better brain health. By giving your body a break from constant digestion, you allow your cells to switch to "maintenance mode," a state where they repair and rejuvenate themselves.

However, fasting isn't a one-size-fits-all solution, especially for women. Extended fasting can sometimes cause hormonal disruptions by raising cortisol levels. If you're new to fasting, start with a simple 12-hour overnight fast (from dinner to breakfast the next day) and see how you feel. The goal is to find a pattern that works for *your* body.

Building a Sustainable, Long-Term Eating Plan
All the best intentions in the world won't help if your plan is too rigid or unrealistic. A sustainable eating plan is one that fits seamlessly into your life, leaving room for indulgences and the occasional glass of wine or slice of cake. It's not about being perfect; it's about creating habits that support your wellbeing in the long run.

I know I'm emphasising the point but think about adding, not restricting. Add more greens, more healthy fats, and more nutrient-dense foods rather than focusing on what to eliminate. When you fill your plate with the good stuff, there's naturally less room (and fewer cravings) for the not-so-good stuff. And remember, balance is key, life is too short to swear off chocolate forever!

Building a Lifestyle of Hormonal Health
Eating for hormonal balance is about more than just the food itself. It's about creating a lifestyle that supports all aspects of your wellbeing. This includes how you manage stress, how much you sleep, and even how connected you feel to the people around you. So while your meal choices are a critical piece of the puzzle, don't overlook the other factors that influence your hormonal health.

Take sleep, for example. Your hormones work on a carefully orchestrated schedule that's heavily influenced by your sleep-wake cycle, or circadian rhythm. If your sleep is erratic or inadequate, this can throw off cortisol production, leading to everything from sugar cravings to irritability. Creating a solid bedtime routine, limiting screen time in the evenings, and getting enough hours of shut eye can do wonders for your hormonal health.

Similarly, managing stress is crucial. When you're in a state of chronic stress, your body pumps out cortisol, a stress hormone that, over time, can interfere with the production of other hormones like thyroid hormones and oestrogen. This can lead to weight gain, low energy, and even digestive problems. Finding stress-relief strategies that work for you, whether that's yoga, meditation, or simply going for a walk in nature, will complement your hormone-friendly eating plan and boost your overall health.

Now's the time for takeaway: A Journey Worth Taking
Eating for hormonal balance isn't about quick fixes or crash diets. It's a long-term strategy that supports not just your hormones but your overall health, helping you feel your best at every stage of life. It's about listening to your body, experimenting with what works for you, and enjoying the process. You don't have to get it perfect right away, small, consistent changes add up over time.

As you explore different foods and see how they impact your energy, mood, and overall wellbeing, you'll start to notice patterns. Maybe that green smoothie in the morning leaves you feeling energised all day, or a hearty vegetable stew helps you feel nourished and calm in the evening. Keep a journal, make notes, and stay curious. This is your journey, and there's no one-size-fits-all solution.

The beauty of this approach is that it's flexible and adaptable. As your body changes, whether due to age, stress, or lifestyle shifts, you can adjust your diet accordingly. Think of it as tuning a musical instrument. Sometimes you might need more protein or healthy fats, while other times, your body might crave a boost of leafy greens or gut-friendly fermented foods.

Above all, remember to be kind to yourself. Your hormones are not your enemies; they're just trying to do their job, responding to the signals they're given. By nourishing your body with the right foods, managing your stress, and getting enough rest, you're setting the stage for a more balanced, vibrant, and healthier you.

So, as you move forward on your journey to hormonal balance, enjoy the process. Explore new foods, experiment with different meal patterns, and notice how even small changes can have a big impact on how you feel. Hormonal health isn't a destination; it's an ongoing relationship with your body that's worth investing in. Because when your hormones are in harmony, everything else just seems to fall into place.

A Final Word of Encouragement

By now, you might be thinking, "That's a lot to keep track of!" And yes, it can feel overwhelming at first. But take a deep breath and remind yourself that you don't have to do it all at once. Start small. Maybe begin by incorporating one hormone-friendly food into your diet each week or trying a new recipe that features healthy fats and lean protein. Little by little, these small changes will add up, creating a lifestyle that supports not only your hormonal health but your overall wellbeing.

You deserve to feel energised, balanced, and happy at every stage of life. Eating for hormonal health is just one piece of the puzzle, but it's a powerful one. With the right foods, a bit of patience, and a willingness to listen to your body's cues, you'll be amazed at what a difference it can make.

And remember, there's no "perfect" way to eat for hormonal health. Some days you'll have kale smoothies and salmon salads, and other days you'll reach for that slice of cake because, well, life's too short to skip dessert every time. And that's okay. The goal is balance, not perfection. This is about creating a way of eating and living that's sustainable, enjoyable, and supports your health for the long haul.

So go ahead, dig into that avocado toast, sprinkle those chia seeds on your breakfast, and toast to your health with a glass of kombucha.

Here's to a life of hormonal harmony, where every meal is a chance to nourish not just your body but your spirit too. Because when you eat well, you feel well. And when you feel well, you truly thrive.

In the end, that's what it's all about, living your best, most vibrant life, at every age and every stage. So grab your fork, embrace the power of food, and let's get those hormones dancing to the right tune! Cheers to a balanced, happy, and healthy you.

Lifestyle Wellness Plan: Eating for Longevity

Small Lifestyle Change	Current Habits	Goal/Action to Implement
Increase Nutrient-Dense Foods	Eat processed snacks during the day	Swap for nuts, seeds
Include Anti-Inflammatory Foods	Rarely eat fish or plant-based fats	Add fatty fish (salmon) or chia seeds twice a week to meals
Practice Mindful Eating	Often eat or snack while watching TV or working.	Set aside 20 minutes for mindful interrupted meals

How to Use This Table:
1. **Identify your current eating habits:** Are you reaching for unhealthy snacks during the day or skipping essential nutrients? Write it down.
2. **Set an achievable goal:** Pick one or two small changes to start with. For example, add a handful of berries or leafy greens to your meals or swap a sugary snack for something more nutrient-dense.
3. **Track your progress:** Keep an eye on how these changes make you feel. The goal is to create habits that will enhance your healthspan and be enjoyable enough to maintain in the long term.

By consistently making small, conscious choices, you'll be well on your way to eating for longevity and living a healthier, more vibrant life.

CHAPTER 3
Movement Matters

Building a Strong Body: The Foundations of Exercise
Imagine this: it's a bright morning, and you step out of bed feeling light, limber, and ready to take on the day. Your muscles are strong, your joints are supple, and your energy levels rival those of your younger self. You breeze through your morning routine, your mind sharp and focused, your mood uplifted. This isn't a dream, but a realistic vision of what regular exercise can do for you, no matter what age or stage of life you're at.

For too long, the conversation around exercise has focused on appearance, getting toned abs or losing a dress size. But in reality, exercise is so much more than that. It's about maintaining your independence, your mobility, and your mental sharpness well into your 70s, 80s, and beyond. It's about creating a strong body that can support you through all the adventures and challenges life throws at you, so you're able to enjoy the things you love without limitation.

Why Exercise is Crucial for Extending Healthspan
The benefits of exercise are practically endless. It's like the Swiss Army knife of health interventions, improving your physical, mental, and emotional wellbeing all at once. For starters, exercise keeps your heart, muscles, and bones strong. It boosts your energy levels, sharpens your focus, and even helps you sleep better. But its real magic lies in its ability to slow down and even reverse some of the effects of aging.

Regular physical activity has been shown to reduce the risk of chronic diseases like heart disease, diabetes, and osteoporosis. It also helps maintain muscle mass, which is crucial for keeping you steady on your feet and avoiding those dreaded falls that can lead to a cascade of health issues. And for the brain? Exercise is like a power-wash for your neurons, keeping your memory sharp and your mind agile.

If healthspan is all about living well for as long as possible, then exercise is a non-negotiable part of the equation. It's what helps you keep doing the things you love, whether that's playing with your grandchildren, travelling, dancing, or simply walking up the stairs without feeling winded. And it's never too late to start. No matter your age or fitness level, there's an exercise routine that can help you build strength, resilience, and vitality.

The Best Types of Exercise for Every Age Group
Now that we've established just how crucial exercise is for extending healthspan, let's look at what types of movement are best suited for each stage of life. Because as you move through the decades, your body's needs change. What worked in your 20s might not cut it in your 50s. And that's perfectly okay. The goal is to find the right balance for *where you are now.*

20s to 30s: Laying the Foundation
In your 20s and early 30s, you're at your peak in terms of strength, flexibility, and endurance. This is the perfect time to build a solid foundation that will set you up for a lifetime of health. Focus on a mix of cardiovascular workouts, strength training, and flexibility exercises.

Strength training, in particular, is crucial at this stage. Building muscle not only tones your body but also boosts your metabolism, strengthens your bones, and helps you avoid injuries. Aim to hit the gym or lift weights two to three times a week, targeting all major muscle groups. You don't have to go heavy, bodyweight exercises like push-ups, squats, and lunges work just as well.

For cardio, think high-energy activities that keep your heart pumping: running, cycling, swimming, or your favourite dance class. And don't forget flexibility! Yoga and Pilates are excellent for keeping your muscles long and supple, and they'll help you maintain good posture and prevent those niggling aches and pains down the line.

30s to 50s: Managing Time and Building Strength
By the time you hit your 30s, life tends to get a bit hectic, doesn't it? Between careers, children, managing a home, and all the other commitments that crop up, carving out time for yourself can seem like a luxury. But this is when staying active becomes even more crucial. As we get older, we naturally start losing muscle mass, at a rate of about 3-5% per decade, beginning in our 30s. This isn't just about looking toned; maintaining muscle is vital for bone health, joint stability, and overall strength.

But here's the good news: you don't have to sign up for a gym membership or commit to a gruelling routine to counteract these changes. If the idea of working out in a gym filled with complicated machines and people in Lycra isn't your thing, that's completely fine! What really matters is finding ways to build strength and stay active within your *everyday life*. In fact, there are plenty of simple, effective ways to do this that fit seamlessly into your daily routine.

The Power of Everyday Movement
For many, the idea of "strength training" brings to mind pumping iron in a sweaty gym, but that's not the only path to staying strong. Consider all the ways you can work your muscles without even thinking about it. Got a garden? Digging, planting, and pulling out weeds all require strength. If you have lifts (elevators) at home or at work, just decide to take the stairs.

These seemingly small activities count more than you might realise. Even playing with your kids or tackling household chores can become a mini workout if you approach it with intention. Think about all the lifting boxes you do, moving furniture around, or cleaning the windows, whatever you're doing, if you're using your muscles, you're building strength. With a bit of creativity, your daily tasks can double up as a workout, giving you that strength training without an official "exercise" session in sight.

Use Your Bodyweight: The Built-In Gym
If you do fancy doing some daily exercises, you don't need to hit the gym to work on resistance training. One of the best tools at your disposal is your own bodyweight. Exercises like squats, lunges, and push-ups can all be done anywhere, in the living room, the garden, in front of the Antiques Roadshow on TV or even the office (if you don't mind a few curious glances!). These exercises target multiple muscle groups at once, improving both strength and coordination. You can start small, perhaps adding in a few squats before brushing your teeth in the morning or doing calf raises while waiting for the kettle to boil.

The beauty of bodyweight exercises is that they're easily adaptable. You can do them at your own pace, with no equipment needed, and they're easy to slot into your day, whether it's 5 minutes in the morning, a quick stretch in the afternoon, or a more structured session in the evening. Start with just a few reps and build up gradually as you get stronger. The goal is consistency, not intensity.

Resistance Bands: A Compact Solution
If you want to add a bit more challenge but aren't keen on investing in weights, resistance bands are a fantastic option. These stretchy bands can be looped around legs or arms to add extra resistance to simple movements. They're portable, affordable, and easy to store in a drawer, making them perfect for home workouts or even packing in your bag if you're travelling. Plus, they offer a way to build muscle without putting too much strain on the joints, which is especially useful if you're just starting out or dealing with any aches and pains.
Try using them for squats, bicep curls, or even to add a bit more resistance to your regular stretches. They're an excellent way to keep your muscles guessing, and they're so versatile that you can use them while watching TV or listening to a podcast. Just a few minutes a day can have a big impact on maintaining and building muscle strength over time.

Making Movement a Priority
Consider adopting a "movement mindset." This simply means looking for little ways to incorporate more activity into your regular routine. Walk or cycle instead of driving whenever possible and use commercial breaks on TV as a prompt to move. Even standing up

while on the phone, shifting your weight from leg to leg, can help engage your muscles. It's these small, consistent actions that add up over time.

Household Activities That Double as Workouts
Have a pet? Take your dog for longer walks or try carrying your cat for some extra weight training (if the cat is cooperative, of course!). Got kids? Turn playground visits into your personal fitness session, climb, run, and play alongside them. Every bit of movement counts, and it's a win-win: you get stronger, and they see the importance of staying active, too.

The Big Picture: It's All About Building Habits
Ultimately, the best exercise routine is the one that *fits into your life*, whether that's in a gym or at home, with weights or just bodyweight. The goal is to make strength training a regular, sustainable habit. It's not about how heavy you lift or how long you exercise but about building a routine that keeps your body strong and capable for years to come.

Think of strength training as your personal investment in your future self. It's what will keep you climbing the stairs with ease, carrying your shopping bags without strain, and playing with your grandchildren well into your later years. So, forget about perfection, ditch the "gym guilt," and find ways to move that feel good for *you*. Because when you focus on making movement a joy instead of a chore, that's when it becomes a habit for life.

50 and Beyond: Staying Active, Staying Independent
Once you reach your 50s and beyond, the focus shifts again. Now it's all about maintaining your independence and mobility. The key here is to keep moving, in a way that supports your body without overdoing it.

Strength training is still essential, but you may want to opt for lighter weights and more repetitions to protect your joints. Resistance bands and functional exercises (think squats, lunges, and pushing or pulling movements) are brilliant for keeping your body strong and balanced. For cardio, choose low-impact activities like brisk walking, swimming, or cycling. These will keep your heart healthy without putting too much strain on your joints. And don't underestimate the power of balance training! As we age, our balance tends to decline, which can lead to falls and injuries. Incorporate exercises like single leg stands, tai chi, or even dancing to improve your stability.

Yoga and Pilates remain invaluable, helping to maintain flexibility, reduce stress, and promote mindfulness. The goal is to stay active, stay engaged, and keep your body and mind moving.

Creating a Balanced Fitness Routine
With so many different types of exercise to choose from, it's easy to feel overwhelmed. But building a balanced routine doesn't have to be complicated. Think of it as creating a recipe for a healthy, vibrant life, one that includes a pinch of cardio, a sprinkle of strength training, and a dash of flexibility.

Cardio is like the main ingredient; it strengthens your heart and lungs and keeps your energy levels high. Strength training is the protein of your routine, building and maintaining muscle mass and bone strength. And flexibility is the spice that keeps your body agile and your movements smooth.

Aim for at least 150 minutes of moderate aerobic activity or 75 minutes of vigorous activity a week, combined with two to three strength training sessions. Add in flexibility exercises two or three times a week, and you've got a well-rounded plan that covers all the bases.

Avoiding the Trap of Overtraining and Burnout
Finally, let's talk about something that often gets overlooked in the world of fitness: *overtraining*. While it's easy to focus on pushing yourself harder, faster, stronger, there's a point where too much of a good thing can backfire. Overtraining can leave you feeling exhausted, mentally drained, and more prone to injuries, not exactly the recipe for longevity!

Balancing family, work, and social obligations can make it tempting to view exercise as another box to tick off the list, a goal to smash through. But exercising too much, without adequate rest, can lead to burnout. The key to sustainable, long-term health is to think of exercise not as a sprint, but as a marathon. You want to pace yourself, take care of your body, and allow it time to recover.

So how do you know if you're overtraining? Watch out for signs like persistent muscle soreness, fatigue that just doesn't go away, or a drop in performance. Even mood swings and trouble sleeping can be your body's way of signalling that it needs a break. If this sounds familiar, give yourself permission to take a rest day (or two!). Remember, rest is just as important as movement. Your muscles need time to repair and grow stronger, and your mind needs time to relax and reset.

One of the best ways to avoid burnout is by mixing things up. Varying your workouts keeps things fresh and fun, and it helps you avoid overuse injuries. If you've been pounding the treadmill every day, try swapping in a swim or a Pilates class. If you usually lift weights, try a low-impact yoga session instead. Balance your high-intensity workouts with gentler activities, like a leisurely bike ride or a walk in the park. This variety not only keeps your body guessing, but it also keeps you engaged and excited about staying active.

Make Exercise a Lifestyle, not a Chore
The ultimate goal of this chapter is to help you create a fitness routine that fits seamlessly into your life, rather than feeling like a burden. Forget the "no pain, no gain" mentality; exercise should enhance your life, not detract from it. The best kind of exercise is the one you *enjoy*, the one that makes you feel alive, energised, and empowered.

Maybe that's dancing around your living room to your favourite tunes, or a Sunday morning run with your dog. Maybe it's joining a local netball team or finding a yoga class that feels more like a community than a workout. Whatever it is, find your *thing* and run with it (literally, if that's what you love!). Because when you enjoy what you're doing, it's not just a workout, it's a form of self-care, a way to connect with your body, and a chance to celebrate everything your amazing body can do.

Talking of dancing, joining a dance class is one of the most enjoyable ways to weave fitness into your life. But it's so much more than just exercise; it's a full-body experience that benefits not only your physical health but also your mental well-being. Imagine stepping into a lively dance studio filled with music that makes you want to move, surrounded by people laughing, sharing stories, and getting lost in the rhythm. That's the magic of dance.

The Physical Benefits of Dance ~ Without Feeling Like a Workout!

Dance is one of those sneaky workouts that doesn't *feel* like a workout. It improves your cardiovascular health, strengthens muscles, and enhances flexibility and coordination, all without the monotony of gym equipment. Every twirl, step, and beat helps to tone and sculpt your body. Whether it's salsa, line-dancing, ballroom, or a high-energy Zumba class, dancing provides a mix of aerobic exercise (getting your heart pumping) and resistance training (engaging your muscles), which means you get a balanced workout in a single session.

One of the most surprising benefits of dance is how it challenges your brain. Learning new routines, remembering steps, and staying in time with the music keeps your mind sharp. This makes it a fun way to build cognitive function, which is especially beneficial as we age. Plus, dance forces you to stay present, focus on coordination, and lose yourself in the rhythm. It's a great way to press pause on the everyday stresses of life.

Then there is balance. Dancers are 50% less likely to fall over, except maybe on the dance floor itself.

But let's be honest: it's not just about the fitness. The best part of a dance class is often the camaraderie that comes with it. Imagine the bonds you form when you and your dance partner finally nail a tricky step or when you share a laugh after a misstep that lands you both out of sync. These shared experiences create a sense of community and belonging. Whether you're an extrovert looking for a social outlet or someone who feels a little isolated and could do with expanding their social circle, a dance class is a fantastic way to meet like-minded people.

Dancing is a universal language; there's something about moving in unison to a beat that builds connections quickly. Even if you come in as a shy newcomer, by the end of the class, you'll have shared smiles, high-fives, and maybe even swapped a few stories over post-class coffee. And it's not just the friendships that make a difference; studies show that dancing with others can release feel-good chemicals like oxytocin and endorphins, which help to reduce stress and boost your mood. So, you're not just building a fitter body, you're nurturing a happier mind too.

Now, what if you're not quite ready to jump into a dance class? That's where "story strolls" come in, a simple yet transformative way to add some movement to your day without it feeling like a chore. The idea is simple: combine walking with a gripping audiobook or podcast to create a ritual you'll actually look forward to. The secret is to pick something *so good* that you can't wait to lace up your trainers and head out the door.

Think of story strolls as your own personal mini adventure. The suspense of a good thriller or the inspiration from a motivational podcast can make the minutes and miles fly by. By the time you're caught up in the latest plot twist or lost in the soothing voice of a favourite narrator, you've likely covered more ground than you ever thought possible. And because your mind is engaged, you're less likely to get bored or feel like you're forcing yourself to exercise.

Story strolls are more than just a way to pass the time, they also have numerous mental and physical health benefits. Walking is a low-impact activity that's gentle on the joints but still great for your heart and lungs. Pair that with an engaging story, and you have a recipe for lower stress levels and a boosted mood. It's a brilliant way to practice mindfulness too, helping you stay present and focused on the here and now, rather than worrying about your to-do list.

And don't underestimate the motivational boost of a good narrative. People who listen to audiobooks or podcasts while walking often find they're more consistent with their exercise routines. Why? Because they're not just going for a walk, they're catching up with characters they love or delving into new ideas. It's no longer a walk; it's an experience.

So, whether you're getting lost in the intrigue of a murder mystery or soaking up the wisdom from a TED Talk, story strolls turn a simple walk into something far more meaningful—and that's when habits start to stick.

Making Exercise Enjoyable ~ For the Body *and* Soul
Ultimately, whether it's through dancing with friends or losing yourself in an audiobook, finding enjoyable ways to move is the key to making exercise a sustainable part of your life. Forget the idea that workouts have to be punishing or boring. Instead, seek out the joy, the fun, and the little moments that make your body, and your spirit, feel alive.

One thing is certain: exercise is not just about living longer; it's about living *better*. It's the energy to keep up with your kids (or grandkids), the strength to carry your shopping bags without strain, and the agility to join in on all those adventures you've got planned for your golden years. It's not just about adding years to your life but about adding life to your years.

So, let's make a pact. From this day forward, you're going to think of exercise not as something to endure, but as a way to show your body some love. A way to build a strong, resilient foundation that will carry you through the decades with grace, strength, and vitality. Because you deserve to live younger, longer. And it all starts with taking that first step. Whether it's a five-minute walk or a 30-minute strength session, every bit counts. And every bit is worth it, because *you* are worth it.

Now, put on those trainers and get moving!

Lifestyle Wellness Plan: Movement Matters

Small Lifestyle Change	Current Habits	Goal/Action to Implement
Incorporate daily movement into routine tasks	Sedentary during work hours, relying on car for short trips	Walk or cycle, take stairs rather than lifts/elevators
Gentle bodyweight exercises like squats or push ups	No structured exercise that is a routine	Start with short bodyweight exercises and increase intensity gradually
Adopt a movement mindset by seeking opportunities for physical activity	Limited awareness of incorporating movement into daily tasks	Set reminders to stand or move every hour. Integrate stretching while watching TV

CHAPTER 4
Mental Wellness and Emotional Resilience

When we think about health, most of us picture the physical side of things, eating well, staying active, and getting enough sleep. But there's another part of the equation that's just as important, if not more so: mental wellness and emotional resilience. We often hear phrases like "mind over matter" and "the power of positive thinking," but when it comes to living longer and feeling good while we're doing it, these sayings hold more truth than we realise. The mind-body connection is real, and learning to nurture it can not only improve how we feel each day but also add years to our healthspan.

The Mind-Body Connection
It's a phrase that's thrown around a lot these days, but what does "mind-body connection" really mean? In short, it's the concept that our mental and emotional health is deeply intertwined with our physical well-being. You've probably noticed this yourself—when you're stressed or anxious, you might get a headache, feel nauseous, or even break out in a rash. On the flip side, when you're feeling joyful and optimistic, you likely have more energy, sleep better, and get sick less often.

The relationship between our mind and body goes much deeper than just feeling good or bad. Scientific research shows that our mental health has a direct impact on our immune system, heart health, and even how we age. Stress, anxiety, and depression aren't just emotional states—they create physical changes in the body. So, taking care of your mental wellness isn't just about feeling happier (though that's certainly a nice bonus); it's also about ensuring your body functions at its best.

The Science Behind Stress and Aging

Let's talk about stress. It's one of those inevitable parts of life that we all experience, whether it's the stress of work deadlines, juggling family responsibilities, or just trying to navigate the daily chaos. In small doses, stress isn't necessarily a bad thing—it's what motivates us to get things done. But chronic stress, the kind that lingers and becomes a constant companion, is a whole different beast.

When we're stressed, our bodies produce cortisol, the "stress hormone." In short bursts, cortisol helps us manage tough situations by giving us a jolt of energy. But when cortisol is constantly pumping through our system, it starts to wear us down. Think of it like keeping your car revving at high RPMs all the time—it's going to cause wear and tear over time. High cortisol levels over a long period can lead to issues like high blood pressure, digestive problems, and a weakened immune system.

More importantly, chronic stress accelerates the aging process. That's right, all those sleepless nights spent worrying don't just leave you feeling tired, they can actually make you age faster. The stress hormone cortisol has been linked to the shortening of telomeres, which are protective caps on the ends of our DNA strands. When telomeres get too short, cells can't divide properly, which leads to aging and the development of age-related diseases. In essence, stress is one of the biggest culprits in the premature decline of our healthspan.

Understanding the Mind's Role in Healthspan

So, how do we prevent stress and other mental health issues from taking years off our healthspan? First, we need to recognise that mental health is just as important as physical health. If we neglect our minds, our bodies will eventually pay the price. That's why it's crucial to understand that the mind plays a key role in our overall well-being.

When we talk about healthspan, we're really talking about how long we can live without experiencing major health problems that interfere with our quality of life. It turns out that mental wellness plays a huge part in this. Research shows that people with better mental health tend to live longer, healthier lives. They're less likely to develop chronic diseases, and when they do face health challenges, they're better equipped to manage them.

But it's not just about avoiding illness. Positive mental health also makes life more enjoyable. It's what helps us cope with difficulties, find joy in the little things, and build meaningful relationships, all of which are essential for a fulfilling life.

Managing Anxiety and Depression Naturally

Anxiety and depression are two of the most common mental health issues that can seriously impact our well-being. They're also notorious for being sneaky, creeping up on us in ways we don't always recognise until we're deep in it. The good news is that there are natural, everyday ways to manage these feelings before they take over.

For starters, regular exercise is a fantastic tool for managing anxiety and depression. Not only does physical activity release endorphins, the body's natural feel-good chemicals, but it also gives you a sense of accomplishment. Plus, exercise can act as a form of moving meditation, giving you time to clear your head and focus on something positive.

Nutrition is another powerful tool. Eating a balanced diet rich in omega-3 fatty acids, like those found in fish, flaxseeds, and walnuts, can help reduce inflammation in the brain and improve mood. Studies have shown that diets high in fruits, vegetables, whole grains, and lean proteins can significantly lower the risk of depression. On the flip side, processed foods high in sugar and unhealthy fats can exacerbate anxiety and mood disorders. So, what you eat doesn't just fuel your body—it fuels your mind too.

Sleep also plays a vital role in mental wellness. Anyone who's ever had a sleepless night knows how much it can affect your mood the next day. Chronic sleep deprivation can lead to increased feelings of anxiety, irritability, and even depression. Making sleep a priority, whether that means setting a regular bedtime, cutting down on caffeine, or creating a calming bedtime routine, can work wonders for your mental health.

Finally, don't underestimate the power of mindfulness and meditation. Even just a few minutes of deep breathing or meditation each day can help reduce anxiety and bring a sense of calm. It's all about finding what works for you—whether it's sitting quietly, going for a walk, or practising yoga.

How Positive Thinking Can Improve Your Health

We've all heard the phrase "look on the bright side," and while it might sound like a cliché, there's actually a lot of truth behind it. Positive thinking doesn't just make you feel better in the moment—it has real, long-term benefits for your health.

Studies have shown that people who maintain a positive outlook on life tend to live longer, healthier lives. Why? Because positive thinkers are more likely to take care of themselves. They're more motivated to exercise, eat well, and engage in healthy behaviours. Plus, they're better at managing stress, which, as we know, plays a huge role in how our bodies age.

But it's not just about putting on a happy face. True positive thinking is about developing a mindset that sees challenges as opportunities for growth, rather than setbacks. It's about being resilient in the face of difficulties and believing that things will get better. This doesn't mean ignoring negative emotions—it's important to feel all our feelings—but it's about not letting them define us or our future.

One easy way to start cultivating a positive mindset is by practising gratitude. Simply taking a few minutes each day to think about or write down things you're grateful for can shift your focus away from what's going wrong to what's going right. Over time, this practice can help rewire your brain to look for the good in every situation.

Building a Resilient Mindset

At the heart of mental wellness is resilience, the ability to bounce back from adversity, to keep moving forward even when life throws you a curveball. Building a resilient mindset doesn't mean that you'll never feel stressed, anxious, or sad again. It means that when those feelings come, you have the tools to manage them and move through them.

One of the best ways to build resilience is by focusing on what you *can* control. When life feels overwhelming, it's easy to get bogged down in the things that are out of your hands. But by shifting your attention to the things you can change, whether it's your attitude, your daily habits, or how you react to situations, you'll start to feel more empowered.

Another key to resilience is self-compassion. We're often our own worst critics, especially when things go wrong. But learning to treat yourself with kindness and understanding, as you would a close friend, can help you recover from setbacks faster. Remember, nobody is perfect, and everyone has bad days. What matters is how you respond and take care of yourself along the way.

Lastly, building a support system is essential. No one should have to go through life's challenges alone. Whether it's family, friends, or a therapist, having people you can talk to and lean on makes a world of difference.

Mental wellness and emotional resilience are just as important to your healthspan as eating well or staying active. By taking care of your mind, managing stress, and cultivating a positive outlook, you're not only improving your quality of life but also giving yourself the best shot at a long, healthy future. After all, the mind is a powerful tool, when we harness its strength, there's no limit to what we can achieve And if that means living longer, healthier, and happier? Well, that's something to smile about.

Morning and Evening Routines for Mental Health: Setting the Tone for Your Day

Let's start with the bookends of your day, your morning and evening routines. These are the moments that frame everything in between, so getting them right can set you up for success both mentally and emotionally.

In the morning, how you wake up can affect your mood for the rest of the day. I know the temptation is strong to reach for your phone and dive straight into emails but giving yourself a few moments of peace before you get caught up in the world's demands can be a game-changer. Why not try waking up a little earlier and carving out time for yourself? Even just five or ten minutes to sip your tea, stretch, or simply breathe can make all the difference. It's a moment for you to ease into the day on your terms, not your inbox's.

A gentle morning routine can be as simple as a few stretches, a gratitude practice (more on that later!), or even just opening the window to let in some fresh air and natural light. Anything that feels good to you is a great start. If you've got more time, try journaling or doing a few minutes of mindfulness meditation, it's a way of centring yourself before the world pulls you in all directions.

Evenings, on the other hand, are all about unwinding. After a long day, your brain needs to switch off from the constant stimulus. A bedtime routine that helps you wind down is not just for children, adults need it too! Try to avoid screens at least 30 minutes before bed (yes, that means putting your phone down!). Instead, read a book, take a bath, or practice some light yoga. The idea is to send signals to your body and mind that it's time to relax, which can improve your sleep and, in turn, your mental health.

Mindfulness and Meditation: Getting Out of Your Head and Into the Moment
If you're new to mindfulness and meditation, you might think it sounds a bit, well, woo-woo. But trust me, there's nothing mystical or complicated about it. At its core, mindfulness is simply about being present in the moment, something that's easier said than done in today's fast-paced world.

How often do you find yourself worrying about the future or replaying conversations from the past? Mindfulness helps to break that cycle by bringing your focus back to the here and now. And the benefits?

Reduced stress, improved focus, and even better emotional regulation. Not bad for something that requires nothing more than your own breath!

A simple way to get started is with mindful breathing. Sit comfortably, close your eyes if that feels right, and take a few slow, deep breaths. Focus on the sensation of the air entering and leaving your body. When your mind inevitably wanders, gently bring it back to your breath. That's it. This practice can be done anywhere, while you're waiting for the kettle to boil, sitting in traffic, or even at your desk. The beauty of mindfulness is that it's portable and accessible, no fancy equipment or lengthy time commitment required.

For those who want to dive deeper, guided meditations are a great way to develop a regular practice. There are plenty of apps like Headspace or Calm that offer beginner-friendly sessions, and before you know it, you'll start noticing the benefits in your daily life.

Journaling for Self-Reflection and Growth: Putting Pen to Paper
If meditation isn't your thing, that's okay, there are plenty of other ways to process your thoughts and emotions. One of the best? Journaling. It's amazing how simply writing things down can clear the mental clutter, provide perspective, and even spark creativity.

Journaling is like having a conversation with yourself, and it's especially helpful when you're feeling overwhelmed or stuck. There's no right or wrong way to do it. Some people like to keep a structured journal with prompts, while others prefer a more free flowing "brain dump" where they write down whatever's on their mind. The act of writing helps to process your thoughts and emotions, and over time, you'll start to notice patterns that can help you make positive changes.

A good place to start is with simple prompts like:
- What am I feeling today, and why?
- What am I grateful for today?
- What's one thing I can do tomorrow to make it a great day?

These prompts help to focus your attention on both your emotional state and the positive aspects of your life, which can lift your mood and provide clarity. Plus, it's a great way to track your growth over time. Looking back at old journal entries can be a powerful reminder of how far you've come.

How to Create a Stress-Management Toolkit: Dealing With Life's Curveballs

We all experience stress, but the key to maintaining mental well-being is how we manage it. And since we can't always control the things that stress us out, what we can do is build a toolkit to help us cope when stress inevitably shows up.

First off, let's talk about having a mental health "toolkit." Think of it as your go-to list of strategies and activities that help you de-stress. Everyone's toolkit will look a little different, but some tried-and-true options include deep breathing exercises, physical activity, mindfulness practices, and taking time for hobbies that bring you joy. The goal is to have a variety of options to choose from, so you're not relying on just one method.

For instance, when you're feeling stressed, sometimes a quick 10-minute walk can help clear your head and shift your perspective. Other times, a long chat with a friend might be just what you need. Or maybe you find that cooking a meal or diving into a good book is the perfect way to unwind. The key is to experiment with different activities and see what works best for you. And don't forget, it's okay to reach out for professional help when needed, there's no shame in that at all.

Building a Support Network: You Don't Have to Go It Alone

We often hear the phrase "it takes a village" when it comes to raising children, but honestly, it takes a village to navigate life. Having a strong support network is crucial for mental well-being. This can include friends, family, colleagues, and even online communities where you feel seen and heard.

The key here is to surround yourself with people who lift you up and provide positive energy. Having a friend you can call for a chat or someone who understands what you're going through can make all the difference. It's not about having a huge group of friends but about having meaningful connections that offer support when you need it most.

And here's the thing, building a support network isn't just about reaching out when things are tough. It's also about offering your support to others. Relationships are a two-way street, and being there for someone else can often help boost your own mood and sense of well-being.

The Power of Gratitude Practices: A Simple Shift with Big Results

Finally, let's talk about gratitude. It might sound a bit cliché, but practising gratitude is one of the simplest and most effective ways to improve your mental well-being. When you make a habit of noticing and appreciating the good things in your life, it shifts your focus away from the negatives, even if only for a moment.

Gratitude doesn't have to be some grand, sweeping declaration. It can be as simple as noticing the warm sun on your face, appreciating a delicious cup of coffee, or being thankful for a kind word from a friend. The point is to train your mind to look for the positives, no matter how small.

One easy way to start is by keeping a gratitude journal. At the end of each day, write down three things you're grateful for. They don't have to be big, just things that made you smile or feel good. This simple practice can change your mindset over time and help you cultivate a more positive outlook on life.

Bringing It All Together: A Daily Routine for Mental Well-Being

By integrating these strategies into your daily life, you'll start to notice how your mental well-being improves. It's about creating small, sustainable habits that add up over time—morning mindfulness, evening wind-downs, journaling, stress-management techniques, and gratitude practices all play their part. And remember, it's not about perfection or doing everything at once. Pick one or two strategies to start with and gradually build from there.

Life can be unpredictable and stressful, but with a few daily strategies, you can face whatever comes your way with resilience, positivity, and a little humour. Because let's face it, sometimes laughter is the best mental health tool of all.

Reframing Aging

Aging has had a bit of a PR problem for quite some time, hasn't it? It's as if society has collectively agreed to view getting older as something to dread, like a looming shadow in the background that slowly encroaches as we pass certain milestones: turning 30, 40, 50, and beyond. But let's pause for a second and ask ourselves: Why should aging be something we fear? Why is it that we tend to focus so much on what we're losing instead of recognising the incredible things we gain with every year? Here's the secret no one really tells you: aging is not the end of the story, it's merely a new chapter, one that comes with its own challenges, sure, but also a lot of hidden perks.

The truth is, the way we think about aging can radically affect the way we experience it. That's where the concept of reframing aging comes into play, specifically by cultivating a growth mindset. Let's shift away from viewing life as a slow decline after a certain age and start seeing it as a constantly evolving process, one where there is always room for growth, learning, and even transformation. Who says your best days have to be behind you? Honestly, the best might just be ahead, waiting for you to reframe the way you see the whole concept of growing older.

Overcoming Negative Beliefs About Aging

Let's start with the elephant in the room: those nagging, negative beliefs about getting older. We've all heard them (or possibly even thought them). "I'm too old to try something new." "It's too late for me to change." "What's the point now?" If those sound familiar, congratulations, you're human. But here's the thing about those thoughts: *they're all wrong.*

Research shows that a lot of the things we attribute to aging, things like loss of energy, cognitive decline, even aches and pains, are not inevitable. Much of it comes down to lifestyle choices, mental health, and, critically, mindset. Think of aging less as a relentless conveyor belt and more as a garden. If you plant seeds of negativity, self-doubt, and defeat, then sure, that's what you'll get in return. But if you water your garden with positivity, curiosity, and a sense of purpose, guess what? You'll start to bloom at every stage of life.

A growth mindset, coined by psychologist Carol Dweck, is about believing that our abilities and intelligence can develop through effort, learning, and persistence. Applied to aging, this means embracing the idea that you *can* continue to grow, change, and flourish at any age. Aging doesn't mean you're fading away; it means you're evolving into a more seasoned, nuanced version of yourself.

Reframing Midlife Transitions

Midlife is often portrayed as a crisis, cue the stereotypical image of someone buying a sports car, making dramatic career changes, or feeling generally lost and confused about their place in the world. But here's the good news: midlife is not a crisis; it's an opportunity. It's a time to reassess, to recalibrate, and to take stock of where you've been and where you want to go. Sure, there may be some things you need to let go of, perhaps that dream of becoming a rock star didn't quite pan out (but hey, who knows?). However, there are so many new paths to explore, especially with the wisdom and experience you've accumulated.

Instead of seeing midlife as a time when doors close, start seeing it as a time when new doors can open. You're no longer the person you were in your 20s or 30s, and that's not a bad thing. In fact, it's quite freeing. By reframing this transition, you can allow yourself to explore new interests, pursue passions you might have put on the back burner, or even embark on an entirely new career. It's not about what you can't do anymore; it's about what you *can* do now, with a little more clarity and purpose than you might have had in your younger years.

Building Self-Compassion and Acceptance

Now, I know what some of you are thinking: "Reframing sounds nice, but what about the parts of aging that are hard to accept?" And that's fair, aging comes with its share of changes, some of which can be challenging. But here's the thing: building a strong foundation of self-compassion is key to navigating these transitions with grace.

Self-compassion is the ability to be kind to yourself, especially during times of difficulty. It's about recognising that you're not perfect, that no one is, and that it's okay to have moments where things feel tough. But instead of beating yourself up, you approach those moments with understanding, patience, and a little kindness.

As we age, our bodies change, and sometimes, our capabilities shift. Rather than criticising yourself for not being able to do something you once could, celebrate all that your body and mind *can* still do. There's a quote I love: "Don't focus on the wrinkles, focus on the smile." That sums it up. It's about accepting the changes with grace and acknowledging that these changes are a natural part of life. They're not signs of failure; they're signs of experience.

The Benefits of Lifelong Learning
One of the most exciting aspects of reframing aging is embracing the idea of lifelong learning. Who ever said that education had to stop when you left school? In fact, learning new skills, picking up new hobbies, and staying mentally engaged are all linked to greater longevity and better cognitive health. It's like giving your brain a little workout—and just like any muscle, the more you use it, the stronger it becomes.

The beauty of lifelong learning is that it's entirely up to you what direction you take. Always wanted to learn French? Now's your time. Curious about painting? Grab that brush. Want to master sourdough bread baking or explore the world of photography? Go for it. The world is full of opportunities to learn, and in this age of technology, there are more ways to access information than ever before. Whether through online courses, community workshops, or just picking up a book, there's no limit to the knowledge you can acquire—and the benefits go far beyond mental stimulation.

Lifelong learning isn't just good for your brain; it's also a fantastic way to connect with others. Many lifelong learners form new social connections through the classes or hobbies they pick up. And in an age where maintaining social ties is proven to extend our healthspan, that's another win-win.

Finding Purpose and Passion at Every Age

One of the most transformative ways to reframe aging is to realise that having a sense of purpose and passion is vital at any stage of life. This sense of purpose could be related to your career, your family, your community, or something entirely personal, like a creative project or spiritual growth. The key here is that *purpose* doesn't retire when you do. In fact, many people find a deeper sense of purpose later in life when they have more time and space to explore what truly makes them happy.

Purpose is a bit like rocket fuel for your mental and emotional well-being. Studies have shown that having a sense of purpose can reduce the risk of disease, improve cognitive function, and even add years to your life. It's not about what you *should* do; it's about what you *want* to do and finding something that sparks joy, curiosity, and fulfilment.

The trick is to allow yourself the time and freedom to explore. You don't have to have it all figured out by a certain age. Give yourself permission to try different things, explore new passions, or dive deeper into something you've always loved. Purpose is fluid, not fixed, and it can evolve with you over time.

Creating a Personal Mantra for a Positive Mindset

Lastly, let's talk about the power of words. A personal mantra can be a simple but powerful tool to help you keep a positive mindset as you navigate the process of aging. Think of it as your guiding phrase, something to ground you when doubts creep in or when you need a little boost.

Your mantra could be something like, "I am growing and evolving every day," or "I embrace the changes that come with wisdom and grace." The key is to find a phrase that resonates with you personally, something that reminds you to stay positive, stay open to growth, and embrace each new chapter with curiosity and joy.

This mantra can become a touchstone you return to whenever life feels overwhelming, a little like having your own personal cheerleader in your head, reminding you of all the reasons why you're doing great, exactly where you are, right now.

Now I can see there will be many of you skip past this bit but write your mantra in the margin of this book, yes think about it and then write it down, as writing it down helps you remember and makes it real.

The Joy of Aging with a Growth Mindset
In the end, reframing aging is about more than just flipping a mental switch, it's about adopting a whole new way of seeing your life and the world around you. Aging is not a battle to be won or lost; it's a journey to be embraced. By cultivating a growth mindset, developing self-compassion, staying curious, and finding purpose, you can transform the way you experience aging.

The years ahead are not something to fear but something to look forward to with excitement and anticipation. Life, at any stage, is full of possibility. And isn't that something to smile about?

Lifestyle Wellness Plan: Mental Wellness and Emotional Resilience

Small Lifestyle Change	Current Habits	Goal/Action to Implement
Start day with 5-10 minutes of mindfulness or deep breathing	Get up and rush to work or arranging other people	Avoid looking at phone as soon as you wake up. Get up 10 minutes earlier and wake up with breathing exercises.
Unwind after work. Stretch you mind muscle in the same way you might stretch after exercise.	Switching modes without unwinding	Introduce a 10 minute walk with ear phones in that clears the brain of the days junk.
Gratitude practice	Going to sleep with all the bad things or worries of the day, without realising the good.	On paper if possible, if not mentally, note 3 things you have been grateful for today, good things about your day or the people within it.

CHAPTER 5
Mastering Sleep: The Ultimate Healthspan Pillar

Sleep is often seen as a luxury, something we squeeze in between busy days and long nights. But the truth is, mastering sleep is like finding the ultimate healthspan elixir, a kind of secret potion that can help you live a longer, healthier, and more vibrant life. Sleep isn't just about feeling rested; it's about laying the foundation for everything else you do. Whether you're training for a marathon, trying to eat better, or simply aiming to feel more focused at work, sleep plays a critical role in your success. It's the cornerstone of physical and mental well-being, and if you can master your sleep, you can unlock the potential for a better life, full stop.

Let's be real for a second: how often have you bragged about "only needing four or five hours" of sleep? It might sound heroic, but the truth is, consistently short-changing yourself on sleep is like driving a car with a slow leak in one of the tyres. Sure, you can keep going for a while, but eventually, that tyre is going to give out, and it's probably going to happen at the worst possible moment. Sleep is non-negotiable, and the sooner we accept that, the sooner we can start reaping the benefits it offers.

Sleep 101: Why It Matters for Health and Longevity
Let's start with the basics: why does sleep matter so much? Well, for starters, it's during sleep that your body does some of its most

important work. Think of sleep as the time your body uses to go into repair mode. During the night, your body is busy restoring damaged tissues, regulating your hormones, and even clearing out toxins that build up in your brain throughout the day. Yes, sleep is when your brain takes out the rubbish, so to speak!

Getting enough quality sleep doesn't just make you feel more refreshed; it's directly linked to how well you age. Research shows that people who sleep well are more likely to have a longer healthspan—the number of years you live without chronic diseases or major health issues. In other words, good sleep helps you stay young, inside and out. It's like an anti-aging treatment you don't have to pay for, and yet most of us are skipping out on it!

But it's not just about the number of hours you spend in bed; it's about the quality of your sleep. You need to be cycling through the various stages of sleep, especially the deep sleep stages, for your body and mind to get the full benefits. Deep sleep is when your body does most of its physical repair, while REM sleep, the stage where you dream, is crucial for cognitive function and emotional well-being.

How Poor Sleep Affects Your Hormones, Mood, and Weight
One of the biggest misconceptions about sleep is that it only affects how tired you feel the next day. In reality, poor sleep has a profound impact on almost every aspect of your life. Take hormones, for example. When you don't get enough sleep, your body produces more of the stress hormone cortisol. This isn't just bad for your mood; it can also lead to weight gain, particularly around your middle. And as we all know, that stubborn belly fat is the hardest to shift!

Sleep deprivation also messes with the hormones that control hunger: ghrelin and leptin. Ghrelin tells you when you're hungry, and leptin tells you when you're full. When you're sleep-deprived, your body produces more ghrelin and less leptin, which means you're more likely to overeat. That's why after a bad night's sleep you suddenly find yourself reaching for that extra biscuit or feeling ravenous for a plate of chips. Sleep deprivation basically turns your body into a snack-seeking missile, which is another reason it's so important for maintaining a healthy weight. And let's not forget the mood swings.

Have you ever noticed how everything seems a bit more dramatic after a bad night's sleep? The smallest inconvenience becomes a major crisis. That's because sleep plays a huge role in emotional regulation. When you're well-rested, you're better equipped to handle stress and stay positive. But when you're sleep-deprived, your brain is less capable of managing emotional responses, which is why you might feel more irritable or anxious when you're running on empty.

Understanding Sleep Stages and Cycles

Okay, so we've established that sleep is crucial, but what actually happens when we sleep? Sleep isn't a one-size-fits-all kind of thing. It's a complex process that moves through several stages, each of which has its own unique role to play in your health.

There are two main types of sleep: REM (rapid eye movement) sleep and non-REM sleep. Non-REM sleep is divided into three stages, with each stage serving a different purpose.

1. **Stage 1** is the lightest stage of sleep. It's that feeling when you're just starting to drift off but can easily be woken up. This stage is like the prelude to real sleep—it doesn't do much for your health on its own, but it's important because it transitions you into deeper sleep.
2. **Stage 2** is where your body temperature drops, your heart rate slows, and your brain waves start to change. This is where your body begins to relax and prepare for the deeper stages of sleep. It's important for overall rest and recovery, but the real magic happens in Stage 3.
3. **Stage 3** is deep sleep, and it's essential for physical repair. This is when your body goes into full-on recovery mode, repairing tissues, strengthening your immune system, and even building muscle. If you're trying to get fit or recover from a workout, deep sleep is non-negotiable.

Then there's **REM sleep**, which usually occurs about 90 minutes into your sleep cycle. This is when your brain is most active, and it's also when you dream. REM sleep is crucial for memory consolidation, emotional processing, and cognitive function. If you've ever woken up feeling mentally foggy, it's probably because you didn't get enough REM sleep.

The Link Between Sleep and Cognitive Health
Let's talk brains for a second. Your brain is a marvel, and sleep is when it does some of its most important work. During sleep, especially REM sleep, your brain processes all the information you've taken in throughout the day. It's like your brain is filing everything away into its proper place. This is why good sleep is crucial for memory and learning. If you don't get enough sleep, your brain doesn't have time to properly store and organise information, which can leave you feeling forgetful and unable to focus.

But that's not all. Sleep is also when your brain clears out harmful toxins that can build up over time. There's a lot of research showing that poor sleep is linked to cognitive decline and diseases like Alzheimer's. When you don't get enough sleep, these toxins aren't cleared away as efficiently, which can accelerate cognitive decline as you age.

So, if you want to keep your mind sharp, whether you're 30 or 80, sleep needs to be a priority. It's like a nightly brain detox that helps you stay focused, alert, and mentally agile.

The Role of Sleep in Immune Function
Here's something that might surprise you: sleep is one of the best things you can do to boost your immune system. During sleep, your immune system releases proteins called cytokines, which are essential for fighting off infections and inflammation. If you're not getting enough sleep, your body produces fewer of these cytokines, which means you're more susceptible to illness.

Think about the last time you were sleep deprived. How quickly did you catch a cold or feel run down? That's no coincidence. Your body needs sleep to function at its best, and your immune system is no exception. This is why one of the first things doctors recommend when you're feeling unwell is to rest. It's not just because they want you to take it easy, it's because sleep is your body's most powerful weapon against illness.

The Benefits of Good Sleep Hygiene

So how do we ensure we're getting the best quality sleep possible? It all comes down to sleep hygiene, which is just a fancy term for the habits and environment that contribute to good sleep. Think of sleep hygiene as setting the stage for your body to get the best possible rest.

First things first, create a routine. Your body loves routines and going to bed at the same time every night helps regulate your internal clock. This means you'll fall asleep faster and wake up feeling more refreshed.

Next, consider your environment. Your bedroom should be cool, quiet, and dark. Avoid bright screens before bed, they mess with your body's production of melatonin, the hormone that regulates sleep. And yes, that includes your phone! Scrolling through Instagram right before bed is a one-way ticket to a restless night.

And finally, give yourself time to wind down. You can't go from 100 miles an hour to falling asleep in an instant. Try reading, listening to calming music, or doing some gentle stretches before bed to signal to your body that it's time to sleep.

In the end, sleep isn't just something we do to pass the time until morning, it's one of the most important things we can do for our health. It affects everything from how we look to how we feel, and it's the ultimate foundation for a long, healthy life. So, let's stop treating sleep as a luxury and start giving it the attention it deserves. After all, there's no better way to invest in your future than by getting a good night's sleep. And who doesn't love the idea of waking up feeling energised, focused, and ready to take on the world, knowing that while you were dreaming, your body was busy working miracles?

By giving sleep the priority it deserves, you're not just investing in how you feel tomorrow but setting yourself up for years of good health. The benefits of sleep ripple out into every aspect of your life, your mood, your relationships, your work, and your ability to stay active and engaged as you age. And the best part? It's something that doesn't require any fancy equipment, costly memberships, or drastic life changes. You can start tonight, in the comfort of your own bed!

Incorporating a sleep-friendly routine is simpler than you might think. It's about making small adjustments—putting down your phone an hour before bed, setting the room to a cooler temperature, or even trying a bedtime tea. You'll notice the difference not just in how well you sleep, but in how vibrant and alive you feel the next day. And the day after that.

Mastering sleep is like unlocking a secret weapon for healthspan, one that makes you sharper, happier, healthier, and more resilient. So tonight, instead of seeing sleep as the end of your day, think of it as the beginning of a better tomorrow. Because that's exactly what it is.

Let's get a little science on the topic
Sleep is more than just a time for our bodies to rest; it's a critical process for maintaining cognitive function, particularly when it comes to memory. The brain's nightly task of processing, storing, and consolidating information is akin to a highly sophisticated computer, where data is sorted, saved, and sometimes erased to optimise performance. While we sleep, our brain is hard at work, and the science behind this has fascinated researchers for decades. Studies show that sleep is essential for everything from learning new skills to recalling emotional experiences. To better understand this process, we can turn to specialists who have studied the brain's activity before, during, and after sleep.

Sleep as the Brain's Filing System
One of the pioneering researchers in this field, Dr. Matthew Walker, a professor of neuroscience and psychology at the University of California, Berkeley, explains that sleep, particularly REM (Rapid Eye Movement) sleep, plays a crucial role in consolidating memories. Walker has noted that during sleep, the brain moves memories from short-term holding areas into long-term storage, much like a computer transferring files from a temporary folder to a more permanent archive.

Walker states, "Sleep is the greatest legal performance-enhancing drug that most people are probably neglecting." He explains that without adequate sleep, the brain's ability to consolidate information is significantly impaired, leading to forgetfulness, difficulty in learning new information, and cognitive decline over time. This idea is supported by numerous studies that have recorded brain activity during sleep, revealing how different stages of sleep play distinct roles in memory formation.

The Science Behind Brain Activity and Sleep
Using advanced neuroimaging techniques such as functional magnetic resonance imaging (fMRI) and electroencephalography (EEG), researchers can observe brain activity during sleep in real time. These studies have revealed that sleep consists of different stages, each contributing uniquely to memory processing.

For example, slow-wave sleep (SWS), which is the deepest stage of non-REM sleep, is when declarative memories (facts and knowledge) are consolidated. EEG studies have shown that during SWS, there is a marked increase in brain waves called delta waves, which are associated with deep, restorative sleep. This stage is when the hippocampus, a region of the brain crucial for memory, communicates with the cortex to transfer memories. Dr. Jan Born, a sleep researcher at the University of Tübingen, Germany, conducted experiments showing that people who experienced more SWS after learning a new task performed significantly better on recall tests the next day compared to those who were sleep deprived.

Born's research has highlighted how critical this slow-wave sleep is in "cementing" our experiences. He describes sleep as "offline processing time," where the brain revisits and strengthens neural connections formed during waking hours. His experiments showed that people who took naps after learning demonstrated up to 30% better recall of information than those who didn't nap.

Then comes REM sleep, often referred to as "dream sleep." REM sleep is associated with emotional memory processing and creativity. Brain activity during REM sleep is similar to waking levels, and it is during this time that the brain integrates emotional experiences, strengthens problem-solving skills, and supports learning that requires creativity. A 2017 study by scientists at Harvard Medical School, led by Dr. Robert Stickgold, found that students who entered REM sleep after studying complex information performed better on creative problem-solving tests compared to those who remained awake or only experienced non-REM sleep.

Stickgold's work has been fundamental in linking sleep stages to specific types of memory consolidation. "When you sleep, your brain is going through all the stuff that's happened during the day," Stickgold explains. "And it's trying to figure out what's important, what's not, and how all these things fit together." His research underscores the idea that sleep doesn't just solidify memories but also reorganises them, allowing us to connect previously unrelated ideas—crucial for creativity and problem-solving.

Memories Before and After Sleep
The changes in brain activity during sleep have been measured extensively, and the differences between a sleep-deprived brain and a well-rested one are stark. In one of Walker's studies, participants were asked to memorise a series of facts. Half of them were allowed to sleep for eight hours, while the other half remained awake. Brain scans revealed that the sleep-deprived group had significantly reduced activity in the hippocampus, the brain's memory centre. As a result, their ability to recall information the next day was severely impaired. Walker summarised this by saying, "Sleep deprivation hits the hippocampus like a sledgehammer."

Conversely, those who slept showed enhanced activity in the hippocampus, along with stronger connections to the prefrontal cortex, where complex thought processes occur. The prefrontal cortex is critical for decision-making and executive function, and a good night's sleep helps ensure that these areas are primed for action the next day. This link between sleep and brain connectivity highlights why we often feel more capable of solving problems or making decisions after a good night's rest.

Studies have also shown that even a brief nap can boost memory performance. A study published in the journal *Nature Neuroscience* revealed that a 90-minute nap after learning a task could significantly improve recall, suggesting that sleep rapidly consolidates new information. Dr. Born's research found that during napping, the brain shows a similar pattern of activity to full-length sleep, providing a shorter, more concentrated form of memory consolidation. This is why power naps can be so effective, particularly in high-pressure environments like exam preparation or when learning new skills.

The Sleep-Immune System Connection
In addition to memory, sleep also plays a critical role in maintaining a healthy immune system. When we sleep, the body produces proteins called cytokines, which help combat infections and inflammation. Poor sleep can lower cytokine production, leaving the immune system vulnerable. In fact, a study from the University of California found that people who sleep fewer than six hours a night are four times more likely to catch a cold than those who sleep seven or more hours. This highlights the direct connection between sleep and overall health, a well-rested body is better equipped to defend itself against illness.

The benefits of sleep for the immune system extend to longevity and ageing as well. Research shows that chronic sleep deprivation can accelerate the ageing process, leading to an increased risk of diseases such as heart disease, diabetes, and Alzheimer's. On the flip side, maintaining a regular sleep schedule can help preserve cognitive function and extend healthspan, the period of life spent in good health.

The Nightly Reset
Sleep is not just a time when the brain and body shut down. It's a vital process of renewal, where memories are consolidated, cognitive functions are restored, and the immune system is strengthened. Dr. Matthew Walker's assertion that sleep is a "non-negotiable biological necessity" is backed by years of scientific evidence showing that without it, our ability to learn, recall, and think critically is severely compromised.

By embracing sleep as a priority, not a luxury, we can dramatically improve our cognitive function, mood, and overall health. Much like updating a computer's software overnight, sleep allows the brain to refresh itself, ensuring that it's ready to perform at its best the next day. Without these nightly updates, our "operating system" begins to falter, affecting every aspect of our lives. So, if you're serious about improving your memory, cognitive performance, and overall well-being, getting enough sleep might just be the most important thing you can do.

Not only does sleep enhance memory and cognitive function, but it's also directly linked to longevity. Studies have shown that people who maintain a consistent, healthy sleep schedule tend to live longer and experience better overall health well into their later years. By allowing the brain to process memories and repair cellular damage overnight, sleep acts as a natural defence against the effects of ageing. As Dr. Walker points out, sleep helps reduce inflammation, lowers the risk of heart disease, and protects against neurodegenerative diseases like Alzheimer's. In essence, prioritising good sleep doesn't just make us feel better in the short term, it's an investment in our long-term health, helping us to live longer, more vibrant lives. Getting regular, restorative sleep is one of the most powerful tools we have to ensure a longer healthspan, where we not only add years to our life but also life to our years.

Creating the Perfect Sleep Sanctuary
When was the last time you woke up feeling refreshed, full of energy, and ready to tackle the day? If it's been a while, don't worry, you're not alone. Many of us are familiar with that feeling of dragging ourselves out of bed, groggy and unenthusiastic about the day ahead. And while we often blame busy schedules, stress, or even the wrong pillow, there's one crucial element we often overlook: our sleep environment. If you're not giving your bedroom the attention it deserves, it's time to create the ultimate sleep sanctuary, designed for relaxation and rejuvenation.

Getting a good night's sleep doesn't have to be an elusive dream (pun intended). By making a few adjustments to your environment, routine, and mindset, you can transform your nights and, as a result, your days. Let's dive into how you can create your own sleep haven and wake up feeling like a brand-new person every morning.

Designing a Bedroom for Optimal Sleep
Let's start with the basics: your bedroom. If it's cluttered with laundry, exercise equipment, and stacks of books you're "going to get around to reading," it's time to rethink the space. Your bedroom should be a

calming, restful place, an escape from the busyness of life. This isn't just about aesthetics; it's about signalling to your brain that when you step into this space, it's time to unwind.

The first step in creating the perfect sleep environment is decluttering. Remove anything that isn't related to rest and relaxation. Your bedroom isn't an office or a gym, so get rid of those distractions. Once you've cleared the space, think about your bedding. If your mattress feels like you've been sleeping on a medieval torture device, it's time for an upgrade. Your bed is the star of your sleep sanctuary, so investing in a supportive mattress and quality sheets is key.

Colours matter too. Opt for soothing, neutral tones like soft blues, greys, or warm whites. These colours are known to promote calmness and relaxation. Avoid bright, bold colours that scream, "Look at me!" when all you want to do is close your eyes. Add some soft lighting (think dimmable lamps or candles) to create a peaceful, cosy vibe. And don't forget about air quality! A stuffy room can make you feel restless, while clean, fresh air helps you sleep better. Keep a window cracked open if possible or invest in a plant that purifies the air, like a snake plant or peace lily, which are low maintenance but high reward when it comes to freshening up your space.

Best Practices for a Bedtime Routine
Creating the perfect sleep sanctuary goes beyond just your physical space. Your bedtime routine plays an equally important role in helping you drift off easily. You wouldn't jump into a big meeting at work without preparing for it, right? Well, sleep is no different. Your brain needs time to wind down, so establishing a pre-bed ritual is a must.

Start by setting a regular sleep schedule. Our bodies thrive on routine and going to bed at the same time every night helps regulate your internal clock. If you're thinking, "But my life's too chaotic for that," I get it, life happens! But aim to be consistent most nights, and your body will thank you.

Next, step away from the screens. I know, I know, those Netflix shows are addictive, but that blue light from your phone or tablet is tricking your brain into thinking it's daytime. Instead, give yourself at least 30 minutes of screen-free time before bed. You can use this time to read (something light and not too gripping), stretch, or practice mindfulness. Lighting a candle or using essential oils like lavender or chamomile can also signal to your brain that it's time to wind down. If you light a candle, do remember to blow it out!

If you've got a racing mind that just won't quit as soon as your head hits the pillow, try journaling before bed. Writing down your thoughts can help clear your mind of worries or tasks, so they don't follow you into dreamland. Think of it as a mental detox.

How Light, Temperature, and Noise Impact Sleep

Even after creating a beautifully designed bedroom and establishing a solid bedtime routine, you might still find yourself struggling to sleep if your environment isn't quite right. Light, temperature, and noise all play pivotal roles in determining whether you'll sleep soundly or toss and turn all night.

Let's talk about light first. Darkness is essential for sleep because it triggers the production of melatonin, the hormone that makes you feel sleepy. Any artificial light, even that pesky glow from your alarm clock or the streetlamp outside, can interfere with melatonin production. Blackout curtains are a game-changer for blocking out unwanted light, or you can try an eye mask for a portable solution.

Temperature is another key factor. Experts agree that the optimal temperature for sleep is around 18°C (65°F). Too hot, and you'll be sweating it out; too cold, and you'll be shivering under the duvet. Both extremes can wake you up in the middle of the night. Invest in breathable bedding that helps regulate your body temperature, and don't be afraid to adjust the thermostat.

Then there's noise. While some people can sleep through a thunderstorm, others are woken up by the sound of a pin dropping. If you're sensitive to noise, you might want to try earplugs or a white noise machine to drown out any disruptive sounds. White noise, or even nature sounds like rain or ocean waves, creates a consistent auditory environment that helps mask any sudden noises that might disturb your sleep.

The Role of Sleep Technology (Trackers, White Noise Machines)

Sleep technology has come a long way, and if you're a tech enthusiast, there's plenty out there to help you optimise your sleep. Sleep trackers are one of the most popular tools, and they can be incredibly helpful in understanding your sleep patterns. These devices, which often come in the form of a wristband or a phone app, can track your sleep cycles, heart rate, and even how often you toss and turn.

While a sleep tracker can't solve all your sleep problems, it can give you valuable insights into what might be disrupting your rest. For example, if you notice that you tend to wake up at the same time every night, it could point to an environmental factor, like noise or temperature, that needs adjusting.

White noise machines, as mentioned earlier, can be a great addition to your sleep sanctuary. These devices produce soothing sounds that help mask other disruptive noises and create a calming backdrop for sleep. Some machines even offer customisable soundscapes like rainforest sounds or gentle waves, so you can tailor your sleep environment to your personal preferences.

Managing Night-Time Wakefulness and Insomnia

We've all been there—lying awake at 3 a.m., staring at the ceiling, and wondering why sleep is playing hard to get. Whether it's due to stress, hormones, or just one too many cups of coffee, insomnia and night-time wakefulness can be frustrating. But before you start worrying about lost sleep, take a deep breath. There are ways to manage those restless nights.

First and foremost, avoid clock-watching. Constantly checking the time only heightens your anxiety about not sleeping, making it harder to fall back asleep. Instead, try practising deep breathing or progressive muscle relaxation to calm your mind and body. If you're still wide awake after 20 minutes, it's okay to get out of bed. Go into another room and do something calming, like reading or listening to soft music, until you feel sleepy again. The key is not to stay in bed tossing and turning, as this can condition your brain to associate your bed with wakefulness.

Caffeine, as much as we love it, can be a major culprit in sleep disturbances. Try cutting back in the afternoon and evening and opt for herbal teas like chamomile or valerian instead. These teas have natural calming properties that can help ease you into sleep.

If stress is the main reason you're waking up at night, you might benefit from mindfulness or meditation. Apps like Headspace or Calm offer guided meditations specifically designed to help with sleep. Over time, these practices can train your brain to relax more easily when it's time for bed.

Creating a Personalised Sleep Plan

Now that you've learned about all the elements that contribute to a good night's sleep, it's time to pull everything together into a personalised sleep plan. This plan should be tailored to your specific needs and preferences, making it easy to stick to.

Start by reviewing your current sleep habits. How much sleep are you getting each night? How often do you wake up during the night, and how do you feel in the morning? Tracking these patterns will give you a clearer picture of what's working and what needs tweaking.

Next, decide on a bedtime routine that works for you. Whether it's stretching, journaling, or simply reading a book, find activities that help you relax and wind down. Stick to the same routine every night to signal to your brain that it's time for sleep.

Finally, make sure your bedroom is optimised for sleep. Adjust the lighting, temperature, and noise levels to suit your needs. If you're interested in sleep technology, experiment with a tracker or white noise machine to see if they make a difference.

Remember, getting quality sleep is a journey, and like all journeys, it's about progress, not perfection. You won't always sleep perfectly, and that's okay. But with a little effort and some mindful adjustments, you'll be well on your way to creating the perfect sleep sanctuary and waking up feeling refreshed and ready for whatever the day brings.

Sleep Strategies as we get older
Whether you're in your 30s, 40s, or 50s, the relationship between you and a good night's sleep can be as complicated as any long-term relationship. At first, in your younger years, it's effortless, sleep just happens. But as time goes on, it starts playing hard to get and the eight hours you used to take for granted seem like a luxury. If you've ever spent a night tossing and turning, staring at the ceiling, you'll know what I mean. Let's break it down and tackle the biggest sleep challenges in each decade, because, spoiler alert, they evolve as we do.

The Sleep Struggles of Your 30s
By the time you hit your 30s, life is often a busy balancing act of career, family, and personal commitments. This is the decade where sleep usually takes a backseat because there's just so much to do. If you're juggling a full-time job with young children, sleep might start to feel more like a rare treat than a daily necessity. And let's not forget about the rise of stress. This is also the age when financial pressures, career growth, and adult responsibilities start to weigh heavily.

Sleep challenge number one in your 30s? *Finding the time.* The day feels short, and your mind feels long. You might stay up too late just trying to squeeze in some "me time," which is great, but then your alarm goes off at 6 a.m. for work, and you're left sleep deprived. Or maybe you have kids who don't quite grasp the concept of sleep being for everyone. If they're up at night, so are you.

Sleep in Your 40s ~ Shifting Hormones and New Priorities
Now, let's talk about the 40s. Ah, the hormonal roller coaster. For women, this is the decade when perimenopause might rear its head, bringing along symptoms like night sweats and insomnia. For men, testosterone levels begin to decline, which can also affect sleep quality. The changes can be subtle at first, but as the years roll on, the impact on your sleep becomes more noticeable.

Night sweats aren't just uncomfortable; they can wake you up repeatedly during the night, leaving you feeling tired and cranky the next day. You might find yourself waking up more frequently, and it's harder to fall back asleep. If you're in this phase, your sleep routine might start to feel like a constant battle with your hormones.

Sleep challenge number two in your 40s: *managing hormonal changes*. This is where you need to start being proactive about your sleep. It's a time to learn about your body's new rhythms and adjust accordingly. Hormonal shifts might not be avoidable, but the way you approach sleep during these years can make all the difference.

The Sleep Conundrum in Your 50s
When you reach your 50s, your body's internal clock might start to shift even more. You may find yourself waking up earlier, even if you haven't adjusted your bedtime. You might not feel as tired as you used to during the night, but then come mid-afternoon, you're ready for a nap. And let's not forget that as we age, we tend to get less deep sleep, the kind that's most restorative.

For many, this is also the age when snoring or sleep apnea may enter the picture. If your partner has started complaining about your loud snoring, it might be worth looking into, because sleep apnea doesn't just affect your sleep; it affects your health too.

Sleep challenge number three: adjusting to changing sleep patterns. Instead of fighting against the clock, it's better to work with it. Accept that your body is going through natural changes and adjust your schedule accordingly. Maybe your perfect sleep window is now 10 p.m. to 5 a.m., and that's okay!

The Hormone-Sleep Connection: Understanding the Impact
We've already touched on how hormones can disrupt your sleep, but let's dig a little deeper into what's happening inside your body. For women, perimenopause and menopause are the big culprits, with a decline in estrogen and progesterone wreaking havoc on sleep. Estrogen helps regulate your body's temperature and is tied to the production of serotonin, the "happy hormone" that also regulates sleep. When levels drop, you're more prone to night sweats, mood swings, and yes, sleepless nights.

Men don't get a free pass either. Testosterone levels decline gradually with age, and lower levels can lead to a reduction in deep sleep, as well as increased awakenings during the night. It's easy to brush off sleep issues as "just part of getting older," but there's more you can do.

Sleep and Stress: How They're Inextricably Linked

Ever notice how when you're stressed, sleep becomes even more elusive? Stress and sleep are like frenemies, constantly getting in each other's way. Stress, whether from work, relationships, or life's challenges, triggers your body's fight-or-flight response, which isn't exactly conducive to winding down and falling asleep. Elevated levels of cortisol, the stress hormone, keep your body alert, which is why you often find yourself wide awake at 2 a.m., going over tomorrow's to-do list in your head.

This becomes a vicious cycle: you're stressed, so you don't sleep, and then because you haven't slept, you feel more stressed the next day. Breaking the cycle requires being mindful of how you handle stress. Deep breathing, meditation, or even simple relaxation techniques before bed can go a long way in reducing cortisol levels and improving your ability to fall asleep.

The Power of Natural Remedies: A Holistic Approach to Better Sleep

If you're someone who prefers a more natural approach to health, you'll be pleased to know there are plenty of natural remedies that can enhance your sleep quality. Lavender, for instance, has been shown to calm the nervous system. Whether you use it in essential oil form, spritz it on your pillow, or sip it as a tea, lavender is a fantastic natural sleep aid.

Magnesium is another powerful sleep booster. This essential mineral helps regulate neurotransmitters that promote relaxation. You can increase your intake through diet, think leafy greens, nuts, and whole grains, or opt for a magnesium supplement.

If you're looking for a plant-based option, valerian root has been used for centuries as a sleep aid. It's known to help reduce the time it takes to fall asleep and improve the quality of sleep overall. The same can be said for chamomile, which has mild sedative properties. While herbal remedies won't solve all your sleep issues, they can help create a more relaxing environment to support better rest.

When to Seek Professional Help

Sometimes, no matter how hard you try, sleep doesn't come easily. And that's when it's important to know when to seek help. If sleep challenges become chronic, think insomnia lasting more than a few weeks, sleep apnea, or severe snoring, it's time to see a doctor or sleep specialist. There's no shame in reaching out for help; sleep is too important to your overall health to ignore.

It's also worth considering professional guidance if you've tried every sleep hygiene trick in the book and still find yourself struggling. Sleep disorders can often be a symptom of an underlying condition, such as anxiety, depression, or a thyroid issue, that needs addressing.

Long-Term Strategies for Sleep Health

So, what's the secret to long-term sleep success? Consistency. It may sound simple, but sticking to a consistent sleep routine is one of the best ways to regulate your body's natural sleep-wake cycle. Go to bed and wake up at the same time every day, even on weekends, and you'll notice an improvement in the quality of your sleep.

Create a bedtime ritual that tells your brain it's time to wind down. This could include reading a book, taking a warm bath, or practising relaxation exercises. And don't forget about the environment you sleep in. Your bedroom should be a sanctuary, dark, cool, and quiet. If noise is an issue, invest in earplugs or a white noise machine.

Lastly, limit screen time before bed. The blue light emitted from phones, tablets, and computers can mess with your body's production of melatonin, the hormone that signals it's time for sleep. Try switching off your devices at least an hour before bedtime or use apps that reduce blue light.

Sleep: Your Ultimate Health Ally

When it comes down to it, sleep is the foundation of everything else in your life. It affects your mood, your productivity, your relationships, and your overall health. So, prioritising sleep isn't just about avoiding bags under your eyes (although, let's be honest, that's a bonus), it's about giving yourself the best possible chance to live a vibrant, energetic life.

If you're currently struggling with sleep, know that you're not alone, and that it's never too late to make changes. Whether it's adjusting your bedtime routine, managing stress more effectively, or seeking professional help, there are always ways to improve your sleep. And trust me, when you finally get that good night's sleep you've been craving, you'll feel like a brand-new person.

Lifestyle Wellness Plan: Mastering Sleep

Small Lifestyle Change	Current Habits	Goal/Action to Implement
Create a consistent sleep schedule Set a usual bedtime and wakeup times, even on weekends.	Absence of routine, confuses the body. Look how lack of sleep routine affects your children, It's the same for you.	Use an app or an alarm. If you have a dog they will also help you stick to your wakeup routine.
Create a relaxing bedtime routine	Toss and turn in bed wondering why your not sleeping	Read, stretch, meditate or do light breathing exercises
Optimise your sleep environment, adjust temperature, lighting, noise and clutter	Your body and mind will be in flight mode rather than rest mode, as it thinks it must be alert.	Use a journal or a sleep app and track what works for you

Longevity by Design

CHAPTER 6
Nutrition Beyond the Plate: Supplements, Herbs, and Superfoods

When it comes to nutrition, it's easy to fall into the trap of thinking that a handful of supplements can magically make up for a less-than-perfect diet. As we have discussed before, supplements are just that: *supplements*. They're not a replacement for whole, nutritious food. While they can be incredibly helpful in plugging the occasional gap, the foundation of good health is a well-balanced diet, rich in fresh produce, whole grains, lean proteins, and healthy fats. That's the stuff your body craves and relies on for energy, vitality, and longevity.

The reality, though, is that life isn't always a neatly packaged health food shop. We're all busy, the seasons change, and sometimes you just can't get your hands on the freshest kale or the ripest tomatoes. Maybe you live in a climate where half the year feels like a grey curtain has been pulled over the sun, or perhaps you're juggling a full-time job, family, and social life and can't always prepare every meal from scratch. That's where supplements can step in and help a little, but they're not the whole picture.

Supplements: A Boost, Not a Replacement
Supplements are like the safety net of your nutritional intake. They can fill in the gaps when your diet doesn't quite cut it, but they won't turn a plate of greasy chips into a superfood salad. Think of them as a little boost to help you stay on track, especially when life gets in the way of perfection. For example, Omega-3 supplements can be useful

if you don't eat fish regularly, or a Vitamin D supplement might be essential during the long, dark winter months when sunlight is in short supply.

But even the best supplement can't replicate the complex benefits of eating whole foods. Fruits, vegetables, grains, and pulses provide a wide array of vitamins, minerals, antioxidants, and fibre that work together in ways we're still fully uncovering. Your body loves whole foods because they give you more than just isolated nutrients; they offer a complete nutritional package.

The Power of Herbs: More Than Just a Sprinkle

Now, while we're talking about adding to your diet, let's delve into the wonderful world of herbs. For centuries, herbs have been used not just to flavour food but also to promote health and well-being. From boosting immunity to calming frazzled nerves, herbs are like nature's original medicine cabinet, packed with health benefits.

But here's the best part: herbs are incredibly easy to grow at home. Even if you don't have a sprawling garden, you can start small, perhaps with a windowsill planter or a few pots on a balcony. Fresh herbs like basil, rosemary, thyme, and parsley aren't just great for adding a burst of flavour to your meals, they also come with health benefits.

Growing your own herbs adds something to your lifestyle that's hard to quantify. There's something incredibly rewarding about nurturing plants and knowing that what you're sprinkling on your pasta hasn't travelled halfway across the globe. It's come from your own little patch of nature. These herbs haven't been sprayed with chemicals, packaged in plastic, or shipped across continents. They've travelled a few centimetres from your windowsill to your plate.

Herbs to Boost Your Healthspan

If you're new to the world of herbs, you'll be surprised at just how powerful these little plants can be. Take basil, for example. Not only does it add an aromatic lift to sauces and salads, but it's also known for its anti-inflammatory properties. Rosemary, meanwhile, can help improve circulation and digestion, while thyme is a fantastic natural antiseptic. And don't forget about mint, great for soothing digestion and calming your mind.

Herbs like ashwagandha and rhodiola, known as adaptogens, are particularly powerful when it comes to supporting your body through stress. These herbs help the body adapt to physical and mental stressors, making them a fantastic addition to your wellness routine.

Herbs also invite a sense of creativity into your kitchen. You can explore making your own herbal teas, blending a mix of fresh mint with lemon balm for a calming drink or brewing some chamomile before bed to promote relaxation. Herbal tonics, tinctures, and even herbal-infused oils can all become part of your daily rituals, supporting your health in a natural, nourishing way.

From Supermarket to Garden: Growing Your Own Produce
Now, if you've ever picked up a soggy lettuce from the supermarket, only to discover it's travelled more than you have this year, you'll know the frustration of modern food systems. The idea of growing your own produce may seem daunting, but you don't have to turn into a full-time farmer to make a difference. Starting small can be incredibly impactful.

Imagine having a few pots on your windowsill or in your garden filled with fresh herbs, cherry tomatoes, or even a couple of leafy greens. These simple steps can reconnect you with your food in a way that feels meaningful. Instead of relying on produce that's been shipped halfway around the world, you're taking control of a small part of your food supply.

Growing your own produce also means you know exactly what's gone into your food, no chemicals, no pesticides, just the love and care you've put into nurturing it. Plus, the environmental benefits are a bonus. By growing even a small amount of your own food, you reduce your carbon footprint and packaging waste.

If the idea of growing your own vegetables sounds like a massive leap, start with something simple and small. Fresh herbs, some leafy greens, or tomatoes are great beginner crops. You don't need acres of land, just a few pots, some good soil, and the willingness to give it a go. And before you know it, you'll be harvesting your own ingredients, knowing that they're fresher and more nutrient-rich than anything you could buy.

Adding a Herbal Twist to Your Everyday
Even if you're not growing your own, incorporating more herbs into your diet is easy. Throw a handful of parsley or coriander into your salad, sprinkle some thyme or rosemary over roasted vegetables, or brew up a comforting herbal tea. Herbs are a natural, low-cost way to boost your nutrient intake and support your healthspan without needing to rely heavily on supplements. And there's something truly empowering about learning to use herbs in your daily life. You're tapping into a centuries-old tradition of healing through nature, bringing ancient wisdom into your modern routine. The more you experiment, the more you'll discover how herbs can support not just your physical health but your emotional and mental well-being, too.

Living Closer to Nature, One Step at a Time
At the end of the day, supplements and herbs are just part of a bigger picture. They're tools to support your health, but they're not the whole solution. What matters most is developing a lifestyle that prioritises real, whole foods, fresh, locally grown where possible, and prepared with care.

So, next time you're tempted to buy a bottle of supplements in the hope of magically transforming your health, take a step back. Consider what herbs you can grow on your windowsill, what fresh vegetables you can add to your plate, and how you can take control of your nutrition in a way that feels meaningful and achievable. Supplements can be helpful, but they're no replacement for the real thing.

With a little creativity and effort, you can grow your own fresh produce and herbs, adding richness and vitality to your diet. You're not just nourishing your body, you're also connecting with nature, reducing your environmental impact, and cultivating a sustainable approach to health and well-being that will serve you for years to come. After all, there's nothing quite like eating a meal made with ingredients that you've nurtured and grown yourself, knowing you're giving your body the best possible fuel for a long, healthy life.

Herbal Allies for Health: Nature's Secret Helpers

Herbs are more than just culinary accents; they are powerful tools that can support our overall health and wellbeing. From managing stress and balancing hormones to boosting cognitive function and enhancing vitality, herbs have been used for centuries to promote optimal health. Whether you're a seasoned herbalist or new to the world of natural remedies, there are countless ways to incorporate these powerful plants into your daily life. Let's dive deeper into the wonderful world of herbs and explore how they can help both men and women live healthier, more balanced lives.

Adaptogens: Nature's Answer to Stress and Energy
Adaptogens are a special group of herbs that help the body adapt to stress and restore balance, supporting both mental and physical resilience. They're like nature's built-in support system, helping you maintain energy when you need it most and calming your system when things get overwhelming.

Ashwagandha is one of the most well-known adaptogens, particularly in Ayurvedic medicine. It's often referred to as "Indian ginseng" and is celebrated for its ability to help people manage stress, improve sleep quality, and increase energy levels. Ashwagandha works by regulating cortisol levels, which is crucial because cortisol, the "stress hormone," can wreak havoc on the body when chronically elevated.

How to Use Ashwagandha:
- Tea or Decoction: You can make an ashwagandha tea by simmering a teaspoon of ashwagandha powder in water for 10-15 minutes. Drink it in the evening to support relaxation and better sleep.
- Tincture: Ashwagandha tinctures are available in most health food stores. Add a few drops to water or juice in the morning for an energy boost.
- Capsules: If you prefer a convenient option, ashwagandha capsules offer a standardised dose. These are ideal for taking on the go, especially before stressful situations like a big meeting or a challenging workout.

Rhodiola is another powerful adaptogen, often found growing in cold, mountainous regions. It is excellent for increasing energy levels, reducing fatigue, and improving mental clarity and focus. Unlike caffeine, Rhodiola provides a steady boost of energy without the jittery side effects, making it ideal for those with demanding physical or mental tasks.

How to Use Rhodiola:
- Tea or Infusion: Rhodiola root can be used to make tea. Steep the root in boiling water for about 10 minutes. Drink it in the morning to start your day with a burst of energy and focus.
- Tincture: Add a few drops of Rhodiola tincture to water before a workout or a busy workday to enhance endurance and stamina.
- Capsules or Powder: Rhodiola capsules are a simple way to incorporate this adaptogen into your routine. You can also add Rhodiola powder to smoothies for an energising breakfast.

Hormone-Balancing Herbs: Finding Your Equilibrium

Hormonal balance is crucial for both men and women, influencing everything from mood and energy levels to physical strength and cognitive function. Herbs can offer a natural and gentle way to help restore and maintain this balance, supporting overall health and vitality.

Chasteberry, also known as Vitex, has long been used to regulate the hormonal cycle, particularly for those experiencing PMS, menopause, or hormonal imbalances. It works by influencing the pituitary gland, which controls hormone production, making it useful for both men and women who want to manage hormonal fluctuations.

How to Use Chasteberry:
- Tincture: Chasteberry tinctures are effective for regulating hormones. Take a few drops in the morning with water, especially if you're experiencing symptoms related to hormonal imbalances.
- Capsules: A convenient option, chasteberry capsules can be taken daily. These are particularly beneficial for women who want to manage PMS or menopausal symptoms and for men experiencing hormonal shifts related to aging.

- Tea: Steep dried chasteberries in hot water for 15 minutes to create a tea that supports hormonal balance. Drink once a day for best results.

Black Cohosh is widely known for its benefits during menopause, helping to ease hot flushes, night sweats, and mood swings. However, its benefits extend to men as well, particularly for those dealing with andropause or other age-related hormonal changes. Black Cohosh supports overall hormonal equilibrium, providing comfort during these transitions.

How to Use Black Cohosh:
- Tea or Infusion: Black Cohosh can be brewed as a tea. Simmer a teaspoon of the dried herb in water for 20 minutes. Drink up to two cups a day to help with symptoms like hot flushes or mood swings.
- Tincture: Taking a few drops of Black Cohosh tincture in the morning and evening can be beneficial for consistent support during hormonal changes.
- Capsules: Black Cohosh capsules provide a standard dose and are a practical option for those looking to manage menopausal or andropausal symptoms without the need to prepare tea.

Maca is an adaptogen known for its ability to balance hormones and enhance energy. It's particularly effective for supporting libido, mood stability, and stamina. Maca nourishes the endocrine system, making it a wonderful herb for those experiencing hormonal imbalances, whether due to PMS, menopause, or andropause.

How to Use Maca Root:
- Powder: Maca powder is one of the easiest ways to consume this herb. Add a teaspoon to smoothies, oatmeal, or yogurt for a daily energy and hormone boost.
- Capsules: If you prefer a no-fuss option, Maca capsules offer a convenient way to support hormonal health on the go.
- Tincture: Maca tincture can be added to water or juice and taken once a day for consistent hormonal support.

Cognitive Support: Herbs for a Sharp Mind

Keeping the brain sharp is important for everyone, regardless of age. Herbs like Ginkgo Biloba and Gotu Kola have been shown to improve memory, boost cognitive function, and enhance focus, making them perfect allies for anyone looking to maintain mental clarity.

Ginkgo Biloba is well-known for its cognitive-enhancing properties. It works by increasing blood flow to the brain, improving memory and alertness. It's ideal for those looking to enhance mental performance or maintain memory as they age.

How to Use Ginkgo Biloba:
- Tea: Brew Ginkgo Biloba leaves in hot water for 5-10 minutes to make a tea that supports brain health. Drinking a cup daily can help improve memory and focus.
- Tincture: A few drops of Ginkgo tincture added to water or tea in the morning can provide a quick, convenient boost for cognitive function.
- Capsules: Ginkgo capsules are easy to take daily and are especially useful for those looking to support long-term brain health.

Gotu Kola is celebrated for its brain-boosting benefits and its ability to enhance mental clarity and focus. It also has anti-anxiety properties, making it a dual-purpose herb for both brain health and mood support.

How to Use Gotu Kola:
- Tea: Steep Gotu Kola leaves in hot water for 10-15 minutes for a tea that supports focus and reduces mental fatigue.
- Tincture: Add a few drops of Gotu Kola tincture to water in the morning for a brain-boosting start to your day.
- Powder: Mix Gotu Kola powder into smoothies or herbal blends to create a daily cognitive and mood support drink.

Anti-Inflammatory Herbs: Natural Inflammation Tamers

Chronic inflammation is at the root of many health issues, including arthritis and cardiovascular disease. Herbs like turmeric and ginger act as natural anti-inflammatories, helping to calm inflammation and promote overall health.

Turmeric, known for its active compound curcumin, is a powerful anti-inflammatory and antioxidant. It's particularly beneficial for those dealing with joint pain, arthritis, or general inflammation.

How to Use Turmeric:
- Golden Milk: Make a turmeric latte (golden milk) by simmering turmeric powder with milk (dairy or plant-based) and a pinch of black pepper. The black pepper helps enhance curcumin absorption.
- Capsules: Turmeric capsules are an effective way to consume a consistent dose, especially if you're looking for a convenient option.
- Powder: Add turmeric powder to soups, curries, or smoothies for an easy way to integrate this anti-inflammatory powerhouse into your meals.

Ginger is another anti-inflammatory herb that's both delicious and effective. Known for its ability to ease joint pain and inflammation, ginger also supports digestion and immunity.

How to Use Ginger:
- Tea: Fresh ginger tea is easy to make by boiling slices of ginger root in water for 10 minutes. Add honey and lemon for added flavour and immune support.
- Powder: Add ginger powder to stir-fries, soups, or even baking recipes for a spicy, health-boosting kick.
- Capsules: Ginger capsules provide a targeted dose for those who need anti-inflammatory support, particularly for joint or muscle discomfort.

Incorporating Herbs into Daily Life: Tips for Success

Incorporating herbs into your daily routine doesn't have to be complicated. In fact, it can be as simple as swapping your regular cup of tea for an herbal blend, adding a few drops of tincture to your water, or enhancing your meals with flavourful, health-boosting spices. The key is to start small and find methods that fit seamlessly into your existing lifestyle.

Easy Ways to Add Herbs to Your Routine
1. Herbal teas are one of the simplest ways to enjoy the benefits of herbs. You can purchase pre-made blends tailored for

specific needs, such as digestive support, stress relief, or cognitive enhancement, or create your own using dried herbs like chamomile, peppermint, or turmeric. Experiment with different combinations to find flavours you enjoy and that benefit your particular needs.
2. Tinctures are concentrated herbal extracts, typically made with alcohol as the solvent. They are perfect for busy individuals who need a quick and convenient way to incorporate herbs into their daily lives. Add a few drops of tincture to water, tea, or juice in the morning or before bed, depending on the desired effect. For example, ashwagandha or valerian tinctures can promote relaxation and better sleep, while ginseng or rhodiola can provide an energy boost.
3. Capsules, for those who prefer a more convenient and precise approach, herbal capsules or tablets are a great option. Many herbs, including turmeric, maca, and saw palmetto, are available in capsule form, allowing you to incorporate them into your daily supplement routine without having to prepare teas or tinctures. This is particularly useful if you're travelling or have a busy schedule.
4. Adding Herbs to Cooking. Herbs like turmeric, ginger, and oregano are not only powerful health allies but also delicious additions to your meals. Add turmeric to soups, curries, or scrambled eggs for an anti-inflammatory boost, or sprinkle fresh or dried oregano over salads and pasta dishes for its immune-enhancing properties. Incorporating herbs into your cooking not only boosts flavour but also ensures you're getting their health benefits in an easy, enjoyable way.
5. Smoothies and Tonics. Powders such as maca, ashwagandha, or gotu kola can be blended into smoothies or juices for a quick and nutritious boost. Combine these with other superfoods like berries, spinach, or chia seeds for a powerhouse drink that supports everything from hormonal balance to cognitive function. Herbal powders are especially great for those who prefer a morning or post-workout smoothie as part of their routine.
6. Infused Oils and Salves. Herbs like rosemary, arnica, and calendula are often used in topical preparations. Infused oils or salves made with these herbs can provide anti-

inflammatory and pain-relief benefits when applied to sore muscles, stiff joints, or skin conditions. Making your own herbal-infused oil is as simple as soaking dried herbs in olive oil for a few weeks and then straining it, or you can purchase pre-made versions from health food stores.

Creating a Personalised Herbal Routine

A great way to get the most out of herbs is to develop a routine that aligns with your specific health goals. Whether it's improving energy levels, enhancing cognitive function, supporting digestion, or balancing hormones, you can customise your herbal intake to meet your needs.

Morning Routine:
Start your day with a cup of herbal tea designed for energy and focus, such as green tea with ginkgo or rhodiola. If you prefer a cold drink, add an energising herb like maca to your morning smoothie. This is also an ideal time to take any capsules or tinctures that support your daily energy levels and overall vitality.

Afternoon Boost:
In the afternoon, when energy levels may start to dip, consider having a cup of turmeric tea or a ginger-infused beverage. Both herbs provide an energy lift without the crash associated with caffeine. A few drops of a tincture like ginseng or eleuthero can also help maintain steady energy levels throughout the day.

Evening Wind Down:
At the end of the day, it's important to switch gears and focus on relaxation. Incorporate calming herbs like chamomile, valerian, or ashwagandha into your evening routine. You could enjoy these herbs as a tea, or take them in tincture form. If you struggle with sleep, these herbs can also be consumed as capsules before bedtime to help promote restful sleep and recovery.

Safety and Dosage Considerations: Knowing Your Limits

While herbs are natural, they are also potent, and it's essential to use them wisely. Always start with the lowest recommended dose and monitor how your body responds before increasing the amount.

Consulting with a healthcare professional, especially if you're pregnant, breastfeeding, or taking medication, is crucial to ensure that the herbs complement your health needs and conditions.

1. Quality Matters:
   Choose high-quality herbs from reputable suppliers. Organic and sustainably sourced products are best, as they're free from pesticides and other harmful substances. If you're using tinctures, check that they are made with high-quality alcohol or glycerin and come from trusted manufacturers.
2. Pay Attention to Reactions:
   While herbs are generally safe, everyone's body is different. If you notice any adverse reactions, such as stomach upset, skin irritation, or headaches, stop use and consult a healthcare provider. It's always better to err on the side of caution when introducing new herbs into your routine.
3. Consistency is Key:
   Like most natural remedies, herbs work best when taken consistently over time. Don't expect overnight miracles; instead, view your herbal routine as a long-term strategy for health and wellbeing. Most herbs need at least a few weeks of consistent use to show their full benefits, so patience and persistence are important.

Herbs for Cognitive Support: Ginkgo and Bacopa
Mental sharpness and cognitive health are important for men as they navigate demanding careers, family responsibilities, and personal goals. While physical strength is often the focus, cognitive fitness shouldn't be overlooked. That's where herbs like Ginkgo Biloba and Bacopa Monnieri come into play.

Ginkgo, as mentioned earlier, increases blood flow to the brain, improving memory and cognitive function. It's particularly beneficial for men who want to stay mentally sharp, whether at work or in retirement. Bacopa, on the other hand, is a powerful brain tonic used in Ayurvedic medicine to enhance focus, reduce mental fatigue, and improve memory retention. Together, these two herbs form a strong foundation for cognitive support, helping men and women stay mentally agile as we age.

Embracing the Power of Herbs for Lifelong Wellness
Herbs have long been nature's gift for promoting health, offering us pathways to energy, balance, and vitality. Whether you're seeking to enhance energy levels, balance hormones, sharpen cognitive function, or support overall wellness, herbs provide a versatile and natural approach. They align with the body's innate rhythms, making them an ideal addition to your daily routine.

From adaptogens like Ashwagandha and Rhodiola that help manage stress and increase resilience, to cognitive boosters like Ginkgo, and nutrient-packed options like Sea Buckthorn, herbs cater to a wide range of health needs. These natural allies are not restricted by age or gender; they provide support tailored to the unique requirements of every individual. By welcoming these herbs into your life, you're not merely supplementing your wellness journey; you're building a holistic lifestyle that integrates nature's wisdom and honours your body's needs.

In today's fast-paced world, taking a moment to nurture yourself through nature can be a grounding, transformative experience. Health doesn't have to be complicated or overwhelming—it can be as simple as brewing a comforting cup of herbal tea or adding a sprinkle of turmeric to your meals. The beauty of herbs lies in their simplicity and accessibility; they invite you to slow down and connect with the earth's bounty.

Herbs like Ashwagandha and Rhodiola are perfect for those looking to reduce stress and find balance, while Ginkgo offers cognitive support, keeping the mind sharp as we age. For those seeking a boost in immunity or overall vitality, Sea Buckthorn, rich in antioxidants and vitamins, provides a natural way to support and nourish the body.

By taking the time to explore these options, you're making empowered choices that align with your health goals. The journey doesn't need to be daunting; it can be as simple as a few daily habits, such as a drop of tincture in your morning routine or an evening tea ritual that promotes relaxation.

Embracing herbs is not just about physical wellbeing; it's about creating a holistic approach that includes mental clarity, emotional balance, and a connection to nature. It's about living in harmony with your body and surroundings, using the power of herbs to build a future of vibrant health and wellness. So, why not explore what nature has to offer? By inviting these powerful allies into your life, you step into a lifestyle that promotes balance, energy, and longevity, helping you thrive in a way that feels natural and aligned with your personal journey.

Superfoods

When you hear the term "superfoods," you might picture some rare, exotic fruit plucked from a remote mountain that promises to make you live to 100. While that might sound a little over the top, superfoods do have some pretty amazing health benefits and can be a powerful addition to anyone's diet. So, what exactly makes a food "super"? And is it really as miraculous as the hype suggests?

What Makes a Superfood "Super"?

Let's start with this: the term "superfood" isn't a scientific one. You won't find hard-and-fast rules about what qualifies as a superfood, but it generally refers to nutrient-dense foods that are packed with vitamins, minerals, antioxidants, and other compounds that promote good health. In short, they're nutritional powerhouses, small in size but mighty in delivering health benefits.

Superfoods aren't just about improving your physical health either. They can give you more energy, improve your mood, and even help with those beauty concerns like glowing skin and healthy hair. While superfoods won't turn you into a superhero overnight, they can definitely give you an edge when it comes to feeling and looking your best.

Top Superfoods for Health and Well-being

Let's look at some top superfoods that can benefit anyone, regardless of age or gender. These aren't just any old fruits and vegetables; these are the ones that deserve a special place in your kitchen. If you haven't already added them to your diet, it's time to make space.

Chia Seeds

These tiny black and white seeds are packed with fibre, protein, omega-3 fatty acids, and calcium. They're a great addition for anyone looking to support heart health, digestion, and bone strength. Chia seeds also help with hydration—when mixed with water, they form a gel-like substance that helps retain water, making them a great pre- or post-exercise snack.

The best part? Chia seeds are incredibly versatile. You can sprinkle them on your cereal, mix them into smoothies, or make chia pudding. Simple and effective!

Goji Berries

Goji berries have been used in traditional Chinese medicine for centuries. These bright red berries are rich in vitamin C and other antioxidants that help strengthen the immune system, fight free radicals, and improve skin health. They also contain amino acids and trace minerals that contribute to overall well-being.

A handful of goji berries in your yoghurt or smoothie bowl adds a delicious burst of flavour and a hefty dose of health benefits.

Spirulina

Spirulina is a blue-green algae that is often hailed as one of the most nutrient-dense foods on the planet. It's loaded with protein, vitamins, minerals like iron, and antioxidants. Spirulina is especially popular among those looking to boost their immune system and maintain energy levels. It's also great for anyone looking to up their intake of plant-based protein.

You can add spirulina to smoothies, juices, or even mix it into your water. It has a slightly earthy taste, but the health benefits are worth it!

Superfoods for Skin, Hair, and Nails

What you eat plays a huge role in how you look on the outside. If you're after glowing skin, strong nails, and shiny hair, adding the right superfoods to your diet is key.

Avocado

Avocados aren't just trendy, they're packed with healthy fats, especially monounsaturated fats, which keep your skin hydrated and smooth. They're also high in vitamin E, an antioxidant that helps protect your skin from damage and keeps it looking youthful.

Add avocado to your salads, spread it on toast, or make a creamy guacamole. It's not only tasty but a fantastic way to nourish your skin from the inside out.

Sweet Potatoes

Rich in beta-carotene (which the body converts into vitamin A), sweet potatoes are amazing for skin health. Vitamin A promotes cell turnover, keeping your skin fresh and rejuvenated. Sweet potatoes also provide complex carbohydrates for steady energy, making them a perfect addition to meals.

They're incredibly versatile, you can roast them, mash them, or add them to soups for a healthy, filling dish.

Walnuts

Walnuts are your secret weapon for stronger hair and nails. They're packed with omega-3 fatty acids, which keep your scalp healthy and promote hair growth. They also contain biotin, a B vitamin that strengthens nails and hair. A small handful of walnuts makes a great snack or a crunchy topping for salads.

Immune-Boosting Superfoods for Longevity

Keeping your immune system in top shape is crucial, especially as we age. Superfoods are a great way to support your body's natural defences and promote long-term health.

Turmeric

This bright yellow spice is well-known for its anti-inflammatory properties. The active compound, curcumin, has been shown to support immune function, reduce inflammation, and even help prevent chronic diseases. It's easy to add to your meals, think soups, curries, or even a turmeric latte for a warming drink.

Ginger
Ginger is another superfood with powerful anti-inflammatory and antioxidant properties. It's great for fighting off colds, soothing sore throats, and aiding digestion. Whether you add fresh ginger to stir-fries, sip on ginger tea, or grate some into a smoothie, this root can help keep you feeling well all year round.

Blueberries
These little berries are packed with antioxidants, particularly flavonoids, which help reduce oxidative stress and support your immune system. They're also delicious and easy to add to your diet. Throw them in your morning smoothie, mix them into yoghurt, or just enjoy them on their own.

Making Superfoods Part of Your Daily Life
Incorporating superfoods into your diet doesn't have to be complicated. Here are a few ideas to make it easy and delicious:
- **Chia Pudding:** Mix chia seeds with almond milk and a dash of vanilla, let it sit overnight, and in the morning, you'll have a delicious pudding. Top with fresh fruit for extra flavour.
- **Goji Berry Trail Mix:** Combine goji berries with almonds, walnuts, and a few dark chocolate chips for a snack that's both indulgent and super healthy.
- **Superfood Smoothie:** Blend spinach, a handful of blueberries, a spoonful of spirulina, and half an avocado with some coconut water. It's a refreshing, nutrient-packed way to start your day.

Building a Superfood Shopping List
Stocking your pantry with superfoods doesn't mean you need to overhaul your diet completely. Start small, adding a few key ingredients into your weekly shop.

Here's a quick list to get you started:

- **Chia seeds** – Perfect for breakfasts, smoothies, and healthy snacks.

- **Goji berries** – Great for snacking or topping your morning oats.
- **Turmeric** – Essential for adding flavour and health benefits to meals.
- **Avocados** – Add to salads, sandwiches, or just enjoy them on their own.
- **Spirulina powder** – Ideal for blending into juices and smoothies.
- **Blueberries** – A versatile fruit that can be added to almost anything.

By making these small additions, you'll not only boost your intake of key nutrients, but you'll also be taking active steps towards improving your health and longevity. The great thing about superfoods is that they can be easily integrated into your routine without much effort.

Superfoods for a Healthier, Happier Life
Superfoods may not be magic bullets, but they're a fantastic way to support your overall health and well-being. By focusing on nutrient-dense foods that provide a wide range of vitamins, minerals, and antioxidants, you're giving your body the tools it needs to stay strong, energised, and vibrant.

Whether you're looking to improve your skin, boost your immune system, or simply feel more energetic, incorporating superfoods into your diet can make a big difference. And the best part? They're as delicious as they are healthy.

So why not start adding a few superfoods to your meals today? It's a simple, effective way to take control of your health and live your best, most vibrant life!

Lifestyle Wellness Plan: Beyond the Plate

Small Lifestyle Change	Current Habits	Goal/Action to Implement
Keep track of your weekly meals. Where can you add nutrient dense foods like whole grains or vegetables?	We all have a general routine of meals we repeat. Add something to that routine. EG Chia Seeds	Increase the value of superfood content. Be aware of what you're eating.
Identify 1 or 2 supplements that will bridge nutritional gaps such as Omega-3s or Vitamin D	Unaware what is missing in your diet that could assist longevity	Talk to a healthcare provider if you are unsure what supplements you need.
Start growing your own herbs, like parsley, basil or rosemary	Using few and less impactful herbs. Bland unexciting food	Start small, even a flowerpot on your kitchen windowsill

By consistently making small, conscious choices, you'll be well on your way to enhance your longevity and living a healthier, more vibrant life.

CHAPTER 7
Stress Less, Live Longer: Strategies for Managing Modern Stress

We've all been there: juggling work deadlines, taking care of kids, keeping up with social commitments, and somewhere in the middle of it all, trying to carve out a little "me time." It's a delicate balancing act, and at times, it feels like stress is just part of modern life. But here's the thing, stress isn't just a temporary annoyance; it can sneakily work its way into your body and start doing long-term damage. And while you might brush it off with a "c'est la vie," chronic stress is no laughing matter when it comes to your health and longevity.

But before we delve into strategies for stress management, let's break down exactly what stress is, why it's such a big deal, and how you can kick it to the curb for a longer, healthier life.

The Science of Stress: How It Ages You
Stress is a natural response. It's the body's way of gearing up for a challenge, whether that's running from a natural predator (not something you're likely to face on your way to Tesco!) or handling a tough conversation at work. But while that short-term stress, also called acute stress, is beneficial for giving us the edge in tricky situations, it's the long-term stress that gets us into trouble.

So, what exactly happens when we get stressed? Our bodies have this clever system called the "fight or flight" response. When you encounter something stressful, your brain tells your adrenal glands to release hormones like adrenaline and cortisol. These hormones are your body's way of preparing for battle or escape, heart rate goes up, blood pressure increases, and your muscles get ready to move. All well and good if you're sprinting away from danger, but not so great if you're sitting at your desk stewing over an email.

Now, let's say that stress doesn't go away. Maybe it's work-related pressure, family drama, or the never-ending to-do list. If your body stays in this heightened state for too long, you're essentially marinating in stress hormones. And that's where the trouble starts.

Chronic Stress: The Silent Health Saboteur
Chronic stress isn't just a mental burden; it impacts your body in ways that might surprise you. Over time, this prolonged state of stress leads to wear and tear on your heart, immune system, and even your skin. Yep, that tired, haggard look after a rough week? Stress could be the culprit.

When your body is constantly producing cortisol, it wreaks havoc on several fronts. Cortisol is sometimes called the "stress hormone," but I prefer to think of it as the "age accelerator." It can increase inflammation, raise blood pressure, and throw your metabolism out of whack. This is why long-term stress is so closely linked to aging.

The Inflammation Connection: Why Stress Equals Damage
Inflammation is a bit like your body's defence mechanism. When you get an injury or fight off an illness, inflammation is what helps your immune system do its job. But chronic stress leads to what we call "low-grade inflammation," and this type of inflammation is the slow-burning fire that can cause serious harm over time.

You've probably heard of inflammation in relation to conditions like heart disease, arthritis, and diabetes. Well, chronic stress can be the spark that lights that fire. It's as though your body is in a constant state of alert, responding to a threat that never goes away. And the longer this goes on, the more likely it is to lead to health issues.

The connection between stress and inflammation isn't just physical, it also affects your mood. That's why you might feel more anxious, irritable, or even depressed when you're under prolonged stress. It's a vicious cycle: stress causes inflammation, and inflammation can fuel stress-related conditions like anxiety and depression.

The Hormone Havoc: Why Stress Can Feel So Unbalancing
Hormones are key players in how you feel day to day, and when stress enters the mix, it's like throwing those hormones into a blender on high speed. It doesn't matter if you're male or female, cortisol, the primary stress hormone, can wreak havoc on the delicate balance of other hormones in your body. Stress doesn't just affect one aspect of your health; it can throw your entire system off-kilter.

For both men and women, cortisol disrupts sex hormones, such as oestrogen, progesterone, and testosterone. These hormones are responsible for everything from regulating your mood and energy levels to supporting reproductive health and maintaining muscle mass. When cortisol levels rise due to prolonged stress, it can suppress the production of these crucial hormones, leading to noticeable physical and emotional symptoms.

In women, stress can lead to irregular menstrual cycles, worsened premenstrual symptoms (PMS), and more intense symptoms of perimenopause or menopause, like hot flushes and night sweats. For men, elevated cortisol levels can lower testosterone, leading to reduced libido, energy, and even muscle mass over time. Testosterone is crucial for maintaining physical strength and vitality, so when stress interferes with its production, men can experience fatigue and a dip in overall well-being.

But it's not just about how stress makes you feel day to day, hormonal imbalances caused by chronic stress can also have long-term health effects. In women, lower oestrogen levels are linked to an increased risk of osteoporosis, heart disease, and cognitive decline. Similarly, for men, lower testosterone levels can contribute to muscle loss, decreased bone density, and increased fat accumulation, especially around the abdomen, which raises the risk of cardiovascular issues.

Stress, in short, can mess with the hormones that keep your bones, brain, heart, and overall health in check. This is why managing stress becomes even more crucial as you age, whether you're male or female. It's not just about avoiding the frazzled feeling in the moment but about safeguarding your long-term hormonal health to ensure that your body functions optimally for as long as possible.

The Cortisol Conundrum: How This "Stress Hormone" Affects Aging

High levels of cortisol can lead to fat accumulation around your midsection (the so-called "stress belly"), which isn't just about how your jeans fit. Visceral fat, fat stored around your organs, raises your risk of cardiovascular disease and diabetes. Cortisol also messes with your sleep patterns, leading to insomnia or poor-quality sleep. And without proper rest, your body can't repair itself effectively, which accelerates the aging process.

So, what's the solution? It's all about managing cortisol levels and keeping that stress response in check. The goal isn't to eliminate stress (an impossible task in today's world), but to control how you react to it and how long you stay in that "fight or flight" mode.

The Mind-Body Connection: Why Your Mental Health Matters

There's no separating the mind from the body when it comes to stress. What's happening in your brain directly impacts your physical health, and vice versa. Think of it like a two-way street: chronic stress affects your mental well-being, leading to anxiety, depression, or burnout, and these emotional states, in turn, worsen the physical effects of stress.

But here's the good news: just as stress can wreak havoc on both mind and body, the right strategies can also heal both. Practices like mindfulness, meditation, and yoga have been shown to reduce cortisol levels, lower blood pressure, and improve mood. These techniques tap into the power of the mind-body connection, calming the nervous system and giving your body the chance to recover from stress.

Engaging in stress-reducing activities doesn't have to mean long hours of meditation (unless that's your thing, of course). It could be as simple as taking a walk in nature, practising deep breathing for five minutes, or finding a hobby that allows you to unwind. Whatever works for you, the key is consistency, making time for stress reduction daily, not just when you're on the verge of a meltdown.

How to Stress Less: Practical Strategies
Now that we've unpacked the science behind stress and its effects on aging, you might be wondering how on earth you're supposed to keep your stress in check. The good news is that small changes can make a big difference.

First, get real about identifying your stressors. What's actually causing your stress? Work pressures? Family responsibilities? Social media overload? By pinpointing the source, you can start taking steps to reduce or manage it more effectively.

Next, build stress-relief into your daily routine. It's not just about "finding time" to relax; it's about making relaxation a priority. Whether it's a five-minute morning meditation, a lunchtime walk, or a no-phone policy after 8 pm, find ways to unwind that fit your life.

And don't forget to move! Exercise is one of the best stressbusters out there. You don't have to run a marathon, just get your body moving in a way that feels good, whether that's dancing in your living room or taking a yoga class. Physical activity helps release endorphins, the feel-good hormones that combat stress and boost your mood.

You Have More Control Than You Think
Here's the silver lining: while we might not be able to avoid stress altogether, we *can* control how we respond to it. And that's where the magic happens. By managing stress and finding healthy outlets for it, you can protect your body from its damaging effects and live a longer, more vibrant life. Whether it's through mindfulness, movement, or simply making more time for joy, every small step you take to reduce stress will pay off in dividends for your health and happiness.

So, next time life feels a bit overwhelming, take a deep breath and remember: stress is just a part of life, but it doesn't have to run the show. You've got the tools to manage it—and your future self will thank you for it.

Daily Stress Management

Stress is something that sneaks up on all of us. One minute you're sipping your morning coffee, feeling relatively at peace with the world, and the next, you're spiralling into full-blown panic because your inbox has exploded, the kids are screaming, or the neighbour's dog has decided today's the day for an all-out barkathon. Whether you're navigating through a busy workday, juggling family life, or simply trying to keep your head above water, stress is a constant companion for most of us. But here's the good news: daily stress management techniques can make all the difference. And no, you don't need to retreat to a Himalayan monastery to find your inner calm, though that *does* sound pretty tempting some days.

Breathing Exercises for Instant Calm: When Life Feels a Bit Too Much

Let's start with something we all do, every day, without thinking, breathing. It sounds simple, right? But the truth is, most of us are terrible at it. I don't mean that we're all on the verge of suffocating, but rather that we often breathe shallowly and erratically, especially when we're stressed. This shallow breathing sends signals to the brain that something is wrong, kicking off a chain reaction that leads to more anxiety. So, if there's one thing to master for instant calm, it's breathing. Specifically, controlled, deep breathing.

One technique that works wonders is the *4-7-8 breathing exercise*. It's so simple, you can do it anytime, anywhere, whether you're at your desk, stuck in traffic, or dealing with that family member who knows how to push *all* your buttons. Here's how it works: breathe in quietly through your nose for a count of four, hold your breath for a count of seven, and exhale slowly through your mouth for a count of eight. Repeat this for four breaths and feel your body relax, almost as if someone's hit a 'reset' button.

Another handy technique is box breathing, think of it as breathing with purpose and structure. You inhale for four seconds, hold for four, exhale for four, and then pause for four more seconds before starting again. This pattern helps slow down your heart rate and clears the mind, leaving you with a sense of calm. The great thing about these exercises is that they're discreet, which means you can practice them without anyone noticing. You could be at work, in a crowded room, or even standing in line at the supermarket—wherever stress decides to strike.

Using Movement to Relieve Stress: Yoga, Tai Chi, and Everything in Between

Sometimes, the best way to manage stress is to move through it, literally. When we're stressed, we tend to store all that tension in our muscles, and let's be honest, it's not a good look. We start walking around with hunched shoulders, a clenched jaw, and the general posture of someone who hasn't slept in days.

Movement can help shake that off and release the stress that's trapped in our bodies. Yoga and Tai Chi are fantastic for this because they combine physical movement with mindfulness, a double whammy for stress relief.

Now, I know what you're thinking: *"I'm not flexible enough for yoga!"* Don't worry, yoga is not about pretzeling yourself into impossible shapes; it's about connecting movement with breath. Start with simple stretches like cat-cow or downward dog, poses that help release tension in the back and neck, where we tend to carry most of our stress. Just 10 minutes a day can make a noticeable difference. If yoga's not your thing, Tai Chi might be. Often described as "meditation in motion," it involves slow, flowing movements that help you focus on your body, balance, and breathing. You don't need to be a martial artist to do it, and it's surprisingly gentle on the joints. Plus, the focus on rhythmic breathing and graceful motion is incredibly soothing for the mind.

For those who prefer something less structured, even a brisk walk can do wonders. Taking a stroll, preferably outside where you can get some fresh air, can shake up your energy and help you process stress. Walking has a way of helping your thoughts untangle, leaving you clearer and calmer. Add a good podcast or some music, and suddenly, you've turned stress relief into something you actually look forward to.

Grounding Techniques for Anxiety: Bringing You Back to the Moment

When stress tips over into anxiety, it can feel like you're losing control. Your mind races, your heart pounds, and suddenly, you're thinking of every worst-case scenario imaginable. In these moments, grounding techniques can be a lifesaver. Grounding helps bring you back to the present, cutting through the noise in your head and anchoring you to reality.

One simple technique is called *5-4-3-2-1*. This involves using your senses to ground yourself: start by naming five things you can see, four things you can touch, three things you can hear, two things you can smell, and one thing you can taste. By engaging your senses, you pull your attention away from anxious thoughts and back to the world around you. It's a great trick for those moments when stress feels overwhelming, like before a big presentation or during a tense conversation.

Another powerful grounding technique is to focus on your feet. This might sound odd, but bear with me. By feeling your feet on the ground, whether that's pressing them into the floor or shifting your weight to notice the sensation, you remind yourself that you're *literally* grounded. It's a small, physical reminder that you're here, in the present moment, and that the world isn't spinning quite as fast as your mind thinks it is.

Setting Boundaries to Protect Your Mental Space

Let's face it, we live in a world that demands our attention *constantly*. From the moment we wake up, our phones are pinging, emails are flowing in, and someone always seems to need something. It's no wonder stress has become a daily companion. One of the best things you can do for your mental health is to set boundaries.

Now, boundaries can be tricky, especially if you're someone who's used to saying "yes" to everyone and everything. But learning to say "no" when you need to is one of the most empowering things you can do. It doesn't mean you're being difficult or selfish, it means you're protecting your energy so that you can show up fully for the things that really matter. Start small. Maybe you limit the number of after-work commitments or schedule a "do not disturb" hour in the evening when you can unwind without interruptions.

Setting boundaries also means being mindful of how much time you spend on social media or endlessly scrolling through the news. It's easy to get sucked into a digital vortex, and before you know it, you've wasted hours and feel worse for it. So, give yourself permission to unplug. Your mind will thank you for it, and you might just find that you have more time and headspace to focus on what truly matters.

The Power of Small Breaks and Micro-Practices: Little Acts of Self-Care

When we think of stress management, we often think of big, time-consuming solutions like hour-long yoga sessions or spa days. While those are great, let's be real, not many of us have the luxury of an hour of uninterrupted peace, let alone a whole day. But that doesn't mean you can't carve out small pockets of calm. Enter micro-practices: little moments of self-care that can fit into your day, no matter how busy you are.

Micro-practices can be as simple as stepping outside for a few minutes to breathe in some fresh air, closing your eyes for a quick meditation, or stretching your arms over your head and taking a deep breath. These tiny breaks might seem insignificant, but they have a cumulative effect. Every time you give yourself permission to pause, even for just a minute, you're reducing the build-up of stress.

It could be something as simple as taking a slow, mindful sip of your morning coffee before you dive into the day's tasks. Or maybe you treat yourself to a five-minute stretch before bed. These small acts of self-care remind your body and mind that you're not just running on autopilot—that you're still in control, even amidst the chaos.

Creating a Daily De-Stress Routine: Making It Work for You

Finally, let's talk about the power of routine. There's something incredibly comforting about having a predictable, reliable routine in place, especially when life feels unpredictable. A daily de-stress routine doesn't have to be elaborate; it just has to be consistent.

Start with bookending your day: how you begin and end your day sets the tone for everything in between. In the morning, give yourself five to ten minutes of quiet time before diving into the day. This could be through breathing exercises, a short meditation, or simply sitting with your thoughts and a cup of tea. At the end of the day, wind down with something that helps you transition from "go" mode to "rest" mode. This might be a warm bath, a few gentle stretches, or reading a good book.

The key is to find what works for you and stick to it. Over time, these small daily habits become your foundation, the steady ground beneath your feet that helps keep stress in check. And remember, managing stress isn't about eliminating it entirely—because let's face it, life happens—but rather about building resilience so you can handle whatever comes your way with a bit more ease, grace, and maybe even a smile.

Stress Resilience: Long Term Strategies
It's one of those inevitable parts of life, like taxes or finding leftover socks without a match. No matter who you are, where you live, or what you do, stress will find its way into your life sooner or later. But here's the thing: stress doesn't have to knock you down or leave you feeling frazzled. In fact, with the right mindset and tools, you can build resilience to stress and come out stronger on the other side. This is about not just surviving stress but thriving despite it.

We're not talking about quick fixes here, unfortunately they may be good for coping but sometimes you have to fix the route cause. So, let's explore long-term strategies to help you build a solid foundation of stress resilience that'll hold up over the years. Whether you're juggling work deadlines, family demands, or life's little surprises, these strategies will help you navigate whatever comes your way with confidence, and maybe even a smile.

The Power of a Positive Mindset: Rewiring Your Brain for Resilience
When life throws a curveball your way, it's easy to feel overwhelmed or defeated. But what if I told you that the way you *think* about stress can actually change how it affects you? It sounds a bit like one of those

self-help clichés, but it's grounded in science. Stress isn't inherently bad, what makes it harmful is how we perceive it. If you see stress as a challenge rather than a threat, you're already building resilience.

Think about it like this: your brain is wired to react to stress based on past experiences and learned behaviours. But it's also incredibly adaptable. By practicing a positive mindset shift, you can teach your brain to respond to stress in a more balanced way. Instead of thinking, "This is impossible!" when faced with a challenge, try framing it as, "This is tough, but I can handle it." This simple change in perspective can reduce the impact stress has on your body and mind, helping you bounce back faster.

Of course, it's easier said than done. Nobody's expecting you to walk around like a motivational poster all day. But it's about practising small mindset shifts, day by day. When you start seeing setbacks as opportunities to grow, you take away stress's power to derail you. Plus, the more you practice, the more natural it becomes. Your brain starts to build new pathways, making this positive approach second nature.

Laughter Really *Is* the Best Medicine: The Benefits of Humour and Play

Let's not underestimate the importance of a good laugh. You know those moments when you're caught up in a belly laugh, the kind that makes your sides ache and your eyes water? Those moments aren't just fun; they're incredibly good for your health. Laughter lowers stress hormones like cortisol and boosts endorphins, the body's natural feel-good chemicals. It's a stressbuster that's instantly available, free, and, best of all, fun!

Humour allows us to take life a little less seriously, and sometimes that's exactly what we need. When you're facing a stressful situation, finding the funny side might feel impossible, but seeking out humour in everyday life can help reduce stress in the long term. Whether it's watching a silly comedy, cracking jokes with friends, or even laughing at yourself, humour can shift your perspective and lighten the load.

And don't forget about the benefits of play. Playfulness isn't just for children, it's something adults can (and should) embrace, too. When was the last time you did something purely for the fun of it? Engaging in playful activities, whether it's a spontaneous game of football in the park, doodling in a notebook, or dancing around the kitchen, helps break the cycle of stress. Play gives your brain a break from overthinking, boosts creativity, and gives you a sense of freedom.

The Importance of Social Connections: How a Strong Network Reduces Stress

It's no surprise that having good friends or family around you makes tough times easier to handle, but there's more to it than just moral support. A strong social network actually buffers your body against the effects of stress. When you feel connected to others, your body releases oxytocin, also known as the "cuddle hormone", which helps calm your nervous system and reduces the production of stress hormones.

You don't need a huge group of friends to reap the benefits, either. It's the quality of the relationships that matters. Having a few close connections, people you can turn to in times of need or simply have a good laugh with, can make all the difference. Sometimes, just talking things out with a friend or family member can give you a fresh perspective on whatever's stressing you out.

And let's not forget the power of community. Whether you're part of a local club, a sports team, or even an online group, having a sense of belonging contributes to your emotional resilience. It's comforting to know that you're not going through life's ups and downs alone—there's strength in numbers, even if those numbers come from different areas of your life. So, make time for social interactions, even if it's just a quick chat or a coffee date. Your future self will thank you.

Finding Your Purpose: The Antidote to Burnout

We all know that life can be stressful, especially when it feels like you're running on a hamster wheel, working hard, but not getting anywhere. This is where having a sense of purpose becomes crucial. When you have a clear sense of why you're doing what you're doing, stress becomes easier to manage. Instead of seeing challenges as obstacles, you start to view them as stepping stones toward something meaningful.

Purpose doesn't have to mean a grand, world-changing mission. It's about finding what lights you up, what gets you out of bed in the morning. Maybe it's your career, maybe it's raising your family, or maybe it's volunteering or working on a passion project. Whatever it is, when you feel like you're contributing to something bigger than yourself, the day-to-day stresses of life feel less overwhelming.

Burnout often comes from feeling like we're working hard without seeing the payoff. But when you're aligned with your purpose, you can take on more challenges without feeling drained. It's like having a North Star that keeps you on track, even when things get tough. So, if you're feeling stuck, take some time to reflect on what brings you joy, fulfilment, and energy. Purpose isn't just about the big picture; it's about finding meaning in the little moments too.

Building a Personal Resilience Toolkit: Your Go-To Strategies
Let's talk about tools. When stress hits, having a go-to set of strategies can make all the difference in how quickly you bounce back. This is where building a personal resilience toolkit comes in. Think of it like a first-aid kit for your mental health, filled with practices, activities, and reminders that help you manage stress when it rears its head.

What goes in your toolkit is entirely up to you. It might include simple practices like deep breathing or mindfulness, which help you stay grounded in the moment. Maybe it's journaling, which can help you process your thoughts and emotions. Or perhaps it's taking a few minutes each day to practice gratitude, which is proven to reduce stress and boost well-being.

Physical activity, whether it's a brisk walk or a yoga session, can be another powerful tool. Moving your body helps release tension and gives your mind a break from whatever's weighing on it. And don't underestimate the power of rest, sometimes the best way to deal with stress is to simply step away and recharge.

Your toolkit should be as unique as you are, filled with strategies that resonate with you personally. The key is to build these habits during calmer times, so when stress does show up, you know exactly what to do to handle it.

Long-Term Benefits of Mastering Stress: The Ripple Effect
Building stress resilience isn't just about handling the tough moments; it's about creating long-term benefits that ripple out into every area of your life. When you learn how to manage stress effectively, you're not only protecting your mental health, but you're also boosting your physical health. Chronic stress can lead to all sorts of health issues, from heart disease to digestive problems, so mastering stress resilience has a direct impact on your longevity and well-being.

Over time, these skills become second nature. You'll find that situations that once left you feeling overwhelmed no longer have the same hold over you. Instead of reacting with frustration or anxiety, you'll respond with calm and clarity. It's like training a muscle, the more you practice, the stronger your resilience becomes.

And here's the best part: when you're less stressed, you have more energy and focus to put toward the things that really matter. Whether it's spending time with loved ones, pursuing your hobbies, or simply enjoying life, mastering stress resilience frees you up to live a richer, more fulfilling life.

In the end, stress will always be a part of life, but it doesn't have to control your life. By building resilience, you can learn to navigate life's challenges with grace, humour, and a sense of purpose. You'll find that not only can you handle the tough times, but you can also come out of them stronger, more confident, and ready to take on whatever comes next.

Lifestyle Wellness Plan: Stress Management

Small Lifestyle Change	Current Habits	Goal/Action to Implement
Take time to reflect on what specific stressors are affecting you. Focus on work, relationships, health or financial worries to pin point the source of stress.	Feeling unhappy and not completely sure why.	To identify stressors. If you know what's making you unhappy you can start to put in place a plan to change that.
Build daily stress relief habits, Consistency is key, start with 5-10 minutes and then build from there.	Not controlling stress, letting it control you. Even the fact you recognise it will start to have benefits.	To reduce stress, but also to know you have the power of it. You can then choose to take action.
Create boundaries and time for self-care. Have specific time put aside for self care.	Constant accelerating stress train that doesn't stop at stations.	If you know there is a station ahead you manage your stress before it's a train out of control

You don't have to do everything at once, think of these actions as small, manageable steps that fit into your daily life. It's not about overhauling your routine overnight, but rather making consistent, little changes that add up over time. Each small effort, whether it's a five-minute breathing exercise or a walk during lunch, contributes to a bigger picture of better health and resilience. Taken together, these steps have a huge impact on your overall Healthspan, helping you stress less and live longer with more vitality.

Longevity by Design

CHAPTER 8
The Beauty of Ageing Well

Aging is something we all go through, whether we like it or not. But here's the thing: it doesn't have to be the gloomy, wrinkle-filled process we sometimes see depicted in the media. In fact, it can be something beautiful, empowering, and even, dare I say, fun! Yes, you heard that right. The beauty of aging well is all about embracing who you are, taking care of yourself, and shifting your mindset to see those "laugh lines" as badges of a life well lived.

Rethinking Beauty: Aging Gracefully
Aging is a privilege. Not everyone gets to experience the magic of growing older, so why not own it? For too long, we've been spoon-fed this idea that youth equals beauty, and the further away we get from our 20s, the less we have to offer in terms of attractiveness. Nonsense! The truth is, beauty doesn't have an expiration date. It evolves. We get to redefine what it means to us with each passing decade.

The first step to aging gracefully is letting go of unrealistic expectations. Gone are the days of feeling like we have to chase after some unattainable standard of perfection. Instead, let's focus on celebrating what makes us unique. The lines on your face? They're not "wrinkles." They're your personal roadmap, telling the story of the laughter, tears, and all the emotions in between that make you, *you*.

Aging isn't something to be feared; it's something to embrace, to wear proudly like a well-worn pair of jeans that have been through it all with you.

Understanding the Changes in Skin, Hair, and Body Shape
Let's talk about the changes that come with aging. Yes, they happen, but instead of fighting against them, let's get curious. One of the first things you'll notice is your skin. It might not bounce back as quickly as it used to after a late night, and that youthful glow may need a little extra help. But that's okay. Your skin is still beautiful, it just has different needs now. The trick is to evolve your skincare routine alongside it.

As we age, our skin naturally loses collagen and elasticity. That's science doing its thing. While we can't stop this process altogether, we can give our skin a helping hand. Hydration is key here, both inside and out. Drink plenty of water, slather on moisturisers, and don't forget about sun protection. If you're not already in the habit of using SPF daily, now's the time to start. Your future self (and your future skin) will thank you.

Hair also undergoes its own transformation. Maybe it's a few greys here and there, or perhaps your hair feels a little thinner. This is all part of the process, but it's not all doom and gloom. Grey hair is having a *moment*, and many people are choosing to let their natural colour shine through, rocking silver, white, or salt-and-pepper locks with pride. If you'd rather stick to your old colour, go for it! The beauty of aging well is having options and making choices that suit you, not anyone else.

Let's not forget about body shape. Bodies change as we age, and while it can sometimes feel like a betrayal when clothes don't fit the way they used to, it's important to remember that our bodies are incredible, no matter the shape or size. Instead of focusing on what your body "used to be," why not celebrate all the amazing things it's still doing for you? You've got legs that carry you through life, arms that hug the people you love, and a heart that keeps you going. That's worth celebrating every day.

Redefining Beauty Standards for Midlife

The beauty industry is finally starting to wake up to the fact that aging isn't a problem to be fixed. More and more, we're seeing models, influencers, and celebrities in their 40s, 50s, and beyond redefining what beauty looks like. But it's not just about who's on the cover of the magazine, it's about how we view ourselves.

In midlife, beauty is about confidence, wisdom, and knowing who you are. It's about wearing what makes you feel good, whether that's bold lipstick, comfy trainers, or that fabulous dress you've had for years. It's about doing things that make you feel alive, from dancing around the kitchen to getting outside for a walk in nature.

A big part of redefining beauty is letting go of the idea that there's only one way to look beautiful. Beauty is in diversity, it's in the lines on your face, the scars you've earned, and the strength you've built over the years. Midlife isn't about trying to look like your younger self; it's about becoming your best self.

Embracing Body Positivity and Self-Acceptance

Self-acceptance can feel like a journey, but it's one worth taking. Learning to love the skin you're in, right here and now, is one of the most powerful things you can do for your health and happiness. It's about shifting your focus from what you think you should look like to appreciating what you *are*.

Body positivity doesn't mean ignoring the parts of yourself you wish were different; it means recognising that your body is worthy of love and care exactly as it is. Instead of critiquing yourself in the mirror, try focusing on one thing you love about yourself each day. Whether it's your strong legs, your bright eyes, or your warm smile, start building a mindset of appreciation.

This attitude of self-acceptance does wonders for your mental health, too. When you're not constantly stressing about what's "wrong" with your body, you free up mental energy to focus on the things that bring you joy, connection, and fulfilment. And let's be honest, feeling good about yourself? That's the best beauty secret of all.

How Self-Care Impacts Healthspan

Self-care isn't just about face masks and bubble baths (though we're not knocking those!). It's about taking the time to nurture yourself—body, mind, and soul. And the best part? Prioritising self-care can have a huge impact on your healthspan, which is essentially the number of years you live in good health.

When you invest time in looking after yourself, whether it's through skincare, regular exercise, eating nourishing foods, or just giving yourself a break, you're actively working to extend your healthspan. Think of self-care as preventive maintenance for your body. Just like you'd service your car to keep it running smoothly, taking care of yourself now pays off down the road.

It's also important to recognise that self-care looks different for everyone. For some, it might be a peaceful morning yoga routine, while for others, it could be as simple as saying "no" to things that drain your energy. The point is to find what works for *you* and make it part of your life.

Building a Beauty Routine That Evolves with You

As we grow older, our needs change, and so should our beauty routines. But instead of thinking of this as a chore, think of it as an opportunity to experiment, try new things, and build a routine that makes you feel your best.

Start with the basics: hydration, sun protection, and nourishment. These are the non-negotiables that will keep your skin happy. But beyond that, have fun with it! Maybe you want to explore serums that target specific skin concerns, or perhaps you're more interested in the joy of a little makeup. Your beauty routine should be something that feels enjoyable, not a burden.

Remember, beauty isn't about trying to freeze time, it's about enhancing what you already have and feeling great in your own skin. So go ahead, wear that red lipstick, or take the extra five minutes for your favourite face cream. Embrace your age, and let your beauty evolve with you.

In the end, the beauty of aging well isn't about avoiding wrinkles or hiding grey hair. It's about self-care, confidence, and living fully. After all, the secret to looking good is feeling good, inside and out. So, here's to aging gracefully, and to a life lived beautifully, at every age.

Skincare

Let's talk skincare. Yes, we're all busy with life, careers, families, trying to remember to drink enough water, but your skin is busy too. It's your body's largest organ, after all, and it's constantly working to protect you from the outside world. So, if you think skincare is something you can just "figure out later," let me gently remind you: your skin deserves a bit of TLC right now.

Whether you're in your 30s, 40s, or beyond, your skincare routine is your chance to give back to the loyal friend that's been with you since day one. Don't worry, you don't need a 12-step routine or the latest gold-infused, unicorn-approved miracle cream. What you need is a little knowledge and some consistent care. And let's face it, who doesn't want to feel a little glowier?

Skincare in Your 30s: The "Wait, Is That a Line?" Stage

Your 30s are the time when life starts to settle in a bit, but so do those fine lines (just being honest). It's also when your skin might begin to lose a little of that youthful plumpness you've taken for granted, thanks to a drop in collagen production. But fear not! This decade is all about prevention and keeping things smooth and hydrated.

The golden rule for your 30s? Hydration, hydration, hydration. Your skin's natural oils might start to slow down, leaving you with a slightly drier complexion. This is the time to reach for a good moisturiser, one that keeps your skin hydrated without clogging your pores. Look for ingredients like *Hyaluronic Acid*, which is a hydration superstar, pulling water into your skin like a sponge. Trust me, your skin will drink it up.

While you're at it, introduce *Vitamin C* into your morning routine. Vitamin C is an antioxidant powerhouse that helps brighten the skin and fight off the damage caused by free radicals (think pollution, UV rays, and all the things life throws at your face). It's like a protective shield for your skin, helping to prevent those pesky dark spots that start to creep up as the years go by.

Let's not forget the unsung hero of skincare: *sunscreen*. If you're not already using an SPF daily, now's the time. It's non-negotiable. Seriously, even on cloudy days in the UK, USA or wherever you are, those UV rays are still at work. Sunscreen is your best defence against premature aging and sun damage, which can lead to pigmentation and wrinkles. Opt for a broad-spectrum SPF 30 *or higher* and reapply throughout the day if you're outside. It may be a bit of a burden but believe me, your future self will thank you.

Skincare in Your 40s: The "Okay, Let's Get Serious" Decade

By the time you hit your 40s, your skin might start showing more noticeable signs of aging. Your 40s are a time for reassessment, not panic. Fine lines may start deepening, and skin may lose elasticity. But before you throw your hands up in frustration, know that it's never too late to start a solid skincare routine.

This is the decade when *Retinol* becomes your best friend. If you haven't already incorporated it into your routine, now's the time. Retinol (or its prescription-strength cousin, Retinoids) helps speed up cell turnover, which can slow down with age. It's one of the few ingredients that dermatologists universally agree actually works when it comes to reducing the appearance of fine lines and wrinkles. Just start slow, as retinol can be irritating if you dive in headfirst.

Don't stop at just one powerhouse ingredient, though. Keep up with your *Vitamin C* to brighten and firm and introduce products that help boost collagen production. Look for *peptides* and *ceramides* to help with skin barrier repair, as your skin might feel thinner and drier. Also, hydrating masks and serums packed with hyaluronic acid will have an impact. Hydration is not just for the 30s; it's a lifelong necessity.

Oh, and those peels or exfoliating treatments you've been eyeing? For many of us the prospect of a peel is the last thing on our minds, it's too much fuss, I haven't got time, I'll look silly, it's not what men do, and on we go, but....Your 40s are a great time to try chemical peels or microdermabrasion, which help to slough off dead skin cells and reveal fresher, younger-looking skin underneath. Just make sure not to overdo it, your skin needs time to regenerate. Always follow up these treatments with sunscreen because, yes, your skin will be more sensitive to the sun.

Skincare in Your 50s and Beyond: Embrace the Glow
Your 50s bring another shift, hormonal changes like menopause can cause a whole new set of skincare challenges. Your skin might get drier, more sensitive, and even a little thinner. But here's the thing: age is beautiful, and your skincare routine should focus on enhancing that natural beauty.

In this decade, moisture is everything. Think of rich, nourishing creams as the key to plumping and hydrating skin that's lost some of its natural oils. Oils like jojoba and argan are excellent for restoring hydration. Also, gentle cleansing is more important than ever. Avoid harsh soaps and cleansers that strip away oils and opt for cream cleansers or oil-based formulas that cleanse without drying.

Don't shy away from anti-aging treatments either. Micro-needling and laser treatments can help with skin texture and tone, stimulating collagen and elastin production to firm up sagging skin. If you're hesitant about these more intense treatments, consider professional-grade facials that offer deep hydration and nourishment.

One last thing, don't overlook your neck and hands! They're often the first places to show age and can benefit from the same care you give your face. Use your skincare products on your neck and hands to keep them looking youthful and hydrated.

What to Look for in Natural Skincare Products
If you're inclined to go the natural route (and why wouldn't you?), there are some incredible options out there that won't fill your skin with unnecessary chemicals. But, let's be real, just because a product says "natural" doesn't mean it's automatically good for your skin. Always check the ingredients. Look for products with **botanical extracts**, like **aloe vera**, **chamomile**, and **rosehip oil**, which are soothing and packed with antioxidants. **Shea butter** and **coconut oil** are fantastic for hydration, but make sure they suit your skin type to avoid breakouts.

Be cautious of products with too many essential oils or fragrances, as these can irritate sensitive skin. You want something that nurtures, not something that feels like you're wearing perfume. Brands that prioritise sustainability and use organic farming methods for their ingredients are often a good bet, both for your skin and the environment.

Creating a Non-Toxic Skincare Routine
Creating a non-toxic skincare regimen is easier than you might think. Start with the basics: a gentle cleanser, a moisturiser suited to your skin type, and a broad-spectrum SPF. Build from there with serums that address your specific needs, such as Vitamin C for brightening, Hyaluronic Acid for hydration, and **Retinol** for anti-aging. Stick to a routine and avoid overloading your skin with too many products, it's about consistency, not excess.

Also, keep in mind that what you put into your body affects your skin. Drinking plenty of water, eating antioxidant-rich foods like berries and leafy greens, and getting enough sleep will do wonders for your complexion. After all, skincare starts from the inside out.

Skincare That Ages with You
Skincare isn't about trying to erase the years but about keeping your skin healthy and vibrant at every age. Your 30s, 40s, and 50s all require different approaches, but with a few tweaks and some solid products, you'll find that a little effort goes a long way. Your skin is part of your story—nourish it, protect it, and let it glow.

Alcohol
Alcohol can have a significant impact on your skin, and not in a good way. When you drink, alcohol dehydrates your body, including your skin, which can lead to a dry, dull complexion and the appearance of fine lines and wrinkles. It also dilates blood vessels, particularly on the face, which can cause redness and broken capillaries over time, especially in those prone to rosacea. Alcohol also depletes essential vitamins and nutrients like Vitamin A and C, which are crucial for cell renewal and collagen production. Additionally, alcohol can trigger inflammation, which can exacerbate skin conditions such as acne and

eczema, leaving your skin looking tired and less vibrant. In short, frequent alcohol consumption can accelerate the signs of aging, leaving your skin struggling to recover its natural glow.

While alcohol may have some negative effects on the skin, it's important to balance that with the joy and social connection a nice glass of wine or a night out with friends can bring. As we discussed in the last chapter, happiness, laughter, and strong social bonds are key contributors to a long, healthy life, and sometimes, sharing a drink can be part of that experience. It's not about cutting out alcohol entirely but being mindful of moderation. A glass of wine with a nice meal, or whilst watching Wimbledon, or pint with your mates down the pub can foster connection and create memorable moments, which are vital for our emotional well-being. However, balancing this with good skincare practices, plenty of hydration, and nourishing your body with the right nutrients can help mitigate the impact alcohol may have on your skin, allowing you to enjoy those moments without sacrificing your skin's health.

Enhancing Inner and Outer Beauty
When we talk about beauty, it's tempting to think only of those glossy magazines or Instagram filters, but let's be honest: true beauty is something that radiates from within. It's not just about clear skin or glossy hair, but about how we feel in our own skin, and that's something both men and women can embrace. The beauty we're chasing here isn't fleeting or superficial; it's about creating a glow that lasts a lifetime, inside and out.

Herbal Secrets for Timeless Beauty
If there's one thing nature has never let us down on, it's her ability to provide incredible ingredients that keep us looking and feeling our best. Herbs and essential oils are like nature's little beauty warriors and using them is far simpler than you might think.

Take lavender oil, for instance, a lovely little multitasker. Not only does it smell divine, but it can help soothe irritated skin, balance oil production, and even aid in calming your mind after a hectic day. It's like having a spa in a bottle. And then there's rosehip oil, which is packed with vitamins A and C, perfect for those of us who want to keep our skin supple and reduce fine lines. Dab a bit on before bed and wake up looking like you've had eight hours of sleep (even if the reality involved a Netflix binge and only five).

For men, don't be shy about diving into the herbal beauty world. Chamomile and aloe vera, for example, are great for after-shave irritation, while rosemary oil can help invigorate the scalp and promote hair health. Men's grooming has come a long way, and incorporating these natural remedies into your daily routine isn't just about looking good, it's about feeling good too.

Yoga and Facial Exercises for a Youthful Glow
Now, let's talk about keeping that youthful glow without having to resort to anything drastic. Yoga isn't just about making you bendy and helping you find your zen, it's also fantastic for your skin. The beauty of yoga lies in its ability to increase circulation, which helps bring more oxygen to your skin cells, giving you that dewy, radiant look we all crave.

Think of poses like the Downward Dog or the Camel Pose. They're not just giving your body a great stretch; they're sending blood rushing to your face, plumping up those skin cells. It's a natural way of getting that post-workout glow without the heavy makeup.

Then there's facial yoga, which might sound a little out there, but trust me, it works wonders. Our faces have muscles too, and just like any other muscle in the body, they benefit from a little toning. Simple exercises like puffing out your cheeks, raising your eyebrows, or even the famous "fish face" (you know, where you suck in your cheeks and pucker your lips) can help firm and tone your skin, reducing the appearance of fine lines. I know for some of you I'm stretching this by suggesting doing a fish-face in front of the mirror or whilst watching TV, but give it a go, even if the only result is a giggle at you or your partners expense.

Hair Health and Regrowth Strategies
Whether you're dealing with thinning hair, a receding hairline, or just want to give your locks a little extra love, keeping your hair healthy doesn't have to be a mystery. The first thing to remember is that your

hair health is closely linked to your overall health. What's going on inside your body reflects on the outside, so your diet, stress levels, and even how much sleep you're getting will have an impact.

Herbs like rosemary and peppermint oil are fantastic for promoting hair growth. Rosemary oil, in particular, has been shown to increase circulation to the scalp, which helps with hair regrowth. You can make your own DIY hair tonic by mixing a few drops of rosemary oil with a carrier oil like coconut or almond oil and massaging it into your scalp. Not only will it smell amazing, but it'll give your hair follicles a little wake-up call.

For those facing more significant hair loss, incorporating biotin supplements or foods rich in omega-3s, like salmon and flaxseed, can make a real difference. And don't underestimate the power of a scalp massage, whether you're working in oils or just using your fingertips, stimulating your scalp can encourage healthier hair growth.

To Dye or Not to Dye? The Grey Hair Dilemma
Ah, grey hair, whether it's creeping in gradually or you've woken up one morning to a full silver streak, it's one of those inevitabilities of life. But here's the thing: grey hair doesn't mean you have to panic or rush to the salon with a bottle of dye in hand. In fact, embracing your natural grey is becoming more popular than ever, and for good reason.

For both men and women, grey hair can be a symbol of wisdom, experience, and yes, even elegance. Look at any number of celebrities rocking their silver strands, and you'll see that going grey can be just as stylish as anything. If you've got a natural salt-and-pepper look happening, why not own it?

Of course, if you'd rather keep your original colour, that's totally valid too. There's no right or wrong here, and it's all about what makes you feel confident. If you do decide to dye, consider going for gentler, ammonia-free dyes or even natural alternatives like henna, which can provide a beautiful tint without the harsh chemicals.

Nurturing Your Spirit with Self-Care Rituals
No beauty routine is complete without a little self-care. After all, what's the point of having glowing skin and healthy hair if you're feeling frazzled and burnt out inside? Self-care isn't just about pampering yourself with face masks (though that's definitely part of it); it's about taking the time to nurture your mental and emotional well-being.

For some, this might mean carving out a few minutes each day to meditate or practise mindfulness. For others, it's as simple as curling up with a good book or taking a walk in nature. Whatever it is that makes you feel centred, calm, and recharged, make it a priority.

Creating a self-care ritual that you actually look forward to can do wonders for both your inner and outer beauty. Whether it's lighting a favourite candle and running a hot bath or taking time to journal your thoughts, these small acts of kindness towards yourself add up.

Beauty is More Than Skin Deep
At the end of the day, beauty isn't about perfection. It's about feeling good in your skin, embracing what makes you unique, and taking care of yourself in ways that go beyond the superficial. Whether it's through the use of herbs, yoga, or a simple shift in how we view grey hair, enhancing your beauty is as much an internal journey as it is an external one.

So, embrace the process. Take care of yourself, laugh a little more, and don't be afraid to experiment with new ways to glow, both inside and out.

Lifestyle Wellness Plan: The Beauty of Aging Well

Small Lifestyle Change	Current Habits	Goal/Action to Implement
Embrace the beauty of ageing – not everyone gets the chance	Uncertain or fear of the future	To realise that aging is a privilege and a source of confidence.
Drink more water, hydrate, moisturise, use sunscreen	Considering beauty over health or ignoring one of the most important parts of your body. You may exercise or eat well but forget your largest organ, your skin	Nurture skin and hair and adjust to the changing needs of your body
Prioritise self-care and wellness, incorporate routines than nourish body and spirit	Happily spend 10 minutes on makeup but no time on what can really make you shine.	Understanding that mindfulness and physical care are more important than cosmetics.

Longevity by Design

CHAPTER 9
Stronger Together: Building Social Support and Connection

Stronger Together: Building Social Support and Connection
When we think about living longer and healthier lives, our minds naturally go to the usual suspects: eating well, exercising, getting enough sleep, and managing stress. But there's a secret ingredient that's just as vital, though it's often overlooked in the healthspan conversation: social connection. That's right! Your friendships, family relationships, and even those casual chats with the barista at your local coffee shop could be as important to your health as a green smoothie or a daily jog. And let's be honest, they're certainly more fun.

The Science of Social Connection: Why Your Mates Matter
We humans are, at our core, social creatures. From the earliest days of human history, our survival depended on our ability to connect with others. Whether it was hunting together, gathering around a fire, or protecting the tribe from danger, we thrived through our social bonds. Fast forward to today, and while we may no longer need to gather in groups to chase woolly mammoths (thank goodness), our need for connection hasn't gone away. In fact, science now shows that having strong social ties is crucial for extending our healthspan.

A wealth of research suggests that people who maintain strong social connections live longer and are less likely to suffer from chronic diseases like heart disease, stroke, and even dementia. When you spend time with people you care about, your body releases oxytocin, a hormone that promotes feelings of well-being, reduces stress, and even lowers blood pressure. It's like your body's way of giving you a little pat on the back and saying, "Good job! Keep those connections strong!"

In contrast, loneliness can be as harmful to your health as smoking 15 cigarettes a day. Yes, you read that right, loneliness! It's a silent epidemic that quietly chips away at our health, increasing the risk of depression, anxiety, and even early death. It's no wonder researchers now say that loneliness is one of the biggest public health concerns of our time. But the good news is that the antidote to loneliness, building and maintaining social connections, is completely within our control.

The Link Between Loneliness and Disease Risk
Imagine for a moment that you're feeling disconnected. Maybe you've moved to a new city, started at University without knowing anyone, or your old friends have drifted away as life got busier. It starts as a small feeling, a niggling sense that something is missing. Over time, that sense of isolation can grow, and before you know it, loneliness has crept in, bringing along its harmful effects on both body and mind.

One of the most eye-opening studies in recent years is the "Loneliness Experiment" conducted by the BBC in partnership with the University of Manchester. It showed that chronic loneliness not only makes you feel emotionally down, but it also increases the likelihood of developing conditions like heart disease, high blood pressure, and Alzheimer's. Loneliness actually triggers inflammation in the body, which contributes to the progression of many illnesses. So, while your friends might seem like the cherry on top of a happy life, they're actually more like the foundation, supporting your health in ways you might never have imagined.

And it's not just the deep, lifelong friendships that matter. Even casual interactions with neighbours, co-workers, or the person who sits next to you at your favourite coffee shop can boost your mood and improve your sense of connection. These small moments of social engagement help reduce feelings of isolation, which, in turn, keeps your stress levels down and your health in check.

How Relationships Impact Longevity: Friends for Life
We've established that social connection is essential for your health, but let's dive a little deeper into how relationships specifically impact your longevity. It turns out that having a strong social network doesn't just help you live longer, it improves the quality of those extra years, too.

For instance, researchers have found that people who maintain close relationships into their later years are more likely to stay active, engaged, and mentally sharp. This isn't just about chatting over a cuppa; social interaction helps keep your brain firing on all cylinders. Think of your brain as a muscle that gets a workout every time you engage in meaningful conversation or share an experience with someone. In fact, studies have shown that people with strong social connections have a 50% greater chance of living longer than those who are more isolated.

It's not only about mental stimulation, though. Being part of a social group encourages you to take better care of yourself. You're more likely to eat well, exercise, and see the doctor when you have people around you who care about your well-being. Ever had a friend drag you to the gym or check in on you when you weren't feeling well? That's social support in action, helping you make healthier choices even when you're tempted to slack off.

Understanding Your Social Needs as You Age: Quality Over Quantity
It's important to note that the size of your social circle isn't what matters most. You don't need to have a hundred friends to reap the health benefits of connection (though if you do, more power to you!). What really matters is the quality of your relationships. As we age, our social needs can change, and that's perfectly normal. The number of friendships may shrink, but those remaining tend to be more meaningful, deeper, and built on shared experiences.

Understanding what you need socially as you get older is key to maintaining a fulfilling life. Maybe you've outgrown the need for big, bustling gatherings and instead crave more one-on-one time with close friends. Or perhaps you're feeling the urge to join new social groups to meet people who share your current interests, whether it's a book club, a walking group, or even an online community.

The trick is to stay open to evolving connections. As we go through life's many stages, careers, parenthood, retirement, our relationships will naturally shift. But instead of letting those shifts lead to disconnection, think of them as opportunities to build new, meaningful connections that fit where you are in life right now.

How to Nurture Meaningful Connections: The Care and Feeding of Friendships

Much like a garden, your relationships need nurturing. It's easy to let friendships slide when life gets busy, but staying connected requires a bit of effort. The good news is that it doesn't have to be hard work, it can be as simple as a phone call, a message, or an impromptu meet-up for coffee. Little acts of care and attention can strengthen your social bonds and keep them thriving over time.

Here's a fun fact: researchers have found that people who make time for socialising at least once a week are generally happier and healthier than those who don't. Think of it as emotional maintenance, something that keeps your spirits lifted and your health supported.

If you're unsure where to start, it might be as easy as rekindling old friendships. Send that text you've been meaning to send for months or pick up the phone and reconnect. You might be surprised by how easily the conversation flows, even if it's been a while. And if making new friends feels daunting, start small. Join a club, take a class, or attend a local event. Remember, it's not about forming instant, lifelong bonds, it's about giving yourself the opportunity to connect.

Creating a "Circle of Care" in Midlife: Your Social Safety Net

As we move into midlife, building a "circle of care" becomes increasingly important. This doesn't just mean having friends who will join you for brunch or a pint at the pub (though that's certainly nice, too). It's about cultivating a group of people who support you in a more holistic way, emotionally, practically, and socially. These are the people who will cheer you on when you're trying to reach your goals, lend a sympathetic ear when things aren't going so well, and help out in times of need.

Think of your circle of care as your personal support team, made up of different people who fill different roles in your life. You might have friends you turn to for emotional support, family members who are your rock in times of crisis, or colleagues who keep you motivated and inspired. Nurturing this circle means giving as much as you take, being there for others, and allowing others to be there for you. It's a mutual exchange that benefits everyone involved.

Building this circle in midlife is particularly important as you start to face new challenges, whether they're related to career transitions, health changes, or family dynamics. Your circle of care can provide the resilience you need to navigate these challenges while also reminding you that you're never alone in your journey.

At the heart of a long and healthy life is connection. While we often focus on individual health goals, like eating well or staying active, it's equally important to prioritise our social well-being. After all, we're stronger together. By building and nurturing meaningful relationships, we not only add years to our lives, but we also make those years richer, happier, and more fulfilling.

So, reach out to that friend, make time for the people who matter, and remember that every shared laugh, heartfelt conversation, and small moment of connection is helping to boost your healthspan. And what could be more rewarding than that?

Building a Supportive Community

You might think of community as something abstract or distant, but it's much more personal than that. Your community could be your lifelong best friend, the neighbour you wave at each morning, your book club, the fitness class you go to every week, or even the people you chat with online about your favourite hobbies. The beauty of building a supportive network is that it's entirely customisable to your life and your interests, and it can happen at any stage of life. So, let's dive into the why, the how, and everything in between about finding and nurturing your tribe.

Finding Your Tribe: Building a Social Network That Fits

First things first: *finding your tribe* sounds a bit mystical, right? Like you're about to embark on a quest with a map and a compass. But in reality, it's much simpler and, thankfully, less dramatic. Finding your tribe just means surrounding yourself with people who lift you up, understand you, and share your values, interests, or sense of humour. These are the people you feel comfortable with, the ones who get you without much explanation, and who support you through thick and thin.

Now, finding these magical humans might take some time. You don't just stumble upon them overnight. Start by considering your interests. Do you love hiking, dancing, painting, or perhaps you're a bookworm who can't resist a good novel? Whatever it is, there's probably a group or club out there for it. The great thing about joining groups cantered around activities you already enjoy is that you'll automatically have something in common with the people you meet, which makes conversation flow naturally.

If you're the shy type, dipping your toe into new social circles can feel intimidating. Here's a little secret: most people feel exactly the same way. Everyone's just waiting for someone to break the ice. You don't need to arrive with a grand speech prepared; a simple "Hi, I'm new here" is usually enough to get things going. Remember, you're not alone in wanting to connect, others are looking for their tribe too.

The Benefits of Friendships for Health

For women in particular, friendships can be lifelines. In fact, research has shown that female friendships play a significant role in reducing stress and boosting mental health. There's something uniquely powerful about the way women support each other. You know those conversations that start with "I just need to vent" and end with a feeling of pure relief? That's not just emotional, it's science. When women engage in supportive social interaction, their bodies release oxytocin, a hormone that reduces stress and promotes feelings of bonding and trust. So, those long chats over coffee or wine are more than just pleasant; they're good for your health!

Of course, these benefits aren't exclusive to women. Men, too, can gain tremendous health benefits from having close, supportive friendships. However, studies suggest that men often rely more heavily on their romantic partners for emotional support, which can lead to a smaller social circle. This is why it's important for everyone, men and women alike, to cultivate diverse social relationships. Whether it's a mate you've known since school, a colleague turned confidant, or a friendly neighbour, having people outside of your immediate family to talk to, laugh with, and rely on is key to your overall well-being.

Joining Clubs, Groups, and Social Circles
One of the easiest ways to build a supportive community is by joining clubs, groups, or classes that align with your interests. The beauty of group activities is that they create an instant sense of belonging. Whether it's a yoga class, a running club, a book group, or a cooking workshop, these activities provide a built-in social structure. You might not immediately feel like you're part of a tribe, but over time, as you attend more sessions, chat with more people, and share more experiences, that sense of community will start to grow.

The great thing about groups is that you can also learn new skills while making friends. Take a pottery class, for instance. Not only will you end up with a wonky bowl or two, but you'll also have a laugh over the mess with the person next to you. Or try a hiking group. As you trek through forests or mountains, conversations naturally flow, and friendships develop without the pressure of formal socialising. These kinds of shared experiences build strong bonds because they're rooted in something you both enjoy.

If you're looking to dip your toes into social waters without too much commitment, you can also explore online communities. There are countless forums, Facebook groups, and even local Meetup events for every interest under the sun. These can be a great way to connect with like-minded people and, if you're up for it, meet in person for events or gatherings.

Volunteering as a Way to Connect and Contribute

If you're looking for something deeper than just joining a group, volunteering is an incredibly fulfilling way to build connections. When you volunteer, you're not only doing something good for your community, but you're also creating meaningful relationships with people who share your passion for a cause.

Whether it's at a local charity, an animal shelter, or a community garden, volunteering brings together people from all walks of life. You'll meet others who are committed to making a positive difference, which can often lead to some of the most genuine, long-lasting friendships.

There's a certain camaraderie that comes from working alongside others for a shared cause. Whether it's organising a charity run or serving meals at a food bank, the bonds you form during these experiences are often incredibly strong. Plus, it gives you a shared purpose, something bigger than yourself, which can make conversations flow more naturally. And let's face it: it's hard to be shy when you're busy walking dogs or planting trees!

Navigating Changes in Relationships

Building a supportive community doesn't mean relationships stay static. Friendships can ebb and flow, and that's perfectly normal. As you grow and change, so do your relationships. Sometimes, you might drift apart from people you were once close to. That can be tough, but it's a natural part of life. As we evolve, our needs change, and so do the people we connect with.

If you find yourself in a situation where some relationships are no longer serving you, it's okay to step back. That doesn't mean cutting people out dramatically but recognising that certain friendships may not fit into your life as they once did. This can open up space for new, more aligned relationships to enter your life.

Change can be difficult, but it also brings opportunities for growth. When you move into new circles or experiences, don't be afraid to bring new people into your community. Each stage of life presents a chance to meet others who will support and enrich your journey.

Avoiding Toxic Relationships and Negative Influences
While building a supportive community, it's crucial to recognise and avoid toxic relationships. We've all been there: stuck in a friendship or relationship that drains our energy rather than refilling our emotional tank. Toxic relationships, whether they're based on manipulation, negativity, or constant drama, can harm your mental and emotional health. One of the greatest acts of self-care is learning when to step away from people who bring you down or create stress in your life.

Boundaries are important. It's okay to say no, to step back, and to protect your own well-being. Surround yourself with people who lift you up, inspire you, and make you feel good about yourself. Life is too short to waste time on relationships that don't bring joy or positivity.

The Power of Community for a Longer, Happier Life
In the end, building a supportive community is about creating a life filled with connection, laughter, and shared experiences. It's about finding those people who celebrate your wins, support you through challenges, and offer a shoulder to lean on when times get tough. It's also about reciprocating that support, giving back to the people around you, and nurturing the relationships that matter most.

Whether you find your tribe through hobbies, volunteering, or shared passions, remember that these connections are essential for a long, healthy, and fulfilling life. Social bonds aren't just pleasant extras, they're vital components of our well-being. So go ahead, say yes to that club, that class, that coffee with a friend. The community you build today will be the foundation of the vibrant, supportive life you live tomorrow.

Creating a Legacy of Connection
There's something magical about the idea of leaving behind a legacy, isn't there? It conjures up visions of lives touched, wisdom shared, and a ripple effect that extends far beyond our years. For many of us, though, the word "legacy" feels like it belongs to grand figures in history books, people who built empires or wrote bestsellers. But the truth is, we all create legacies, every single day. And more often than

not, the most enduring legacies are the ones built on love, connection, and the moments we share with others. It's the kind of legacy that doesn't get etched into stone but, instead, is written on the hearts of the people we care about.

Let's dive into the very human need to connect and share, to leave behind something meaningful, not in a flashy, look-at-me sort of way, but in the quiet, powerful, and profoundly human way of building lasting bonds. And let's be honest: we all want to feel like we've made a difference in someone's life, don't we?

Mentoring Younger People: Passing the Torch Without the Lecture

Remember when you were young, fresh-faced, and totally convinced you knew it all? Now that we've gathered a little more wisdom (and perhaps a few more grey hairs), it's easy to look back and laugh at how much we didn't know. That's where mentoring comes in. It's not about sitting down and giving out a TED Talk on life (though, hey, if you've got the chops for it, why not?), but rather sharing those hard-earned lessons in a way that's relatable, helpful, and most importantly, non-patronising. After all, no one likes a lecture.

Mentoring can take many forms. Maybe it's your niece or nephew who's just starting out in their career, or perhaps it's the younger colleagues at work who seem to be running into the same walls you did at their age. The key is to listen as much as you talk. Remember, no one likes being told what to do, but they appreciate guidance, especially when it's delivered with a dash of humility. After all, none of us have it all figured out, and that's okay.

Think of mentoring like offering a map. You're not telling someone exactly where to go, but you're showing them some routes that worked for you—and maybe pointing out the potholes and dead ends along the way. And, if you're lucky, they'll do the same for you when you find yourself navigating unfamiliar terrain. It's a two-way street, and that's what makes it so powerful.

Why not look at The Kings/Prince's Trust at https://www.kingstrust.org.uk/

Staying Connected to Family and Loved Ones: The Balancing Act

Family dynamics can be tricky, can't they? Whether it's keeping in touch with siblings, managing the whirlwind of grandkids, or just making time for those family Zoom calls, it can sometimes feel like a full-time job. But staying connected with the people who matter most is one of the best ways to build a legacy of love.

One of the keys here is recognising that connection doesn't always have to be big and showy. It's the little things that count. Sending a quick message to check in, dropping off a batch of cookies, or simply making time for a phone call, it all adds up. And sometimes, the quieter moments of connection, like sitting together in comfortable silence, can be the most meaningful.

But let's be real: life gets busy. Between work, personal commitments, and everything in between, staying connected can feel like just one more thing on the to-do list. That's where setting realistic expectations comes in. You don't have to be available 24/7, and you certainly don't have to attend every family event. What matters is the quality of the connection, not the quantity. So, when you do show up, whether in person or virtually, make sure you are really there, fully present, and engaged. That's what people will remember.

Supporting Others Without Burning Out: The Delicate Dance of Giving

Let's talk about one of the toughest balancing acts of all: supporting the people you care about without burning yourself out in the process. It's easy to get caught up in the idea that being a supportive friend, family member, or mentor means always being available, always putting others first. But the truth is, if you don't take care of yourself, you're not going to be much help to anyone else in the long run.

Supporting others is like being on an aeroplane when the oxygen masks drop: you've got to put on your own mask first before you can help anyone else. That might mean setting boundaries, saying no sometimes, or even stepping back when you need to recharge. It's not selfish, it's essential. You can't pour from an empty cup, as the saying goes.

When it comes to supporting others, it's also important to recognise the limits of what you can do. You can't fix everyone's problems, and you're not responsible for their happiness. What you can do is offer empathy, a listening ear, and sometimes a shoulder to cry on. And if someone you care about is really struggling, don't be afraid to suggest professional help. Sometimes the best way to support someone is by helping them find the right resources.

Hosting Gatherings and Rituals for Connection: More Than Just a Party
There's something timeless and deeply human about gathering together, isn't there? Throughout history, people have come together to share food, stories, and experiences. Whether it's a family meal, a holiday celebration, or just a casual get-together, these gatherings help strengthen bonds and create lasting memories. Plus, who doesn't love a good party?

But here's the thing: gatherings don't have to be formal or elaborate. In fact, some of the most meaningful connections happen in the simplest settings. A Sunday roast with the family, a backyard BBQ with friends, or even a virtual happy hour, what matters is the time spent together, not the decorations or the menu. And if you're the one hosting, don't stress about making everything perfect. People remember how you made them feel, not the matching napkins.

If you want to take things up a notch, consider creating rituals that you can return to year after year. Maybe it's an annual gathering to celebrate a shared passion, or perhaps it's a simple weekly tradition like Sunday dinners or Friday night board games. These rituals give people something to look forward to, a sense of continuity and connection that can help strengthen relationships over time.

Using Technology to Maintain Bonds: Bridging the Distance
In today's world, staying connected doesn't always mean being physically present. Thanks to technology, it's easier than ever to keep in touch with loved ones, no matter where they are. Whether it's a quick video call, a group chat, or even sharing memes or funnies on social media, technology can help bridge the gap when distance or time constraints get in the way.

That said, it's important to use technology mindfully. Just because we can be connected 24/7 doesn't mean we should be. The goal is to use tech to enhance your connections, not replace real-world interactions. And let's be honest, sometimes there's no substitute for a face-to-face chat over a cup of tea.

But when in-person isn't possible, embrace the digital tools at your disposal. Set up regular video calls with far-flung family members, start a group chat with your closest friends, or even create a shared photo album where everyone can upload pictures and memories. These small gestures can help keep relationships strong, even when life gets busy or people move away.

Leaving a Legacy of Love and Support: The Lasting Impact of Connection

At the end of the day, the legacy you leave behind won't be measured in material possessions or professional accomplishments, it will be reflected in the lives you've touched, the love you've shared, and the connections you've nurtured. And the best part? You don't have to wait until you're gone to start building that legacy. Every kind word, every moment of support, and every connection you make today becomes a part of that legacy.

A legacy of love and support is something that lives on long after we're gone. It's in the memories of the people whose lives you've touched, the lessons you've passed down, and the bonds you've helped create. It's in the way you've shown up for others, not as a superhero who's always got it together, but as a fellow human being who's willing to share, listen, and care.

So, go ahead, create your legacy of connection. Mentor the next generation, host those family dinners, check in on your friends, and be there for the people who matter. Because in the end, it's not about what we have; it's about who we have and how we've loved them along the way.

Lifestyle Wellness Plan: Stronger Together

Small Lifestyle Change	Current Habits	Goal/Action to Implement
Identify key relationships and focus on those	You spend time nurturing the relationships that are not important to you and not watering those that mean everything	These people are on life's journey with you, they make you happy, they support you, or will unless you let the relationship wither
Create regular opportunities for connection. Small moments can mean everything to people, even you.	Too busy. My friends will always be there, may not actually be true unless you make the effort to keep them	Set aside time for regular gatherings, video calls, or just pick up the phone
Build a supportive network, show up and be present	Have the same relationships for the last 10 years, missing out on your new tribe as you've grown	Consider joining clubs, volunteering or something where you meet good people

The connections we build with the people around us are not just an added bonus in life; they are a fundamental part of maintaining a healthy, long, and fulfilling life. We all know the value of eating well, exercising, and getting enough sleep, but social support is an equally crucial factor in extending our healthspan. This action plan encourages you to focus on maintaining and deepening relationships, making time for loved ones, and actively engaging in your community. Because let's face it, life is so much better when shared with others!

CHAPTER 10
Mind over Matter: Cognitive Health and Mental Sharpness

Protecting Your Brain as You Age
We spend a lot of time thinking about how to keep our bodies in top shape, toning muscles, improving heart health, eating the right foods, but what about the brain? That three-pound organ sitting in your skull is arguably the most important muscle you have, and like the rest of your body, it needs care and attention to keep it in tip-top condition as you age. Protecting your cognitive health is all about making conscious choices that nourish not only your physical body but also your mind. And the best part? It's never too late to start!

Understanding Brain Aging and Neuroplasticity
Let's start with a big word: **neuroplasticity**. It sounds complicated, but in simple terms, it's your brain's ability to adapt and change throughout your life. Yes, even as we grow older, our brains can form new connections and pathways—how cool is that? Think of your brain like a road network. When a road gets blocked (or damaged through injury or age), your brain can create a detour—a new pathway to get you where you need to go. That's neuroplasticity in action.

But, just like keeping roads well-maintained, it takes effort to ensure your brain remains agile. As we age, changes happen in the brain, and some of these changes are completely normal. You might notice you're a little slower at recalling names or struggle to remember where you left your keys (spoiler: probably in the fridge). This doesn't mean cognitive decline is inevitable, far from it! With the right strategies, you can keep your brain sharp and flexible.

The Role of Diet and Exercise in Brain Health

What you put in your body has a massive impact on how your brain performs. Let's face it, we all know that eating a burger and fries every day won't do us any favours in the long run. The same is true for your brain. A nutrient-rich diet full of antioxidants, healthy fats, and omega-3s is essential for brain function. Foods like blueberries, nuts, fatty fish, and even dark chocolate are fantastic for cognitive health. So yes, science says you can indulge in that square of chocolate, guilt-free!

Beyond food, *exercise* plays a significant role in protecting your brain. Now, before you sigh at the thought of more fitness talk, here's the good news: you don't have to be a marathon runner to boost your brain power. Even moderate exercise like walking, swimming, or dancing can increase blood flow to the brain, helping it stay oxygenated and nourished. Plus, exercise triggers the release of chemicals that encourage the growth of new brain cells. It's a literal "brain boost." Just think every step on that treadmill is strengthening your brain as much as your body.

Cognitive Decline vs. Normal Aging

It's important to understand that **normal aging** does involve some changes in how our brains function. Just as our skin wrinkles and our hair greys, our brain's processing speed may slow down a little. This is completely natural. You might take a moment longer to retrieve information or get frustrated trying to remember what's on the tip of your tongue. But this is worlds apart from *cognitive decline*.

Cognitive decline refers to a noticeable decrease in mental abilities, such as memory, reasoning, and problem-solving, that disrupts daily life. It's a more serious issue than the everyday "senior moments" we all experience. While cognitive decline can be linked to conditions like Alzheimer's or dementia, it doesn't happen overnight, and there <u>are</u> steps you can take to reduce the risk.

Common Cognitive Disorders in Women (and Men, Too)

Women, it turns out, tend to be at a higher risk for cognitive disorders like **Alzheimer's disease**. In fact, almost two-thirds of Americans living with Alzheimer's are women, but this isn't just a women's issue, men are affected too. Scientists are still working to understand why women are more susceptible, with factors like hormones, genetics, and even life expectancy playing a role. But men are not immune to cognitive disorders. The good news is that with increasing awareness and research, more preventative strategies are emerging for everyone.

Conditions like *vascular dementia,* which is often caused by strokes or other conditions affecting blood flow to the brain, affect both men and women, and both can take the same steps to mitigate risk. The emphasis here is on making proactive changes, long before any signs of decline appear. By nurturing our brains with the right lifestyle choices, we can make a tangible difference to our long-term cognitive health.

Early Signs of Memory Issues to Watch For

We all misplace things or forget why we walked into a room from time to time, it's a universal human experience. But there are some **early signs of memory issues** that are worth keeping an eye on. If you notice you or a loved one:

- Frequently forget conversations or events.
- Struggle to find the right words.
- Have trouble following a storyline (even a Netflix Christmas Prince plot!).
- Lose track of dates or forget appointments.
- Show poor judgement or become confused easily.

These could be early warning signs of more significant cognitive changes. It's important not to panic if you notice one or two of these occasionally, it happens to the best of us! However, if these become frequent and disruptive, it's worth discussing with a doctor. Early detection can make a huge difference in managing cognitive health, and there are many treatments and therapies that can slow the progression of memory loss.

Strategies to Protect Cognitive Function

Now that we've tackled some of the scarier stuff, let's get into the fun part: **how to protect your brain**! The first thing to remember is that keeping your brain sharp doesn't have to be hard work. It's about adding a bit of playfulness and curiosity to your day-to-day life. Here's how:

1. **Keep Learning**: The more you challenge your brain, the better. Learn a new language, pick up a hobby like knitting, painting, or even coding! These activities encourage your brain to form new connections and keep it agile.
2. **Puzzles and Games**: Brain teasers, crosswords, Sudoku, and even board games are excellent for boosting cognitive function. Don't underestimate the power of a good puzzle, solving them is like taking your brain to the gym.
3. **Social Connections**: Chatting with friends is more than just good for your soul—it's good for your brain too! Engaging in conversation, sharing stories, and having a laugh with others stimulates mental activity. So, schedule that coffee catch-up or Zoom call with a mate, it's officially "brain food."
4. **Mindfulness and Meditation**: Taking time to be present can lower stress, which in turn protects your brain from the damaging effects of chronic stress hormones like cortisol. Meditation isn't just about sitting still for hours; it can be as simple as spending a few minutes focusing on your breathing. It's like a reset button for your brain.
5. **Sleep**: Yes, your mum was right, getting enough sleep is crucial for brain health. When we sleep, our brains consolidate memories and clear out toxins. So, next time you're tempted to binge-watch late into the night, remember that those precious zzz's are keeping your brain in tip-top shape.

Leaving a Legacy of Love and Support

Protecting your cognitive health isn't just about you, it's about the people you love too. When you take care of your brain, you're better able to stay present, engaged, and supportive of the ones you care about. There's nothing more valuable than leaving a legacy of love, wisdom, and shared memories. It's the conversations, the advice, the life lessons that you pass down that stay with people long after you're gone.

Think of the stories you'll be able to share, the wisdom you'll impart, and the love you'll spread when your mind is sharp and active well into your later years. Keeping your brain healthy isn't just about preserving memories for yourself, it's about creating a life rich with experiences that you can share with others.

So, whether it's keeping up with your grandkids' latest technology, learning new things to stay relevant, or just being able to sit down and share stories from your life, your brain is your most powerful asset for leaving a lasting impact.

In the end, cognitive health is as much about making memories as it is about keeping them. With a bit of humour, curiosity, and a lot of love for your brain, you can make sure it stays as sharp as your wit well into your golden years.

Learning New Skills: Your Brain's Secret Weapon
We've all heard the saying, "You can't teach an old dog new tricks." But when it comes to our brains, nothing could be further from the truth. In fact, learning new skills is one of the most powerful things you can do to keep your brain in top shape, no matter your age. It's not just about gaining knowledge or mastering a hobby—learning something new literally changes the structure of your brain, making it more resilient, adaptable, and youthful. This is where the magic of building your cognitive reserve comes in.

Imagine your brain as a complex city with a maze of roads connecting all the different neighbourhoods. These roads are like the neural pathways in your brain. When you learn something new, it's like constructing fresh highways, bridges, and shortcuts, giving your brain more routes to take when processing information. The more you challenge yourself with new skills, the more diverse and efficient your mental network becomes. This flexibility is key to maintaining cognitive function as you age, as it allows your brain to adapt even when faced with difficulties like memory loss or injury.

The Science Behind Learning and the Brain
Before we dive into the fun of skill-building, let's explore why learning new things is so beneficial for your brain. Neuroplasticity is the term that refers to the brain's ability to reorganise itself by forming new neural connections. In simple terms, your brain isn't a static organ; it's

constantly changing and adapting based on your experiences. Every time you take on a new challenge, whether it's learning to knit or taking up tennis, you're forcing your brain to create new pathways and connections. The more pathways you create, the stronger and more flexible your brain becomes.

This is especially important as we age. Studies show that cognitive decline is linked to a decrease in these neural connections, but the good news is that by staying mentally active, you can slow down, or even reverse, some of these effects. Learning new skills helps maintain the grey matter in your brain, which is involved in muscle control, sensory perception, and memory. The more grey matter you have, the more cognitive reserve you can build, providing a buffer against the effects of aging and neurodegenerative diseases like Alzheimer's.

Step Outside Your Comfort Zone
So where do you start? The key is to step outside your comfort zone. The brain thrives on novelty and challenge. If you've been doing the same crossword puzzle every day for years, it's time to mix it up. Your brain craves variety, and learning something entirely new is like giving it a surprise workout.

Let's say you've always wanted to learn the piano. You don't need to have visions of playing Beethoven's symphonies to benefit from the process. Simply learning the basics, how to read music, where to place your fingers on the keys, activates parts of your brain that haven't been used before. Not only are you engaging your fine motor skills, but you're also training your memory, spatial reasoning, and even your emotional processing as you interpret the music.

The same goes for learning a new language. When you pick up a language, especially as an adult, your brain has to work extra hard to make sense of unfamiliar sounds, grammar structures, and vocabulary. Apps like Duolingo make the process feel like a game, turning daily practice into an adventure rather than a chore. And the benefits are huge: bilingual individuals tend to have better cognitive function later in life, with a significantly delayed onset of dementia symptoms compared to monolingual people.

The trick is to keep pushing yourself. Mastery isn't the goal; the journey is where the real magic happens. Every time you stretch your mental muscles by learning something new, you're giving your brain a workout that will pay dividends in the long run.

Connecting with Others Through Learning

Learning doesn't have to be a solitary pursuit, either. In fact, one of the most rewarding aspects of taking on new challenges is that it often brings you into contact with others who share your interests. Whether you're signing up for a pottery class or joining a book club, learning something new can help you build meaningful connections with others. This social engagement is another powerful way to boost your cognitive reserve.

Studies have shown that staying socially active is closely linked to better cognitive health. When you're interacting with others, your brain is working hard to process conversations, read social cues, and stay engaged. All of this keeps your mind sharp and alert. Combine that with the benefits of learning a new skill, and you've got a recipe for a healthy brain.

And let's not forget the joy of sharing what you've learned with others. Whether you're showing a friend how to bake bread or discussing the intricacies of Spanish grammar with a language buddy, teaching someone else is a fantastic way to reinforce your own knowledge. It deepens your understanding, sharpens your communication skills, and provides a sense of accomplishment. Plus, it's a lot of fun.

Keeping It Fun: The Importance of Enjoyment in Learning

Let's be honest, if learning isn't enjoyable, it's going to be tough to stick with it. The beauty of building cognitive reserve is that there are endless ways to do it, so you can choose activities that genuinely excite you. Always wanted to learn how to make sushi? Go for it. Curious about photography? Dive in. The point is that the process should feel rewarding and enjoyable.

The more fun you have, the more likely you are to stick with it. And that's crucial because consistency is key when it comes to learning. You don't have to dedicate hours every day, just a little bit of time regularly will have a huge impact on your brain. Plus, when you're having fun, your brain releases dopamine, which not only makes you feel good but also enhances learning and memory. So, find something you're passionate about and dive in.

The Benefits Go Beyond the Brain
While learning new skills does wonders for your brain, the benefits don't stop there. Taking on new challenges can improve your overall well-being in ways you might not expect. For one, learning new skills boosts confidence. There's something incredibly empowering about starting from scratch and gradually improving. It reminds you that you're capable of growth and change, no matter your age.

Learning also gives you a sense of purpose. When you're actively engaged in a new pursuit, you have something to look forward to, a reason to keep going. This is especially important as we get older, when it can be easy to fall into routines that don't challenge us. Having something new on the horizon keeps you motivated and excited about life. And then there's the simple joy of achievement. Whether it's completing a painting, playing a piece of music, or holding your first conversation in French, there's a deep sense of satisfaction that comes with accomplishing something new. These little wins can have a big impact on your mental health, boosting your mood and giving you a positive outlook on life.

Breaking Through the Barriers: Overcoming the Fear of Trying Something New
If you're feeling a bit daunted by the idea of picking up a new skill, don't worry, you're not alone. Many of us hesitate to try new things, especially as we get older. There's a fear of failure, of looking silly, or of not being good at something right away. But here's the secret: it's perfectly okay to be a beginner. In fact, it's one of the best things you can do for your brain.

Remember, the goal isn't perfection, it's progress. Every time you step out of your comfort zone and try something new, you're doing your brain a huge favour. So, let go of the fear of failure and embrace the excitement of learning. Mistakes are part of the process, and they're how we grow. And if you're worried about time, start small. You don't need to dive into a full-blown course or commit hours a day. Even just 10-15 minutes of learning something new can have a positive impact on your brain. The important thing is to get started, and once you do, you'll likely find that the enjoyment of the process keeps you coming back for more.

Why Lifelong Learning Matters
As we get older, it's easy to think that our days of learning are behind us. But the truth is, lifelong learning is one of the best gifts you can give yourself. Not only does it keep your brain sharp, but it also keeps you engaged with the world around you. It fosters curiosity, creativity, and connection, three things that are essential for a happy and fulfilling life.

The benefits of learning new skills go beyond just building cognitive reserve. They enrich your life in ways you might not have imagined. They introduce you to new people, new ideas, and new ways of thinking. They keep you curious and open-minded, qualities that are just as important in your later years as they were when you were younger. And the best part? There's no limit to what you can learn. Whether it's knitting, photography, coding, or playing the guitar, there's always something new to discover. So, why not make lifelong learning a priority? Your brain, and your life, will thank you for it.

Learning new skills isn't just a way to stave off cognitive decline, it's a way to live a richer, more vibrant life. It's about keeping your brain sharp and engaged, yes, but it's also about finding joy in the process of discovery. It's about staying curious, challenging yourself, and embracing the thrill of the new.

So, if you've always wanted to learn something, whether it's painting, playing an instrument, or mastering a new language, there's no better time to start than now. Not only will you be giving your brain a fantastic workout, but you'll also be opening yourself up to new experiences, new people, and new joys. And in the end, isn't that what life is all

The Power of Puzzles, Games, and Memory Exercises: Unlocking Your Brain's Full Potential

Let's face it, keeping your brain sharp is just as important as taking care of your body, but it doesn't have to feel like a chore. In fact, it can be a lot of fun. Whether you're a crossword enthusiast, a lover of jigsaws, or someone who enjoys a quick round of Scrabble, engaging your brain with puzzles, games, and memory exercises is like giving it a workout without the sweat. These activities not only boost cognitive function but also improve your ability to problem-solve, focus, and even stave off the natural cognitive decline that comes with aging. And guess what? It can be downright entertaining too.

Puzzles: Mental Gymnastics for Your Brain

Puzzles, in all their many forms, are much more than a way to pass the time. They are the equivalent of mental gymnastics, forcing your brain to stretch in ways it may not normally do during the course of a routine day. They help develop critical thinking, improve memory, and enhance problem-solving skills. In short, puzzles are like vitamins for your brain, giving it a little extra fuel to stay healthy and vibrant.

Crosswords: Wordplay building connections in the brain

There's a reason crosswords have remained a staple of newspapers and puzzle books for so long. They engage multiple areas of the brain, particularly those associated with language and memory. When you solve a crossword, you're not just recalling facts; you're also working through complex word associations and language mechanics, which help strengthen neural connections in the brain.

A study published in the journal *Neurology* showed that older adults who regularly engaged in word puzzles such as crosswords had better memory function than those who didn't. Even if you're not a whiz at crosswords, starting simple and building up your skills can lead to significant cognitive gains over time. It's all about consistency and keeping that language-processing part of the brain active.

Jigsaw Puzzles: Piecing Together Cognitive Benefits

Jigsaw puzzles, often considered a leisurely activity, have profound benefits for brain health. They require a mix of short-term memory, attention to detail, and spatial reasoning. When you're hunting for the right puzzle piece, you're constantly testing different possibilities, honing your problem-solving skills.

But it doesn't stop there, doing jigsaws also activates both hemispheres of the brain. Your left hemisphere focuses on logic and sequential thinking, while your right hemisphere works on creativity and spatial awareness. This dual-brain engagement boosts overall cognitive function and strengthens brain connections, making it an excellent activity for mental longevity.

Sudoku: Numbers Never Looked So Fun
If words aren't your thing, maybe numbers are. Sudoku, the classic number puzzle, has been shown to improve concentration and logic. By forcing you to think critically about where to place numbers within a grid, Sudoku sharpens your pattern recognition and decision-making skills. It also enhances working memory, which is vital for tasks that require you to hold onto information for short periods of time.

The best part? Sudoku comes in various levels of difficulty, so you can challenge yourself progressively. Even tackling just one puzzle a day can help improve cognitive function and keep your brain in top form.

Games That Push Your Brain to the Next Level
While puzzles are excellent for mental stimulation, let's not forget about games, especially those that require strategy, quick thinking, and coordination. Games, whether they're board games or video games, can provide a host of cognitive benefits while also being a great source of entertainment. The key is to engage with games that require a bit of thought and problem-solving, as they stimulate different areas of the brain and improve overall mental flexibility.

Chess: The Ultimate Brain Workout
There's a reason chess has been around for centuries and continues to captivate millions. It's the ultimate test of strategy and foresight, requiring players to think several moves ahead. When you play chess, you're not only improving your ability to focus and plan but you also strengthen memory and problem-solving skills. Research has shown that regular chess players tend to have higher IQs and better cognitive function, making it an excellent way to keep your brain sharp.

Chess is also a fantastic way to improve decision-making under pressure. Every move requires you to weigh the pros and cons, think about potential outcomes, and make strategic decisions, all within a time limit if you're playing competitively. It's mental agility at its finest.

Not into chess? Don't worry, there are plenty of other strategy-based games that offer similar benefits.

Scrabble: Wordplay Meets Strategy
If chess isn't your cup of tea, how about a good old-fashioned game of Scrabble? Not only does Scrabble challenge your vocabulary, but it also forces you to think on your feet. You're constantly strategizing how to use your letters, maximise points, and block your opponent's moves.

Playing Scrabble regularly helps improve language skills, memory recall, and even arithmetic as you calculate scores. Plus, it's a fun way to engage with friends or family, offering social interaction while giving your brain a solid workout.

Video Games: Fun with a Cognitive Twist
While video games sometimes get a bad rap, not all screen time is wasted time. In fact, certain video games can be incredibly beneficial for cognitive function, especially those that require quick thinking, problem-solving, and hand-eye coordination.

Games like *Portal*, *Tetris*, or even *Zelda* offer puzzles and strategic challenges that require you to adapt and think on your feet. Meanwhile, action games often improve spatial awareness, attention span, and reflexes. The key, of course, is moderation. Too much screen time can be counterproductive, but a bit of gaming here and there can be a fun and stimulating way to keep your brain active.

Memory Exercises: Keeping Your Mind Sharp
Incorporating memory exercises into your daily routine is another excellent way to maintain mental sharpness. These exercises can be as simple as they are effective, requiring just a few minutes each day to give your brain a boost.

Word and Object Recall

One of the simplest but most effective memory exercises is the word or object recall challenge. Start by making a list of random words, numbers, or objects, and then test yourself an hour later to see how many you can remember. This technique helps sharpen short-term memory, making it easier to recall details in everyday life.

Another option is to create mental associations with each word or object on your list. For example, if you have "apple, car, and book" on your list, picture a car with an apple on the roof driving through the pages of a giant book. The more bizarre and creative your associations, the better your memory retention will be.

Visualisation: Mentally Walking Through Memory Lane

If word lists aren't your thing, try this: visualisation. This technique involves mentally walking through a familiar space, like your childhood home, and recalling specific details. How many windows were in the living room? What was the colour of the front door? These mental "walks" challenge your brain to recall spatial and visual details, keeping your memory in fighting form.

You can mix this up by visualising new or imaginary spaces as well, which pushes your brain to both recall and create, enhancing its overall cognitive function.

Memory Palaces: A Time-Tested Technique

The ancient Greeks and Romans used a technique called the memory palace to memorise speeches and vast amounts of information, and it's still incredibly effective today. The idea is to imagine a place you know well, like your home or a familiar walk, and mentally "place" the things you want to remember at various points along your route.

For example, if you're trying to remember a shopping list, imagine putting each item in a different room of your house. When it's time to recall the list, simply walk through the house in your mind, and you'll "see" each item in the place you left it. This technique uses spatial memory to help enhance recall, and it's a fun way to stretch your brain.

The Role of Cognitive Exercises in Preventing Cognitive Decline

Why all this fuss about puzzles, games, and memory exercises? The truth is, engaging your brain in these ways may not just keep it sharp today, it could also help protect it against the cognitive decline that comes with aging. Studies suggest that maintaining an active and engaged brain may lower the risk of dementia and Alzheimer's disease or at least delay the onset of these conditions.

Just as regular exercise strengthens your muscles and bones, cognitive exercises help build brain resilience, or "cognitive reserve." This reserve is essentially your brain's ability to compensate for any damage or deterioration that comes with aging. The more you build your cognitive reserve, the better equipped you are to handle life's mental challenges in the years to come.

The Social Side of Cognitive Engagement

Let's not forget the added bonus of social interaction. Many puzzles, games, and memory exercises can be enjoyed with friends or family, offering a wonderful way to engage your brain while strengthening relationships. Social connection is crucial for mental health, and combining it with brain-boosting activities like a weekly Scrabble game or jigsaw puzzle night gives you double the benefits.

Whether it's a friendly game of chess, a group puzzle-solving session, or even a competitive online Scrabble tournament, you're not only improving your cognitive function, but you're also enjoying the emotional and psychological benefits of connecting with others. And who doesn't love a bit of friendly competition?

Making Puzzles and Games a Regular Part of Your Life

Building cognitive reserve isn't about spending hours a day hunched over a Sudoku book or playing endless rounds of chess. It's about incorporating these activities into your life in a way that feels natural and enjoyable. Maybe you like to do the crossword over your morning coffee or tackle a jigsaw puzzle on a rainy afternoon. Perhaps you challenge yourself to a quick game of Scrabble on your lunch break or play a strategy-based video game in the evenings as a way to unwind. The key is finding the right balance, keeping your brain engaged without feeling like it's a chore. After all, puzzles, games, and memory exercises should be fun. The best part? The more you enjoy it, the more likely you are to stick with it.

Strategies for Making Brain-Boosting Activities a Habit

So how do you make puzzles, games, and memory exercises a regular part of your life? It's easier than you might think, and it doesn't have to be time-consuming or overwhelming. Here are some simple strategies to keep your brain in top shape while enjoying yourself:

1. Create a Routine You Enjoy

Start by incorporating puzzles or games into an existing routine. If you already enjoy reading the paper in the morning, add a crossword puzzle to your ritual. If you like winding down with a cup of tea after work, try tackling a Sudoku or jigsaw puzzle while you relax. The idea is to blend brain-boosting activities into things you already do, so they become an enjoyable part of your daily life.

2. Join a Puzzle or Game Group

If you're a social butterfly, why not join a group of like-minded people who also enjoy puzzles and games? Many communities have Scrabble clubs, chess groups, or jigsaw puzzle meet-ups, where you can combine mental stimulation with social interaction. You can also find online groups where you can connect with others who love solving puzzles or playing games. This adds a layer of fun and accountability, making it easier to stick with your cognitive routine.

3. Make It a Family Affair

Get your family involved! Whether it's a weekly game night with the kids or tackling a huge jigsaw puzzle together over a weekend, involving others can make the experience more enjoyable. Not only does this build cognitive reserve for everyone involved, but it also creates quality time with loved ones, which is just as important for mental health as the games themselves.

4. Set Goals and Challenge Yourself

If you're the competitive type, set personal goals to motivate yourself. Maybe you want to complete a crossword in a certain amount of time or aim to master a chess strategy you've never tried before. Challenging yourself keeps things interesting and pushes you to improve your skills over time. You can even reward yourself with small treats or breaks after accomplishing a particularly difficult puzzle.

5. Try Different Types of Puzzles and Games
Don't limit yourself to just one type of puzzle or game. Variety is the spice of life, and it's also key to keeping your brain on its toes. Mix things up by rotating through different activities, one day it might be a crossword, the next day a memory game, followed by a few rounds of chess over the weekend. This variety keeps your brain guessing and ensures that you're stimulating different cognitive functions.

The Cognitive Payoff: Why It's Worth It
You might be wondering, is all this effort really necessary? After all, puzzles and games can be fun, but can they really make that big of a difference? The answer is a resounding *yes*. Engaging your brain through puzzles, games, and memory exercises builds cognitive reserve, which is like a mental buffer that helps protect your brain against decline as you age.

Researchers have found that people who regularly engage in mentally stimulating activities tend to have better cognitive function later in life. They're more likely to maintain their memory, problem-solving abilities, and decision-making skills well into their golden years. And while nothing can completely prevent cognitive decline, having a robust cognitive reserve can delay its onset and reduce its severity.

Beyond the long-term benefits, there's also the immediate cognitive boost. You may find that after regularly engaging in puzzles or games, you're sharper in your day-to-day life. Maybe you remember things more easily, solve problems faster, or find yourself thinking more creatively. These mental benefits spill over into every aspect of your life, helping you stay sharp, focused, and engaged in the world around you.

Mindful Play: Avoiding Overload
While the benefits of puzzles, games, and memory exercises are clear, it's also important to strike a balance. Just like physical exercise, too much of a good thing can lead to burnout or frustration. The goal is

to keep your brain active, but not to the point of exhaustion. It's perfectly fine to walk away from a challenging puzzle and come back later with fresh eyes. In fact, sometimes taking a break is the best thing you can do to help your brain process information and solve problems more effectively.

Also, remember that not every game or puzzle is for everyone. If you don't enjoy Sudoku or chess, that's okay, find something that excites you. The most important thing is that you're engaging your brain in a way that feels fun and rewarding. The more you enjoy the activity, the more likely you are to stick with it and reap the long-term cognitive benefits.

The Joy of Brain Training
At the end of the day, building cognitive reserve through puzzles, games, and memory exercises should feel more like play than work. It's about discovering the joy in challenging your brain, learning new skills, and staying mentally engaged. Whether you're solving a tricky crossword over breakfast, finishing a jigsaw puzzle on a rainy afternoon, or battling it out in a game of Scrabble with friends, you're doing something wonderful for your brain.

Not only are you sharpening your mind and protecting against cognitive decline, but you're also investing in your mental wellbeing. There's something deeply satisfying about the moment when all the pieces come together, whether it's finding that elusive puzzle piece or nailing a high score in your favourite game. And let's not forget the social benefits, games are a wonderful way to connect with others, have a laugh, and enjoy some friendly competition.

So, why not make brain training a regular part of your routine? With so many fun and engaging ways to boost your cognitive health, you might find that the journey to building cognitive reserve is just as rewarding as the results. And remember, it's never too late to start. Whether you're 30 or 80, your brain is always ready for a challenge—and the benefits will last a lifetime.

The Mindfulness Boost: Calm Your Way to a Sharper Brain

In our always-on world, where multitasking is glorified and taking a break feels almost sinful, the idea of doing nothing can seem, well, counterproductive. But what if I told you that "doing nothing" could be one of the best things you can do for your brain? That's where mindfulness comes in, and the truth is, it's far from doing nothing. It's about giving your brain the space and calm it needs to reset, refocus, and recharge.

Mindfulness is like the secret ingredient to sharpening your mind, enhancing your cognitive reserve, and, let's be honest, feeling a little less frantic about life. The benefits of mindfulness for brain health are both well-researched and incredibly exciting, and what's more, it's something you can start practising right now, wherever you are, and in whatever form suits you best.

The Science Behind Mindfulness and Brain Health

So, what exactly is mindfulness, and how does it help your brain? At its core, mindfulness is the practice of staying present, fully engaged with what's happening in the here and now, without judgement or distraction. It's like giving your mind a mini holiday from the barrage of thoughts, to-do lists, and endless notifications.

When you practise mindfulness, something remarkable happens inside your brain. Studies have shown that mindfulness can increase the thickness of the prefrontal cortex, the part of your brain responsible for decision-making, attention, and self-control. It can also strengthen the hippocampus, which plays a critical role in learning and memory. In essence, you're not just calming your mind, you're actually building a stronger, more resilient brain.

But the most immediate benefit of mindfulness is its ability to reduce stress. Chronic stress is a known cognitive killer, shrinking parts of the brain involved in memory and learning while flooding your system with cortisol, the stress hormone. A little cortisol is fine, but too much can wreak havoc on your mental clarity and focus. That's why just a few minutes of mindfulness each day can make a significant difference. By reducing cortisol levels, mindfulness gives your brain a fighting chance to stay sharp and focused, even during stressful times.

Staying Present: The Art of Mindfulness in Everyday Life
You don't need a meditation cushion or a retreat in the mountains to reap the rewards of mindfulness. The beauty of this practice is that it can be woven into your daily life, no matter how busy you are. It's about bringing your attention back to the moment, whether you're brushing your teeth, washing the dishes, or sipping your morning coffee.

Imagine this: instead of rushing through breakfast while mentally running through your day's to-do list, you take a moment to really *taste* your food. You notice the warmth of the tea, the crunch of the toast, the smell of fresh fruit. This simple act of tuning into your senses brings you back to the present moment and gives your mind a break from its usual constant chatter.

Mindfulness isn't about stopping your thoughts, because, let's face it, that's impossible. Instead, it's about noticing those thoughts without getting swept away by them. When your mind starts racing ahead, mindfulness gently reminds you to pull back and refocus on what's happening right now.

Mindfulness for a Sharper Brain: Building Focus and Attention
One of the major benefits of mindfulness is its ability to improve focus and attention. In a world filled with distractions, being able to concentrate on a task without getting sidetracked is a superpower. Mindfulness helps train your brain to stay on task by strengthening your attention span and teaching you to gently bring your focus back whenever it wanders.

Think of mindfulness as a kind of mental workout. Just like lifting weights builds your physical muscles, mindfulness builds your mental muscles, especially those related to focus. Over time, you'll find that it becomes easier to concentrate on the task at hand, whether that's a work project, a conversation with a friend, or reading a book. You'll also be better at noticing when your mind starts to drift and bringing it back, which is key to maintaining long-term cognitive health.

Breathing Your Way to Calm: Mindfulness in Action

One of the simplest and most effective ways to practice mindfulness is through your breath. You don't need any special equipment, and you can do it anywhere. Just close your eyes (or keep them open if you prefer) and focus on your breathing. Notice the sensation of the air as it enters and leaves your nose. Feel your chest rise and fall. If your mind starts to wander, which it inevitably will, gently bring your attention back to your breath without judgement.

This kind of breathing practice doesn't just calm your mind, it also calms your nervous system. Deep, mindful breaths send a signal to your brain that it's okay to relax. This activates the parasympathetic nervous system, which is responsible for rest and digestion, and shuts down the fight-or-flight response that keeps you in a state of constant stress.

You can try this breathing technique for just five minutes a day. Over time, you may notice that you feel calmer, more focused, and more in control of your thoughts. You'll also likely find that it becomes easier to bring that same sense of calm into other areas of your life, even in the middle of a busy day.

The Magic of Meditation: Training Your Brain to Stay Present

When people think of mindfulness, they often picture meditation, and for good reason. Meditation is one of the most powerful ways to practice mindfulness and boost your brain health. But here's the thing: meditation doesn't have to be about sitting cross-legged in silence for hours on end. In fact, meditation can be done in all kinds of ways, walking, standing, or even while doing everyday activities.

The key is to find a form of meditation that works for *you*. If you're someone who finds sitting still uncomfortable, try a walking meditation. As you walk, focus on the sensation of your feet hitting the ground. Notice how your legs move, how the air feels against your skin, how your breath matches your steps. It's a moving meditation that allows you to combine physical activity with mindfulness, giving you the best of both worlds.

If you prefer to sit, try a guided meditation. There are plenty of apps and online resources that offer short, simple guided meditations that take you through the process step by step. These can be especially helpful if you're new to meditation or find it hard to sit still in silence.

The Mindfulness and Memory Connection
One of the most exciting aspects of mindfulness is its potential to protect and even enhance your memory. As we age, our memory naturally starts to decline, but mindfulness offers a way to slow down this process. By reducing stress, improving focus, and keeping your brain active, mindfulness can help preserve your cognitive function well into later life.

Mindfulness also enhances something called "working memory." This is the type of memory that allows you to hold information in your mind for short periods and use it to complete tasks. Think of it like your brain's scratchpad. For example, when you're trying to remember a phone number long enough to dial it, or when you're holding several items in your head while working through a project, this is your working memory at play. Mindfulness has been shown to improve working memory, making it easier to juggle information and stay mentally organised.

Mindfulness for Emotional Well-Being
It's not just about memory and focus; mindfulness has a profound impact on your emotional well-being too. By staying present and non-judgmental, mindfulness allows you to approach life's challenges with a clearer, more balanced perspective. You become more aware of your thoughts and feelings, but without getting caught up in them.

This emotional regulation can help you navigate stressful situations with greater ease. Instead of reacting impulsively, you learn to respond thoughtfully. This leads to lower levels of anxiety, better stress management, and an overall boost in emotional resilience. In the long run, this emotional clarity supports a healthier brain, as chronic stress and anxiety are known contributors to cognitive decline.

Mindfulness and Creativity: Sparking New Ideas
You might not immediately connect mindfulness with creativity, but the two go hand in hand. By quieting the constant noise in your mind, mindfulness creates the mental space needed for new ideas to emerge. It's like clearing the clutter from a room, once the space is open, creativity has room to flourish.

Many people find that after practising mindfulness, they feel more open to creative thinking. Whether it's solving problems at work, coming up with new ideas for a personal project, or simply approaching a challenge from a different perspective, mindfulness helps you tap into your creative potential. And since creativity itself is a fantastic way to engage your brain, it's a win-win situation.

Mindfulness as a Lifestyle
While mindfulness might start as a practice, a few minutes of meditation here, a bit of focused breathing there, it can eventually become a way of life. The more you practice, the more natural it will feel to bring mindfulness into everything you do.

Imagine approaching your daily tasks with a sense of calm and focus, free from the usual stress and distractions. Whether you're working on a big project, spending time with loved ones, or simply relaxing at home, mindfulness helps you stay fully engaged with the present moment. You become less reactive, more patient, and better able to savour life's small joys.

Final Thoughts: Small Steps, Big Changes
Building your cognitive reserve through mindfulness doesn't require drastic changes or hours of your time. It's all about small, manageable steps that add up to big results. Whether it's a few minutes of deep breathing, a daily walking meditation, or simply taking the time to notice the world around you, mindfulness is one of the most accessible and effective ways to keep your brain sharp and your mind at ease.

So, why not give it a try?

Creativity: Fuel for Mental Sharpness

Think creativity is just for artists? Well, let me stop you right there! You don't need to be a Picasso, a Beethoven, or even a Mary Berry to tap into the brain-boosting benefits of creativity. Whether you're rearranging your living room furniture, writing a short story, or trying your hand at pottery, engaging in creative activities stimulates your brain in all sorts of wonderful ways. It taps into different cognitive processes than solving puzzles or doing mental exercises. Creativity invites your brain to think outside the box, to adapt, and to come up with something new and exciting, keeping those neurons firing.

And here's the best part, you don't have to be a genius or a seasoned artist to reap these benefits. Even something as simple as doodling on a notepad or experimenting with a new recipe can be enough to sharpen your mind and reduce stress. The key is to let go of the pressure to be perfect (which, let's face it, is pretty boring) and dive into the joy of trying something new. The real magic happens when you open yourself up to different creative experiences and stay curious. That's where your brain gets its best workout!

Creativity is for Everyone, Not Just Artists

First things first, let's bust the myth that creativity is reserved for the "naturally artistic." Creativity isn't about drawing a perfect portrait or writing a bestseller. It's about thinking in new ways, solving problems with fresh perspectives, and embracing the fun of experimenting. Every day offers an opportunity for creativity, whether you realise it or not. When you're deciding how to decorate a birthday cake, coming up with a solution to a tricky work problem, or simply organising your garden, you're engaging in creative thinking.

Creativity is something we're all born with. Just think back to childhood, kids are creative without even trying! They paint pictures with wild colours, build forts out of pillows, and make up stories about imaginary worlds. Somewhere along the way, many of us get stuck in the idea that creativity is reserved for "the talented." But that's simply not true. The joy of creativity isn't about being the best, it's about expressing yourself, problem-solving, and finding new ways to connect with the world around you.

And the beauty of it? You can start anytime, with anything. That blank page you've been staring at doesn't have to be intimidating, it's an opportunity to play. Whether you pick up a pencil, a paintbrush, or even a spatula, the act of creating something, no matter how simple, engages different parts of your brain, keeping it sharp and flexible.

The Brain on Creativity: How It Works
So, what's actually happening in your brain when you're being creative? Well, it turns out that creativity lights up multiple areas of your brain all at once. Unlike tasks that focus on specific brain regions (like memory exercises or logic puzzles), creativity requires the brain's left and right hemispheres to work together in harmony. The left hemisphere handles logical, analytical thinking, while the right hemisphere dives into imagination and intuition. When you engage in a creative activity, these two sides team up, creating new neural connections and pathways.

This brain "cross-training" is incredibly beneficial for mental sharpness. It not only helps improve cognitive function but also increases the brain's plasticity, which is its ability to adapt, change, and stay resilient over time. In other words, by being creative, you're not just making something beautiful or interesting, you're actively building a stronger, more flexible brain.

In fact, studies have shown that engaging in creative activities can improve problem-solving skills, boost memory, and even delay cognitive decline. So if you've been looking for an excuse to pick up that guitar or sign up for that pottery class, consider this your invitation. Your brain will thank you for it!

Stress-Busting Through Creative Expression
Now let's talk about one of creativity's most magical side effects: stress relief. We all know that stress is a major factor in cognitive decline and overall health, but finding ways to unwind isn't always easy. Enter creativity! Whether it's sketching, crafting, or even cooking, creative activities have been proven to lower cortisol levels, the pesky stress hormone that wreaks havoc on our mental and physical wellbeing.

The act of creating gives your mind a chance to focus on something other than life's pressures. When you're in the flow of painting a picture or building something with your hands, the world's worries seem to fade away. It's a bit like meditation, but with the added bonus of having something tangible to show for it at the end.

And here's the thing: the finished product doesn't need to be a masterpiece for you to experience these benefits. In fact, embracing the imperfections of the creative process is part of what makes it so relaxing. You don't need to be "good" at something to enjoy it, just the act of doing it is enough to calm your mind and provide a sense of accomplishment. So, if you've ever found yourself avoiding a creative activity because you're worried about not being great at it, it's time to throw that mindset out the window. Dive in, have fun, and enjoy the stress-melting magic of creativity.

Creating Social Connections Through Creativity
One of the often-overlooked benefits of creativity is how it can bring people together. Whether you're joining a painting class, attending a writing workshop, or even cooking with friends, creative activities are a fantastic way to connect with others. And, as we know, staying socially engaged is one of the most important factors in maintaining mental health and cognitive function as we age.

Think about it, working on a creative project with others opens the door for conversations, collaboration, and shared experiences. Whether you're laughing over a failed attempt at baking or sharing tips on how to get the perfect shade of blue in a painting, these moments of connection are incredibly powerful. They not only boost your mood but also strengthen your sense of community and belonging. And let's not forget about the sense of support and encouragement that comes from creative groups. When you share your work with others—whether it's a song, a poem, or even a knitted scarf, you open yourself up to feedback, which can be both rewarding and motivating. The creative process becomes a shared journey, and that sense of camaraderie can do wonders for your emotional and mental wellbeing.

So, if you've ever considered joining a creative group or starting one with friends, now's the time. Whether it's an online book club, a knitting circle, or a virtual art class, these connections can be just as nourishing for your mind as the creative activities themselves.

Creativity as a Lifelong Skill
One of the best things about creativity is that it's not something that fades with age, in fact, it's a skill you can carry with you throughout your life. Unlike some physical activities that might become more challenging as you get older, creativity adapts to where you are. Whether you're 25 or 75, your creative potential never diminishes, and in many ways, it only gets richer with time.

Think of creativity as a muscle. The more you use it, the stronger it gets. And the best part? There's no right or wrong way to be creative. You might find that as you age, your interests shift, maybe you've always loved writing but now feel drawn to photography. Or perhaps you've spent years painting and want to try your hand at sculpting. Creativity is about following your curiosity and staying open to new experiences. As long as you're creating, you're keeping your brain sharp. And let's not forget about the joy that comes from creativity. Engaging in creative activities brings a sense of play and wonder to everyday life. It encourages you to look at the world through fresh eyes and see beauty in unexpected places. That sense of joy and curiosity is something we can all benefit from, no matter how old we are.

Boosting Creativity in Everyday Life
Now, you might be thinking, "This all sounds great, but I'm not exactly sure how to start being more creative." Don't worry, the good news is that there are endless ways to infuse creativity into your daily life, no matter how busy you are.

First, start small. If you've never thought of yourself as a creative person, try setting aside just 10 or 15 minutes a day to do something creative. Maybe that's doodling in a notebook, writing down ideas for a short story, or experimenting with new ingredients in the kitchen. The important thing is to let go of any expectations of perfection and just enjoy the process.

Next, embrace the idea that creativity can show up in surprising places. You don't need a paintbrush or a guitar to be creative: creativity can happen when you're organising your home, planning a garden, or even coming up with new ways to entertain your kids. Look for opportunities to approach everyday tasks with a fresh perspective and a sense of play. And finally, stay curious. Read books you wouldn't normally pick up, explore new hobbies, and challenge yourself to try things that feel a bit outside your comfort zone. Remember, creativity thrives when you're open to new experiences, so give yourself permission to explore and experiment.

At the end of the day, building your cognitive reserve is about more than just doing crosswords or memorising facts—it's about staying curious, playful, and open to new experiences. Creativity, in all its forms, gives your brain the opportunity to flex its muscles, build new connections, and stay sharp as you age.

So, whether you're painting, knitting, writing, cooking, or simply rearranging the furniture in your living room, remember that every creative act is a step towards keeping your mind healthy and resilient. And the best part? Creativity is fun. It's a way to bring joy, fulfilment, and even a little bit of magic into your life, no matter where you are or what stage of life you're in. The more you engage in creativity, the more you'll notice its positive effects on your mental health, cognitive function, and overall sense of well-being. And who wouldn't want that?

So, why not make creativity a regular part of your routine? Think of it as a daily habit, like brushing your teeth or making a cup of tea. It doesn't have to be grand or elaborate, it can be as simple as jotting down a few thoughts in a journal, trying a new recipe for dinner, or spending a few minutes doodling. The key is consistency. Just like physical exercise, the more you do it, the more your brain will benefit.

But here's the thing, creativity isn't just about keeping your brain sharp. It's also about adding richness and depth to your life. It allows you to express yourself, to explore new ideas, and to find beauty and meaning in everyday moments. And in today's fast-paced world, where we're constantly bombarded with information and stress, creativity offers a much-needed escape. It's a way to reconnect with yourself, to slow down, and to experience the joy of creating something new, no matter how simple or small.

The Role of Curiosity in Creativity
At the heart of creativity is curiosity. It's that spark that makes you wonder, "What if?" It's the desire to learn, to explore, to see things from a different angle. And the good news is that curiosity is something we can nurture, no matter how old we are.

When you cultivate curiosity, you open yourself up to new experiences, ideas, and possibilities. You become more engaged with the world around you, and in turn, more creative. So, how do you do it? Start by asking questions, lots of them. When something piques your interest, dig deeper. Read books, watch documentaries, talk to people who know more about the subject than you do. The more you feed your curiosity, the more creative ideas will start to flow.

Curiosity also encourages you to take risks, to step outside your comfort zone. And while that might sound a bit intimidating, it's one of the most important things you can do for your brain. Trying new things, whether it's learning a new language, taking up a new hobby, or travelling to a new place, keeps your mind flexible and adaptable. It forces your brain to work in new ways, strengthening its capacity for problem-solving and innovation.

Creativity as a Lifelong Practice
One of the wonderful things about creativity is that it's not something you "grow out of" or leave behind as you age. In fact, many people find that their creative abilities deepen as they get older. With age comes experience, perspective, and wisdom, all of which can fuel your creativity in ways you might not have expected.

For example, older adults often find joy in creative pursuits they never had time for during their younger years. Whether it's writing memoirs, taking up painting, or even gardening, creativity can be a source of joy and fulfilment at any stage of life. And because creativity is so closely linked to brain health, staying engaged in creative activities as you age can help keep your mind sharp and vibrant.

But here's the thing, creativity isn't just about the big, splashy projects. It's about the little moments of everyday life where you choose to think differently, to approach a problem from a new angle, or to experiment with something new. It's in the way you set the table for dinner, the way you tell a story to a friend, or the way you plan your day. When you start to see creativity in this way—as a mindset rather than a skill, you realise that it's something you can cultivate every day, in every situation.

Creativity for Emotional Health and Well-being
Let's not forget that creativity isn't just good for your brain, it's also great for your heart. Engaging in creative activities can be a powerful way to process emotions, reduce anxiety, and boost your overall mood. There's something incredibly therapeutic about losing yourself in a creative project, whether it's writing, painting, or even gardening. It allows you to express emotions that might be difficult to put into words, and it gives you a sense of accomplishment and purpose.

Studies have shown that people who engage in creative activities report higher levels of happiness and lower levels of stress. Creativity gives you an outlet for self-expression, which is especially important during challenging times. It can help you make sense of difficult emotions, work through problems, and find a sense of peace and balance. And here's a bonus: creative activities often lead to a state of "flow," where you become so absorbed in what you're doing that you lose track of time. This state of flow is incredibly beneficial for mental health, as it allows you to fully immerse yourself in the present moment, leaving behind the worries and stresses of daily life.

Embrace Your Inner Creative Spirit
So, if you've ever thought to yourself, "I'm just not a creative person," it's time to let go of that notion. Creativity isn't about talent or training, it's about curiosity, playfulness, and the willingness to try new things. It's about finding joy in the process, whether you're painting a masterpiece or doodling in the margins of your notebook.

By embracing your inner creative spirit, you're not only boosting your cognitive health but also enriching your life in ways that go far beyond brain function. You're bringing more joy, more meaning, and more connection into your world. And isn't that what we're all striving for?

So go ahead, pick up that paintbrush, start that scrapbook, or rearrange your living room for the third time this month. Your brain, your heart, and your soul will all thank you for it. Creativity truly is the secret to a life well-lived, vibrant, sharp, and full of endless possibilities.

Technology for Cognitive Training: Your Brain's New Best Friend
Let's face it, technology is everywhere. Whether it's our phones, smartwatches, or voice assistants reminding us to pick up milk, we're surrounded by digital gadgets. But instead of letting technology take over our lives, why not let it improve our brainpower? After all, these gadgets aren't just for the young and hip, there's a treasure trove of tools out there designed to help anyone boost their cognitive skills.

When it comes to staying sharp, technology can be your new best friend. The beauty of it is that there are countless apps and platforms out there, making it easier than ever to keep your brain in shape without stepping into a classroom. You've probably heard of apps like Lumosity or Peak. These daily brain-training apps offer exercises that target different cognitive functions, such as memory, attention, and problem-solving. They turn cognitive training into a game, no sweat involved (well, maybe some mental sweat).

Your Brain's Personal Trainer
Think of these apps as personal trainers for your brain. Just like a fitness app guides you through a workout, these cognitive training tools offer daily exercises, guiding you through a range of tasks designed to challenge your mind. And just like a good personal trainer, they keep track of your progress, nudging you to push a little harder, all while reminding you of how far you've come.

Now, let's be honest. At first, "brain training" might sound like it involves sitting at a desk, poring over boring puzzles. But it's not like that at all! These apps make it fun, almost like playing a video game. The challenges are quick, engaging, and designed to give your brain a workout without overwhelming you. And the best part? You can fit them into your day whenever it suits you. Whether you're on the train, waiting in a queue, or simply having your morning coffee, you can squeeze in a brain workout in just a few minutes.

Unlike the repetitive nature of a gym routine, cognitive training apps shake things up by offering a variety of games that stimulate different areas of your brain. Some days, you'll be solving puzzles that enhance problem-solving skills; other days, you might be focusing on memory or attention games. Each task is designed to target a specific aspect of cognitive function, ensuring that your brain gets a well-rounded workout. And because these apps are designed with built-in progress tracking, they're incredibly satisfying. You'll see how you're improving over time, which keeps motivation high. There's something really rewarding about seeing your progress and knowing that your brain is getting stronger and sharper. Plus, these apps often throw in a little healthy competition, allowing you to compare your results with friends or family. After all, who doesn't love a bit of friendly rivalry?

Fit for Any Schedule: Brain Training on the Go
One of the best things about using technology for cognitive training is its flexibility. Whether you've got a packed schedule or just a few minutes to spare, these apps can be tailored to fit your lifestyle. Brain training apps offer short, snappy sessions that you can fit into your daily routine without breaking a sweat.

Let's say you've got a spare five minutes while you wait for your coffee to brew, that's perfect! Open up your brain training app, and you can tick off a couple of exercises. Waiting for the bus? Do a quick memory challenge. These apps don't demand long hours of focus, which makes them ideal for people with busy lives. You get all the benefits of mental exercise without having to carve out a big chunk of time.

The best part? These exercises feel like play, not work. They're designed to be enjoyable, so you might find yourself looking forward to a session the same way you'd anticipate a good book or a favourite TV show. Its cognitive fitness disguised as fun!

Virtual Reality: The Future of Brain Training?

Let's talk about something a little futuristic, virtual reality (VR). While it might sound like something from a sci-fi film, VR technology is making its way into the world of cognitive training, and it's pretty exciting. VR games and exercises can provide immersive experiences that stimulate the brain in ways traditional apps can't. Imagine stepping into a 3D world where you're solving puzzles, navigating mazes, or even learning new skills, all while fully immersed in a virtual environment.

What makes VR special is that it engages multiple senses at once, sight, sound, and sometimes even touch, creating a more holistic brain-training experience. Studies suggest that VR can improve spatial awareness, enhance memory, and even reduce symptoms of cognitive decline in older adults.

While it's still early days for VR in cognitive training, the potential is massive. And who knows? In a few years, you might be donning a headset to take part in virtual brain-training sessions that feel more like an adventure than an exercise routine. The future is looking bright, and smart!

Technology Meets Social Connection

While we're on the subject of technology, let's not forget how it can help keep you socially connected, another crucial factor in maintaining cognitive health. Social interaction stimulates the brain, keeping you sharp and engaged. Technology allows us to stay connected with loved ones, even if they're miles away. Whether it's a quick video call with family, joining an online book club, or connecting with friends on social media, these interactions help ward off loneliness and keep your brain active.

Staying social is more than just a nice-to-have, it's essential for brain health. Loneliness and social isolation have been linked to cognitive decline, so using technology to foster connections is a smart move. You might even combine social interaction with brain training, many apps allow you to challenge friends to cognitive games or quizzes, making the experience even more engaging.

Avoiding the Digital Overload

Now, let's take a moment to talk about balance. With all this technology at our fingertips, it's easy to get caught up in the digital world, but too much of anything isn't always a good thing. While brain-training apps and mindfulness tools are fantastic, it's essential to find a balance that works for you. The key is to use technology to support your cognitive health, not overwhelm it.

Take regular breaks from screens, especially if you find yourself feeling mentally fatigued. Go for a walk, spend time in nature, or engage in some good old-fashioned face-to-face conversations. Just as you wouldn't overtrain your muscles in the gym, you don't want to overtrain your brain with non-stop digital activity.

Lifestyle Wellness Plan: Cognitive & Mental Sharpness

Small Lifestyle Change	Current Habits	Goal/Action to Implement
Engage in creative activities, explore writing, painting or crafting as these stimulate parts of the brain and make us happy	Sitting in front of TV	Creativity strengthens brain plasticity and helps form neural connections. The process matters more than the result, so enjoy.
Play strategy and puzzle games, like chess, sudoku or memory games	Brain absorbs rather than creating connections	Improves cognitive flexibility and attention. Even short daily sessions can have large long-term benefits
Practice Mindfulness and relaxation, such as meditation or deep breathing	Often eat or snack while watching TV or working.	Stress is one of the killers to cognitive health, regular wellbeing sessions open the brain for more connections and help it continue to flourish and grow.

CHAPTER 11
The Power of Purpose: Finding Joy and Meaning in Every Decade

We've all heard the saying, "Find your purpose," as though it's some mystical key to a better life. But here's the thing: science backs it up. Purpose isn't just some lofty, feel-good concept, it's an essential ingredient for a long and happy life. Whether you're in your 30s, 40s, 50s, or beyond, having a reason to get out of bed in the morning can transform not only your mental state but your physical health too. And the best part? It's never too late to find that spark that gives your life meaning.

Let's dive into why purpose is so crucial to your health and longevity, how you can find yours, and how that sense of direction evolves over time. Don't worry, this isn't about grandiose visions of saving the world (unless that's your thing); it's about finding joy, meaning, and fulfilment in the everyday moments of life. And yes, we'll keep it light because this journey, as meaningful as it is, should also be fun!

Why Purpose Can Extend Your Life
Imagine purpose as your personal superpower. Studies show that people with a strong sense of purpose not only live longer but live *better*. Researchers have found that having a sense of direction in life lowers the risk of heart disease, reduces inflammation, and even boosts your immune system. It's like purpose gives your body an internal pep talk, keeping things running smoothly even as the years roll on.

And it makes sense. Think about the days when you've felt adrift, unsure of what you're working toward. Now contrast that with the energy you have when you're excited about a new project or goal. That buzz, that motivation, has a profound impact on your physical health. Purpose-driven people often have lower levels of the stress hormone cortisol and are more likely to engage in healthy behaviours, like staying active, eating well, and sleeping better. Purpose is the fuel that keeps your mind and body running smoothly, helping you live longer, and happier.

Purpose and Mental Health: The Ultimate Dynamic Duo
It's no surprise that purpose and mental health are closely linked. When you have something to strive for, a goal that lights you up inside, it becomes easier to manage the stresses and challenges life throws at you. Purpose acts as a mental health anchor, offering stability during turbulent times.

One of the key benefits of having a sense of purpose is its effect on resilience. When you're focused on something meaningful, setbacks feel less like the end of the world and more like bumps in the road. They become challenges to overcome, rather than reasons to give up. This positive outlook not only helps protect against anxiety and depression but also boosts your overall sense of well-being. Essentially, purpose gives you something to lean on, a steady foundation that keeps you grounded no matter how wild the storm.

How to Discover What Drives You
If you're thinking, "That all sounds great, but I have no idea what my purpose is," you're not alone. Finding your purpose can feel daunting, but it doesn't have to be. Purpose isn't always some grand,

earth-shattering mission. It can be found in small, everyday moments that bring you joy and fulfilment.

The first step is to reflect on the activities, people, and places that make you feel alive. What brings you energy? What makes you lose track of time? Is it helping others? Creating something with your hands? Exploring new places? Purpose often lies in these passions. It's about recognising the things that light you up and leaning into them.

Another helpful tip: look back on your life. What moments have shaped you the most? What are the common threads between the times you've felt happiest or most fulfilled? Sometimes our purpose is something we've known all along but haven't fully embraced.

Remember, purpose can evolve. What drives you in your 20s may not be what excites you in your 50s, and that's okay. We're all works in progress, constantly learning, growing, and adapting.

Purposeful Living in Your 30s, 40s, and 50s

Your sense of purpose is a bit like a house plant, it needs nurturing and attention as it grows. And like any good plant, it will look different at various stages of life. Let's explore how purpose can shape your 30s, 40s, and 50s.

In Your 30s:

This decade is often marked by big life changes, careers, relationships, maybe kids. It's easy to get caught up in the busyness of life and forget to take a step back and ask, "What's this all for?" Your 30s are a great time to focus on personal growth. It's about carving out time to figure out what really matters to you and ensuring that you're spending your time and energy on things that align with those values.

Perhaps your purpose in this decade is about building a family, growing your career, or deepening relationships with friends. Or maybe it's about discovering a new hobby that brings you joy. Whatever it is, purpose in your 30s is about setting a solid foundation for the future, one built on what truly matters to you.

In Your 40s:
Ah, the 40s. Often considered a time of transition, this is when many people start reflecting on where they are in life and where they want to go next. It's a time to reassess what's important and make adjustments. This is when you might find yourself thinking, "Is this what I want to be doing for the next 20 years?" If the answer is no, that's okay. Midlife transitions can be powerful opportunities to redefine your purpose.

Purpose in your 40s might involve a shift, whether that's in your career, your personal life, or even just your mindset. This is the decade for taking stock of your achievements, and if something feels out of alignment, don't be afraid to pivot. Your 40s are about finding fulfilment in new ways and being open to change.

In Your 50s and Beyond:
By the time you reach your 50s, you might feel like you've got things pretty well figured out. But that doesn't mean your purpose is static. In fact, many people discover a renewed sense of purpose later in life. This might be the time to mentor others, to focus on creative endeavours, or to explore the world now that you've got more freedom.

For many, this decade brings a shift from striving toward personal goals to giving back, whether through community work, spending time with grandchildren, or nurturing long-held passions that were put on hold for years. Purpose in your 50s is often about legacy, passing on wisdom, and living in a way that feels deeply authentic.

Redefining Purpose Through Midlife Transitions
Midlife transitions often get a bad rap (cue the cliché images of sports cars and spontaneous tattoos), but they can be incredibly empowering. Yes, they can be uncomfortable as you question long-held beliefs about yourself and your life, but they also provide the perfect opportunity to hit the reset button and realign with your true purpose.

Maybe you've reached a point in your career where you're no longer feeling fulfilled. Or perhaps the kids have grown up and flown the nest, and you're wondering, "What now?" These are the moments when purpose can shift and grow. The key is to embrace change rather than resist it. A midlife transition isn't a crisis, it's a chance to explore new facets of yourself, to redefine your goals and dreams, and to step into the next chapter with renewed purpose.

Turning Challenges into Opportunities for Growth
Life has a habit of throwing us curveballs, and let's be honest, not all of them are fun. But the beautiful thing about having a strong sense of purpose is that it helps you turn those challenges into opportunities for growth. When you're driven by a clear sense of what matters, setbacks become lessons rather than roadblocks.

Think about the tough times in your life, maybe a career setback, a personal loss, or a health scare. Often, these moments are the ones that force us to reflect and grow the most. Purpose acts as a guiding light during difficult times, helping you stay focused on what's important and reminding you that even in hardship, there's room for personal growth and transformation.

The Why
Sticking to a plan is always easier said than done, isn't it? We've all been there, bursting with enthusiasm at the start of a new health routine, promising ourselves this time will be different. But then, somewhere between the good intentions and the reality of daily life, the plan fizzles out. Maybe it's that biscuit with tea, or the allure of the snooze button when you've promised yourself a morning workout. Suddenly, the grand vision of sticking to the plan seems like a distant memory.

So how do we actually make sure we stick to the plan and not just for a week or two, but for the long haul? The truth is, motivation and mindset are the keys. It's not about being perfect, nor about sheer willpower (because let's be real, willpower only gets us so far). It's about understanding *why* you're doing this, embracing small, sustainable changes, and building habits that make healthy living part of your daily routine. Sounds simple enough, right? Let's dive into the details.

Finding Your "Why" to Stay Motivated

The first step to sticking to any plan is to figure out your *why*. This is your personal reason for making a change, and trust me, it needs to go deeper than just wanting to fit into those old jeans. Of course, looking good is always a bonus, but when the alarm goes off at 6 a.m., a pair of jeans might not be enough to get you out of bed. What will? Think about what really matters to you. Maybe it's having more energy to keep up with your kids (or grandkids). Perhaps it's reducing stress or feeling more confident in your own skin. Or maybe it's knowing that you're actively working to prevent long-term health issues.

Your *why* has to mean something to you, deeply. It's the thing you'll hold onto when the going gets tough, when the gym feels too far, or when the sofa and a box set seem a million times more appealing than a salad and a workout. Remind yourself of it regularly. Write it down somewhere visible or use it as a mantra when your motivation starts to waver. Your *why* is the foundation for building lasting motivation, it gives your efforts meaning beyond the surface-level goals.

The Power of Small, Incremental Changes

Now, let's get one thing straight: radical overnight transformations are rare. Most of the time, real, lasting change comes from small, incremental adjustments. And honestly, that's a good thing! If you try to overhaul your entire lifestyle in one go, it's overwhelming. Your brain (and body) will resist, and chances are, you'll find yourself back at square one before you've even had time to enjoy that new gym kit you bought.

Instead, think about small changes you can make today that feel doable. Maybe it's adding an extra 10 minutes to your walk, swapping out one sugary snack for a healthier option, or drinking more water. These might not seem like much, but they add up, and that's where the magic happens. The beauty of small changes is that they're manageable, which means you're more likely to stick with them.

As you get used to each small change, it becomes part of your routine—effortless, even. And before you know it, these little tweaks lead to bigger transformations. Think of it as planting seeds. You don't expect a fully grown tree overnight. You water it, nurture it, and over time, it grows. The same goes for your health. Be patient with the process, and trust that each small step is taking you closer to your goal.

Building Habits That Stick

Ah, habits, those little things we do without thinking that make up the bulk of our day. When it comes to health, building the right habits is crucial. But how do we create habits that stick, especially when life gets busy? The answer lies in making things as easy as possible for yourself. This means reducing friction between you and the healthy choice.

Want to start walking more? Leave your trainers by the door. Trying to drink more water? Keep a bottle on your desk. Planning to eat more vegetables? Make sure your fridge is stocked with pre-cut, easy-to-grab options. The fewer barriers there are between you and the good habit, the more likely you are to stick with it.

Consistency is key here. It's not about being perfect every day but about showing up more often than not. If you skip a workout or have a takeaway, don't let it derail you. The habit will stick as long as you keep returning to it, day after day, week after week. Think of it like brushing your teeth. You don't think about it; you just do it because it's a habit that's ingrained. The goal is to make your healthy choices feel just as automatic.

Overcoming Setbacks and Plateaus

Let's be real: setbacks are inevitable. We all hit bumps in the road, whether it's falling off the wagon after a stressful week at work or hitting a plateau where it feels like no progress is being made. But here's the thing: setbacks aren't failures. They're part of the process. The key is how you respond to them.

Instead of beating yourself up when things don't go as planned, try to approach setbacks with curiosity. What led to the slip-up? Was it stress, lack of time, or maybe not enough planning? Once you identify the cause, you can adjust your approach. Maybe you need to schedule workouts earlier in the day or find healthier ways to manage stress.

As for plateaus, they're completely normal, especially when it comes to fitness and weight loss. Your body adapts, and progress slows. This doesn't mean your efforts aren't working, it just means it's time to shake things up. Change your routine, try a new workout, or focus on a different goal for a while. The key is to keep moving forward, even when progress feels slow. Celebrate the small wins and trust that every effort counts, even when the results aren't immediate.

Celebrating Progress and Milestones
Speaking of small wins, don't forget to celebrate them! Too often, we focus on what we haven't achieved yet, rather than acknowledging how far we've come. Maybe you didn't hit every workout this week, but you still got out for a walk. Maybe you didn't lose as much weight as you hoped, but your energy levels are higher. These are all wins, and they deserve recognition.

Celebrating progress keeps you motivated. It reminds you that you're making a difference, even when it doesn't always feel like it. So go ahead, treat yourself to a non-food reward when you hit a milestone. Buy that new pair of leggings you've been eyeing or take yourself out for a day of relaxation. Whatever feels good to you, do it! You've earned it. And don't forget: progress isn't always linear. There will be ups and downs, and that's okay. What matters is that you keep going, keep learning, and keep moving forward. Each step, no matter how small, is taking you closer to where you want to be.

Creating a Mindset for Lifelong Health
Ultimately, sticking to the plan isn't just about motivation, it's about creating a mindset for lifelong health. This means shifting your focus from short-term goals (like losing weight for a holiday) to long-term benefits (like feeling stronger and more energetic every day). It's about embracing the process, even when it's tough, because you know the rewards are worth it.
A big part of this mindset shift is letting go of perfectionism.

Newsflash: nobody is perfect. Life gets in the way sometimes, and that's okay. What's important is that you don't let one bad day turn into a bad week or a bad month. The sooner you get back on track, the easier it becomes to stay the course.

It's also important to remind yourself that this is *your* journey. Comparing yourself to others, whether it's a friend, a celebrity, or that person on Instagram with the perfectly curated life, is a sure-fire way to lose motivation. Instead, focus on your own progress, your own goals, and what makes you feel good.

Building a healthy lifestyle is about making choices that work for you. It's about creating habits that you enjoy and that fit into your life, not someone else's. And when you approach it with a sense of curiosity, flexibility, and self-compassion, you'll find that sticking to the plan becomes less of a chore and more of a joy.

So, let's ditch the all-or-nothing mentality. Let's embrace the idea that small changes add up, that setbacks are part of the journey, and that progress is worth celebrating, no matter how long it takes. Because at the end of the day, sticking to the plan isn't about being perfect. It's about showing up for yourself, day after day, and building a life that's healthy, happy, and full of vitality.

Lifestyle Wellness Plan: The Power of Purpose

Small Lifestyle Change	Current Habits	Goal/Action to Implement
10 minutes a day to capture activities, people or moments that energise or inspire you. These small reflections can uncover where your true passions lay.	You kinda know what makes you happy, but don't stop to work out why.	To reflect on personal sources of joy and fulfilment
Set a small purposeful goal for the next 6 months	Same routine, Groundhog Day, no advancement that you choose for yourself	Choose one area of your life, relationships, hobbies or career and set a goal that will bring you joy
Integrate purposeful actions into daily routine.	Not particularly proud of the things you do every day.	Find small, actionable ways to live with purpose each day, set aside a passion project, offer to help others, volunteer, or simply engage in mindful moments that align with your values

CHAPTER 12
Healthspan 2.0: Future Trends in Longevity and Aging

As we peer into the future of health and wellness, one thing becomes crystal clear: the traditional boundaries of aging are rapidly changing. The days when aging was seen as an unavoidable decline are fading. Instead, we are entering a new era where maintaining health and vitality deep into our later years is not just a dream, it's becoming a very real possibility. With technological advances and breakthroughs in medicine, the future of healthspan looks more exciting than ever. This isn't about simply living longer; it's about living better, stronger, and more vibrantly for decades beyond what we ever thought possible. Welcome to *Healthspan 2.0*.

In this chapter, we'll dive into the emerging technologies and ideas shaping the future of aging. We'll explore gene editing, personalized medicine, wearables, stem cell therapies, and how artificial intelligence (AI) is revolutionising health management. Whether you're a tech geek, a biohacker, or just someone who wants to stay active and engaged as the years go by, there's something here for everyone. So, buckle up for a fun, optimistic, and slightly futuristic ride through the future of healthspan.

Gene Editing and Longevity: Rewriting the Code of Life

Let's kick things off with something straight out of science fiction: gene editing. Imagine being able to tweak your DNA, the very blueprint of your body, to optimise your health and even extend your lifespan. Well, thanks to CRISPR and other gene-editing technologies, this is no longer the stuff of sci-fi movies, it's happening now.

The idea behind gene editing is simple but revolutionary: by editing out faulty genes or enhancing "longevity genes" like *FOXO3* or *SIRT1*, scientists hope to reduce the risk of age-related diseases and even slow the biological aging process itself. These genes are known for their roles in cell repair, stress resistance, and metabolic regulation, essentially, all the things that keep us functioning optimally as we age.

Now, before you start imagining a world where you can pop into a clinic and order yourself a set of upgraded genes (that day's not quite here yet), know that we're still in the early stages of human trials. But the potential is enormous. Researchers are hopeful that gene editing could one day help us combat diseases like Alzheimer's, heart disease, and even cancer at the molecular level.

Personalized Medicine: Tailoring Your Healthspan

Gone are the days of one-size-fits-all healthcare. Enter personalized medicine, where treatments and interventions are tailored to your unique genetic makeup, lifestyle, and environment. This is medicine that's as individual as you are, and it's becoming a cornerstone of healthspan enhancement.

Imagine your healthcare team crafting a personalised plan for you based on detailed data from your DNA, biomarkers, gut microbiome, and even your daily habits. Whether it's choosing the right diet, exercise routine, or preventative care, personalized medicine ensures you get what *you* need to thrive. It's like having a bespoke health programme designed to help you age as healthily and gracefully as possible.

For example, certain people metabolise caffeine differently based on their genes. While some can sip on espresso all day and sleep like a baby, others might find themselves wide awake at 2 AM after just a single cup.

Personalised medicine can help you navigate these quirks in your biology, giving you actionable insights into how to live your healthiest life. It's an approach that promises to take healthcare from reactive (treating illness after it strikes) to proactive (preventing illness before it ever takes root).

Wearables and Tech for Aging Well: Gadgets That Keep You Going

Technology has long been a friend to the fitness world, but now it's revolutionising how we approach aging itself. Wearable tech, like smartwatches, fitness trackers, and even sensor-embedded clothing, is no longer just for counting steps. It's evolving into a sophisticated toolkit that can monitor heart rate variability, track sleep quality, and even detect irregularities in movement that might predict future health issues.

Imagine this: You wake up in the morning and your wearable device tells you not only how long you slept but how well you slept. It suggests modifications to your evening routine based on your body's metrics, perhaps a little more magnesium, fewer late-night Netflix binges. Your watch can even predict the onset of health conditions like atrial fibrillation (AFib) or high blood pressure, allowing you to intervene *before* it becomes a serious problem.

The beauty of wearables is that they bring health management to your fingertips, literally. You don't need to wait for your annual GP appointment to know how you're doing; your tech can give you real-time feedback on everything from stress levels to calories burned. The future of aging well may very well involve a tech-savvy partnership between you and your wearable gadgets. The best part? These technologies are becoming more user-friendly and affordable. So whether you're a fitness enthusiast tracking every heartbeat or just someone trying to get a little more movement into your day, there's a device for you.

Stem Cell Therapies and Regenerative Medicine: The Fountain of Youth?

Stem cells are like the body's natural repair kits. They have the unique ability to develop into many different types of cells, which makes them invaluable for healing damaged tissues and organs. In recent years, stem cell therapies have been touted as one of the most promising advancements in the quest to extend healthspan.

Regenerative medicine, powered by stem cells, offers the tantalising possibility of repairing aging tissues, regrowing damaged cartilage, and even reversing some of the signs of aging. Imagine going into a clinic in the future, getting a boost of your own rejuvenated cells, and walking out feeling (and looking) a decade younger. While we're not there yet, the strides being made in stem cell research are nothing short of breathtaking.

For instance, researchers are exploring the use of stem cells to treat everything from degenerative diseases like osteoarthritis to cosmetic concerns like skin aging. What if we could use our own cells to regenerate youthful, vibrant skin or restore strength to weakened muscles? The possibilities are endless—and exciting.

The Role of AI in Health Management: Your New Digital Doctor

Artificial Intelligence (AI) is poised to transform healthcare in ways we're only beginning to understand. From predictive analytics to personalised treatment plans, AI is already making waves in medical research and health management. And when it comes to healthspan, AI is shaping up to be an indispensable tool.

AI algorithms can sift through mountains of data far faster than any human could, spotting patterns and correlations that can help predict diseases before they happen. Imagine an AI assistant monitoring your health metrics, diet, exercise, sleep, stress levels, and providing recommendations tailored specifically to you, based on thousands of data points from people just like you. It's like having a GP on call 24/7, but with the power to process data from millions of patients in real time.

What's particularly exciting about AI is how it can revolutionise preventative care. No more waiting for symptoms to crop up, AI could alert you to potential issues well before they become serious. Whether it's spotting early signs of heart disease or predicting a future joint injury based on your movement patterns, AI could help extend your healthspan by making interventions at the earliest possible stage.

Women's Healthspan: What's on the Horizon?
The future of healthspan for women is particularly exciting. Historically, much of medical research has been skewed towards male subjects, but that's changing. We're seeing an explosion of research into areas specifically relevant to women, such as hormonal health, menopause management, and gender-specific risk factors for diseases like osteoporosis and cardiovascular issues.

In the future, women's healthspan could be significantly enhanced by breakthroughs in personalised medicine and hormone therapies. For example, targeted hormone replacement therapies could be developed to minimise the impact of menopause on bone density and cardiovascular health. We might also see advancements in treatments for conditions like polycystic ovary syndrome (PCOS), which affects millions of women worldwide and has far-reaching effects on long-term health.

Moreover, as more women enter the research field, we're likely to see a broader focus on how lifestyle factors, diet, stress, exercise, specifically impact women's health and aging. The future of women's healthspan will involve bespoke treatments that address the unique challenges women face as they age.

Men's Healthspan: What's on the Horizon?
When it comes to extending men's healthspan, the future looks just as promising as it does for women. Historically, men have faced unique health challenges that weren't always addressed with the same focus or nuance in healthcare research and treatment. However, as the understanding of gender-specific health risks deepen, more attention is being directed towards ensuring men can enjoy longer, healthier lives. The exciting thing is that the innovations being

developed now, and those on the horizon, are designed to tackle the specific issues that men face as they age.

One of the most significant areas of focus in men's healthspan is hormonal health. Just as women experience menopause, men experience a gradual decline in testosterone levels, often referred to as "andropause." This drop in testosterone can lead to fatigue, reduced muscle mass, and changes in mood, factors that significantly impact men's quality of life as they age. Fortunately, new research into hormone replacement therapies and lifestyle interventions is making strides in helping men maintain more balanced hormone levels as they age, which can support both physical and mental well-being.

Testosterone replacement therapy (TRT) is gaining traction as a potential tool for extending men's healthspan. By managing testosterone levels, TRT may help combat the decline in muscle mass, cognitive function, and libido that often accompanies aging. However, much like hormone therapies for women, the future of TRT lies in personalisation. Advances in personalised medicine are likely to provide men with more tailored treatments, ensuring the therapy meets their unique physiological needs while minimising potential risks.
Beyond hormones, cardiovascular health remains a central concern in men's healthspan. Men have long been at higher risk for heart disease compared to women, with lifestyle factors such as diet, stress, and physical activity playing a key role. But the good news is that new approaches in heart health, driven by advances in genetics, AI-driven diagnostics, and wearable technology, are set to revolutionise how we monitor and manage cardiovascular risk. In the future, men will have access to real-time insights into their heart health, allowing them to make adjustments in diet, exercise, and medication before problems develop into serious conditions.

Another critical area for extending men's healthspan is muscle maintenance. Men are often able to build muscle more easily than women due to higher levels of testosterone, but the natural decline of this hormone means that muscle mass deteriorates with age. Maintaining muscle mass is crucial not just for physical appearance, but for metabolism, mobility, and overall health. In the coming years, we may see innovative fitness regimes tailored specifically for older men, incorporating resistance training, mobility exercises, and recovery strategies that are designed to combat age-related muscle loss.

Mental health is another crucial component of men's healthspan, and one that has traditionally been overlooked. Men, especially older men, are less likely to seek help for mental health concerns, yet they face higher rates of depression and suicide. This is changing, with more focus being placed on encouraging men to open up about mental health, and more accessible mental health services being developed. The future of men's healthspan will undoubtedly include increased emphasis on mental well-being, with holistic approaches that include therapy, stress management techniques, and even emerging treatments like psychedelic-assisted therapy.

Prostate health is another area where men face specific challenges as they age. Prostate cancer is one of the most common cancers among men, and while screening techniques have improved, future advancements will likely see even more precise diagnostic tools and less invasive treatments. Research into genetic markers and early detection will help men manage prostate health with greater accuracy, potentially catching problems long before they become life-threatening. Furthermore, advancements in less invasive surgical techniques and therapies like immunotherapy offer hope for more effective treatments with fewer side effects.

Beyond traditional medicine, lifestyle factors like diet and exercise continue to be critical in men's healthspan. We're seeing more research into how specific dietary patterns, like high-protein diets or intermittent fasting, affect men's metabolism and muscle retention as they age. As personalised nutrition plans become more sophisticated, men will be able to tailor their eating habits to maximise longevity, taking into account their individual genetic make-up, activity levels, and overall health status.

Additionally, the future holds exciting possibilities in the realm of aging-in-place technologies. As men age, maintaining independence and mobility becomes a priority. New technologies designed to support aging at home, such as smart home devices, fall detection systems, and wearable health monitors, will play a significant role in extending healthspan. These devices will not only help prevent accidents but will provide continuous health monitoring, giving older men and their families peace of mind while supporting a more active, independent lifestyle.

Lastly, we can't overlook the impact of social connections on men's healthspan. Research shows that men are more likely to experience social isolation as they age, particularly after retirement or the loss of a spouse. The importance of fostering social networks and meaningful relationships is increasingly recognised as a pillar of longevity. Future initiatives will likely focus on creating community-based programmes and digital platforms that encourage social interaction and camaraderie among older men.

The future of men's healthspan is full of promise. From hormonal therapies and heart health innovations to muscle maintenance, mental well-being, and advanced technologies, men today can look forward to living longer, healthier lives with the help of these emerging strategies. The key, as always, will be a balanced approach that combines cutting-edge treatments with proven lifestyle habits. As research progresses, men will have more tools than ever to ensure that their later years are as fulfilling and vibrant as possible. Whether it's through personalised medicine, innovative fitness regimes, or simply fostering stronger social connections, men have the opportunity to embrace a future where aging well is not just possible, but the norm.

The Mindset of Longevity: Creating a Lifelong Health Approach
All the technology in the world won't help if we don't approach healthspan with the right mindset. The future of aging well starts between your ears, your attitude towards health and longevity plays a massive role in how well you age. Developing a proactive, optimistic outlook on your health and making the commitment to care for your body and mind is key.

Cultivating a mindset that embraces the future of healthspan means accepting that aging doesn't have to be synonymous with decline. It's about maintaining curiosity, staying engaged, and being open to new possibilities, whether it's trying a new fitness trend, exploring the latest in wearable tech, or embracing the advances in gene therapy.

Above all, it's about understanding that health is a lifelong journey. Every step we take towards improving our physical and mental health today builds the foundation for a healthier, longer future. And the best part? You don't have to wait for some futuristic breakthrough. You can start improving your healthspan right now with the choices you make every day.

A Future Full of Promise
Ultimately, *Healthspan 2.0* isn't just about extending the years of life we get, it's about ensuring those years are filled with vitality, energy, and happiness. The emerging technologies we've discussed, from gene editing to AI-powered health management, are making it more possible than ever to imagine a future where growing older doesn't mean growing weaker. Instead, it means staying strong, mentally sharp, and full of life.

What makes this journey so exciting is that, while science is advancing rapidly, there are still so many things we can do in our everyday lives to start reaping the benefits of a longer, healthier life right now. The tools for improving our healthspan are not just confined to cutting-edge labs, they're in the decisions we make about how we move, what we eat, how we sleep, and how we think.

Even better, this is a journey we don't have to take alone. Whether you are using a smartwatch to track your fitness, joining a community of like-minded people focused on wellness, or simply staying open to the latest health insights, you are part of a global movement that is reshaping the future of aging. And that's something truly extraordinary.

As we step into this new era of healthspan, we're learning that the key to longevity isn't just about adding years to our lives but about adding life to our years. The future is one where we can hope not only to live longer but to stay active, engaged, and joyful throughout those extra years. Whether through tech innovations, medical breakthroughs, or simply adopting a mindset of lifelong health, we are entering a period where aging doesn't have to mean decline.

It's a future filled with possibility, and it's one we can all be a part of. So, let's embrace it, stay curious, and keep exploring the many ways we can live better, longer. After all, the future of healthspan is not just something to look forward to, it's something we can start building today.

The New Longevity Economy: A Thriving Market for Health, Wellness, and Aging Well

We live in exciting times, where the dream of living longer and living better is becoming more and more attainable. There's a growing shift from simply extending lifespan to truly extending healthspan, those vital, active years when you can enjoy life to the fullest. With this shift comes an entire industry built around enhancing health and well-being, known as the "Longevity Economy." But this isn't just about surviving longer; it's about thriving in ways our grandparents never could have imagined.

The New Longevity Economy is like a booming marketplace where businesses are racing to meet the needs of an aging yet vibrant population. And it's not just retirees who are benefiting from these trends; more and more people in their 30s, 40s, and 50s are jumping on board to future-proof their health. In this chapter, we're going to take a closer look at the rise of healthspan-enhancing businesses, trends in skincare, fitness, aging technologies, workplace wellness, and even financial planning for the long haul. Buckle up—because the future looks bright!

The Rise of Healthspan-Enhancing Businesses

First up, let's talk about the businesses that are tapping into this new market of longevity enthusiasts. From startups focused on personalised health solutions to big brands transforming their product lines, companies everywhere are pivoting toward one goal: helping people live healthier for longer. These aren't just health spas or juice bars, although, let's be real, a good green juice never hurt anyone. We're talking about businesses revolutionising everything from genetic testing to AI-powered health trackers that monitor your body 24/7.

Think about services like personalised supplements that are tailored to your DNA or fitness programs that adapt as you age. Companies are now offering meal plans designed to optimise brain health, gut health, and everything in between. Even the beauty industry is stepping in, with a wave of products that claim to "turn back the clock" or at least slow it down a bit. And it's not just individuals who are buying into this. Healthspan-enhancing services are being integrated into employee wellness programs, insurance plans, and even community initiatives. Gone are the days when the goal was simply to live a long life, the new mantra is about quality, vitality, and keeping up with your life's passions, whether you're 35 or 75.

New Approaches to Fitness for Aging Well
Let's face it, as we get older, our bodies don't bounce back quite as quickly as they used to. But that doesn't mean we should throw in the towel on fitness. In fact, staying active is one of the best ways to maintain a long, healthy life. And here's the good news: fitness is evolving to meet us where we are.

Gone are the days when fitness was all about "no pain, no gain." Today, there's a greater focus on balance, flexibility, and functional movement—all of which help support mobility and prevent injury as we age. For example, Yoga and Pilates have surged in popularity not just because they build strength, but because they improve flexibility and balance, two things we tend to lose as we get older.

Another exciting trend is the rise of fitness tech. From smartwatches that monitor your heart rate and oxygen levels to apps that guide you through personalised workouts, technology is making it easier than ever to stay on top of your fitness goals. And let's not forget the role of virtual classes, which have exploded in popularity since the pandemic. Now, you can join a live yoga session or spin class from the comfort of your living room, making it easier than ever to fit fitness into your busy life.

Whether it's strength training, low-impact cardio, or mobility work, the key is finding a routine that feels sustainable and enjoyable. After all, you're much more likely to stick with something you love than a gruelling workout you dread.

The Future of Aging-in-Place Technologies
One of the most fascinating areas in the New Longevity Economy is the rise of aging-in-place technologies. The goal here is simple: to help people live independently in their own homes for as long as possible. This is about more than just smart thermostats or voice-activated assistants; we're talking about AI-powered devices that monitor your health, predict falls, and even remind you to take your medications.

Imagine a world where your home is equipped with sensors that alert your family or doctor if something seems off, like a sudden change in your walking pattern or a missed pill. This kind of technology not only empowers older adults to maintain their independence but also gives peace of mind to their loved ones.

It's not just about health. These technologies are also enhancing quality of life by making daily tasks easier and more accessible. From robotic vacuum cleaners to smart lighting systems that adjust based on your needs, the future of aging in place is looking pretty high-tech, and it's all geared toward helping people live longer, more fulfilling lives in the homes they love.

The Wellness Revolution in Workplace Design
It's not just homes that are changing; the workplace is undergoing a wellness revolution too. As people work longer and retire later, there's a growing recognition that workplace design needs to support health and well-being. Companies are beginning to realise that happy, healthy employees are more productive and less likely to burn out, and they're investing in wellness programs and ergonomic office designs to help make that happen.

Think standing desks, yoga breaks, and even nap pods. The modern workplace is shifting away from the sedentary 9-to-5 grind and moving toward a more holistic approach that values mental and physical health. There's a reason Google has meditation rooms and on-site fitness classes, healthy employees are simply better employees. And it's not just the tech giants getting in on the action. More businesses are recognising the value of integrating wellness into the workspace, making it easier for workers to balance their health with their careers.

Financial Planning for Extended Healthspan
Living longer sounds fantastic, until you realise that it also means needing more financial resources. If you're going to live well into your 90s or beyond, you need to plan for it. The rising cost of healthcare, housing, and long-term care can be daunting, but with the right financial planning, it's entirely possible to live comfortably throughout your extended healthspan.

This is where savvy investing and strategic saving come into play. It's no longer enough to plan for a retirement that lasts 20 years; today's financial planners are helping people prepare for 30, 40, or even 50 years of post-work life. And it's not just about pensions or savings accounts, there are new tools like longevity annuities and reverse mortgages that can help stretch your finances further.

The key is to start early, whether you're in your 30s or already in your 50s, and to work with professionals who understand the challenges and opportunities that come with a longer life. It's not just about saving for retirement; it's about planning for the life you want to live, well into your later years.

The Risks of Extreme Anti-Aging Strategies
Finally, a word of caution: in the pursuit of longevity, it's easy to fall into the trap of extreme strategies. Whether it's crash dieting, over-exercising, or taking untested supplements, these approaches can do more harm than good. In fact, extreme anti-aging strategies can backfire, leaving you more exhausted, stressed, and potentially less healthy than if you had just stuck to a more balanced approach.

Take extreme dieting, for example. Sure, calorie restriction has been linked to longevity in some animal studies, but that doesn't mean severely restricting your food intake is a good idea for humans. In fact, overly restrictive diets can lead to nutrient deficiencies, lower energy levels, and even psychological harm like disordered eating. Your body needs fuel to function optimally, and depriving it of what it needs can do more damage than aging itself.

Similarly, over-exercising can wreak havoc on your body. While regular exercise is one of the most powerful tools for maintaining a long, healthy life, pushing yourself too hard can lead to injury, burnout, and chronic fatigue. There's no need to train like a professional athlete to stay healthy. In fact, it's the small, consistent efforts, daily walks, moderate strength training, or even a weekend bike ride, that keep your body strong without overloading it.

When it comes to supplements, many promise the world but deliver very little. Some anti-aging supplements can be beneficial, like omega-3s for heart health or vitamin D for bone strength. But others lack the scientific backing or are downright dangerous. Always consult a healthcare provider before diving into a new supplement regimen. Remember, your health is built on balance, not on the extremes.

A Balanced Approach to Healthspan
So, what's the key takeaway from all this? The New Longevity Economy is giving us unprecedented access to tools, products, and services that can help us live longer and healthier lives. From personalised skincare to fitness tech, from aging-in-place innovations to financial planning, the future of aging well is full of promise. But with all this innovation comes responsibility, the responsibility to be discerning, to avoid extreme strategies, and to focus on the fundamentals of health and well-being.

The good news is that the things that truly enhance healthspan aren't hidden in expensive products or extreme diets. They're often simple, sustainable habits that you can start today. Eating a balanced diet full of whole foods, moving your body regularly, nurturing social connections, managing stress, and getting enough sleep, these are the foundations of a long, healthy life.

While there may not be a real-life fountain of youth, we do have something just as powerful: the ability to make informed choices every day that contribute to our long-term health. In the end, healthspan isn't about a one-time fix; it's about creating a lifestyle that supports your well-being for decades to come.

So, embrace the excitement of this new era in longevity, but keep your focus on what really matters. With the right mindset, a little savvy, and some good old-fashioned self-care, you'll not only live longer, but you'll also live better. And that's what the New Longevity Economy, and this journey toward extending your healthspan, is all about.

Lifestyle Wellness Plan: Eating for Longevity

Small Lifestyle Change	Current Habits	Goal/Action to Implement
Incorporating Wearable Technology	Currently relies on annual health check-ups and occasional manual tracking of activity levels.	Start using a smartwatch to monitor daily activity, sleep quality, and stress levels to receive real-time health insights and adjust routines accordingly.
Exploring Stem Cell Therapy Options	Manages joint pain and skin health with conventional treatments and topical creams.	Research and consult about emerging stem cell therapies that could offer long-term benefits in joint regeneration and anti-aging treatments.
Utilising AI-Powered Health Monitoring Apps	Uses traditional apps for tracking fitness and diet but lacks integrated AI features or predictive analytics.	Transition to an AI-powered health app that offers personalised recommendations based on diet, exercise, sleep, and overall health metrics for a proactive approach to health management.

Longevity by Design

CHAPTER 13
Designing Your Personal Lifestyle Wellness Plan.

How to Live Well and Help Others Do the Same

Congratulations! If you've made it to this point, you're already well on your way to transforming your life and extending your healthspan. You've absorbed countless tips and strategies, learned the importance of balancing nutrition, sleep, and exercise, and even discovered how stress and social connections play a critical role in your wellbeing. But now it's time to put everything together into a clear, actionable plan.

It's time to design your own personal Lifestyle Wellness Plan. And here's the good news: you don't have to be a health expert or wellness guru to create one. All you need is a little self-reflection, a dash of enthusiasm, and a willingness to tweak your habits as you go. Think of it like this, just as you wouldn't design a house without laying the foundation, you shouldn't aim for a longer, healthier life without building a solid personal plan. Let's take this final chapter together, step by step, and make sure you're equipped to live your best life for as long as possible—and maybe help a few friends along the way.

Assessing Where You Are Today

Before you embark on creating your personal Lifestyle Wellness Plan, it's essential to start by assessing where you stand right now. After all, you wouldn't head out on a long journey without first checking your map and packing the right supplies. This is your chance to take a clear-eyed look at your current health, habits, and mindset, and determine where there's room for improvement. You've been collecting notes throughout the book, and now is the time to bring them all together.

How to Measure Your Current Healthspan Status

First, let's assess your current healthspan status. The healthspan is about the quality of life you have while you're alive, not just how long you live. So ask yourself: how well are you living right now? Think about how often you feel energised versus exhausted, how many days you spend feeling good versus days where aches, stress, or illness get in the way. This is your current baseline, and understanding this is crucial. Maybe you've got excellent fitness levels but struggle with stress. Perhaps your diet is impeccable, but you're not sleeping well. Identify your strengths and weaknesses honestly, this is the starting line of your healthspan journey.

Creating a Baseline Health Profile

Now, it's time to gather the hard data. If you've been avoiding your GP for a while, this might be the nudge you need to book a check-up. Knowing your blood pressure, cholesterol levels, body mass index (BMI), and other key metrics provides the foundation for understanding your health risks. It's also worth reflecting on the small, everyday habits that impact your health. Do you get enough sleep? How often are you active? How's your diet? Are you managing stress effectively? These questions will help create your baseline health profile.

Identifying Areas for Improvement

Once you have that profile, you'll be able to see where you're thriving and where you could use a bit of help. Maybe you're already smashing your daily steps target but could stand to cut back on those late-night snacks. Perhaps you're diligent about staying active but could benefit from a bit more mindfulness or stress management.

Identifying these areas isn't about self-criticism, it's about self-empowerment. After all, how can you get to where you want to go if you don't know where you're starting from?

Prioritising Key Healthspan Goals

Now that you've assessed your current status and pinpointed areas for improvement, it's time to set some goals. Here's where the fun starts! Your Lifestyle Wellness Plan is all about choosing goals that align with how you want to feel as you age. Do you want more energy to play with your kids or grandkids? Maybe you're eyeing that half-marathon, or perhaps you just want to be able to travel, dance, or walk around the park without feeling winded. Prioritise the goals that matter most to you, and don't be afraid to dream big.

Addressing Your Biggest Health Risks

We can't talk about a Lifestyle Wellness Plan without addressing potential risks. This might not be the most glamorous part, but it's crucial. If your baseline profile reveals any significant health risks, such as high cholesterol, elevated blood sugar, or a sedentary lifestyle, it's essential to tackle those head-on. The good news? With the knowledge you've gained, you're well-equipped to start making changes. Whether it's adjusting your diet, adding more movement into your day, or adopting better sleep habits, addressing these risks is about setting yourself up for success.

Setting Your Vision for a Longer, Healthier Life

Finally, let's get a little visionary. Imagine yourself a decade from now, what does your healthiest, happiest self look like? Picture that person clearly. Are you hiking mountains? Running your own business with boundless energy? Playing with your grandchildren? Whatever the vision, use it as your north star. This vision will keep you motivated and serve as a reminder that every positive step you take today leads to a better tomorrow.

Building Your Personal Lifestyle Wellness Plan

With your assessment in hand, you're ready to start building your personalised Lifestyle Wellness Plan. This is where all the individual pieces you've collected come together into a cohesive strategy for living a longer, healthier, more joyful life. And remember, this plan isn't just a to-do list, it's a dynamic, evolving approach that will grow with you as you age. It's not about achieving perfection from day one, but about making small, sustainable changes that lead to lasting improvements.

Mapping Out Your Healthspan Journey

Your healthspan journey will have many stages, just like any long road trip. The key is to map out what each leg of that journey looks like. Think of it as a flexible roadmap where you can set milestones along the way. Start by breaking it down into achievable steps. Maybe in the first month, you focus on getting your diet in check, while in the second month, you start integrating more exercise into your routine. This journey is yours to shape.

How to Set Realistic Short- and Long-Term Goals

The biggest mistake most people make when starting a health plan is setting overly ambitious goals. Let's avoid that! Instead, think of short-term goals as stepping stones that lead to your bigger, long-term visions. Maybe your first short-term goal is to walk for 30 minutes three times a week. That's achievable, right? Over time, these small goals will build up to long-term results, such as maintaining strong bones and a healthy heart well into your 80s. Set both types of goals, and remember, it's about progress, not perfection.

Creating a Holistic Plan for Nutrition, Exercise, and Sleep

A true Lifestyle Wellness Plan isn't just about eating better or exercising more, it's about bringing everything together in a balanced way. Think of your body as a well-oiled machine. To function optimally, it needs the right fuel (nutrition), regular maintenance (exercise), and enough downtime (sleep). Your plan should address each of these areas holistically. Start with simple changes: swap processed snacks for fruit and veg, take the stairs instead of the lift, and set a bedtime that gives you at least seven hours of rest. With time, these small shifts become habits, and those habits become the foundation of your long-term health.

Building a Support Network for Accountability

We're not meant to go through life alone, and the same goes for our health journey. Finding a community or support network is key to staying on track. Whether it's a close friend, a family member, or even a virtual group with similar goals, having others cheer you on can make a massive difference. Accountability partners help you stay motivated on tough days and celebrate your wins with you. It's like having your own personal cheering squad. Don't be afraid to ask others for support, chances are, they'll want to join you in improving their health, too.

Using Trackers and Journals to Monitor Progress

Technology can be a helpful companion in your healthspan journey. Fitness trackers, apps, and even old-fashioned journals can help you stay organised and keep track of your progress. Whether you're tracking your steps, monitoring your heart rate, or just jotting down how you feel after a good night's sleep, these tools provide insight into what's working and where you might need to tweak your plan. Seeing your progress over time can be incredibly motivating.

Making Adjustments as You Age

As we've discussed throughout this book, aging is a natural part of life, but that doesn't mean you're powerless in the process. The beauty of your Lifestyle Wellness Plan is that it's adaptable. As you grow older, your body's needs will change, and so should your plan. Maybe you'll need more focus on flexibility and balance in your 60s, or perhaps you'll want to try new hobbies or activities to keep your mind sharp. Whatever changes come, remember that the key to a long, healthy life is staying flexible and willing to adjust along the way.

The Power of Sharing Your Lifestyle Wellness Plan

Finally, let's talk about the impact your journey can have on those around you. You might not realise it yet, but by designing and sticking to your Lifestyle Wellness Plan, you'll become a beacon of inspiration for your friends and family. People around you will start noticing your increased energy, your positive outlook, and your resilience. And here's the thing: when you make positive changes, it often encourages others to do the same.

Sharing your health journey isn't about preaching or pushing others to follow the same plan, it's about showing them what's possible. By sharing your successes, challenges, and lessons learned, you create a ripple effect that can motivate others to take control of their health too. Whether it's simply talking about your progress during a catch-up with friends or sharing your experiences online, your journey could be the spark that helps someone else make a lasting change. Remember, health is contagious, in the best possible way.

Leading by Example
We've all had that friend or family member who inspires us to make better choices, whether it's because they radiate positivity or they're always the first to try something new. By committing to your Lifestyle Wellness Plan, you become that person. You'll likely find that when others see you taking care of yourself, eating well, staying active, managing stress, they'll be more inclined to follow suit. And who doesn't want to surround themselves with people who are thriving?
It's not about showing off, but about quietly leading by example.

Maybe you'll start organising Sunday morning walks or suggesting healthier options when meeting up for a meal. You might even inspire someone close to you to make their own Lifestyle Wellness Plan. And when you do, the rewards will be twofold, not only will you benefit from living your best, longest life, but you'll also have the pleasure of watching others grow and flourish alongside you.

The Healthspan Community: A Shared Journey
As much as we focus on individual action plans, it's important to remember that no one is an island. We thrive on connection, and your healthspan journey can become a shared experience. This book isn't just a guide for you, it's an invitation to bring others along for the ride. Whether it's your partner, children, friends, or colleagues, you have the opportunity to create a health-conscious community around you.

Perhaps you'll start a group chat where everyone shares their weekly progress or even a fitness challenge to keep things fun. As you move forward, you'll likely find that those who support you also become your biggest motivators. It's a beautiful cycle: you inspire them, they inspire you, and together you all achieve more than you ever thought possible.

Keeping the Momentum Going
The truth is, designing your Lifestyle Wellness Plan is just the beginning. The real magic happens as you start living it. Each day brings new opportunities to make small improvements and adjust your habits. Some days, you'll nail it, hitting your fitness goals, cooking a delicious and nutritious meal, getting eight hours of sleep. Other days, life will get in the way. And that's perfectly okay.

The beauty of the Lifestyle Wellness Plan is that it's flexible and forgiving. It's about long-term progress, not short-term perfection. If you have an off day, or even an off week, remember that it's all part of the journey. You're not starting from scratch; you're building on a foundation that will continue to grow stronger over time.

Reflecting on Your Journey
As you work through your plan and make changes, take time to reflect. What's working well for you? What areas need more attention? Do you feel more energised and empowered than when you started? Reflection isn't just a way to celebrate your wins (though that's important too); it's a tool for making adjustments as you go.

And let's not forget the joy that comes from looking back and realising how far you've come. In six months, a year, or five years, you'll be amazed at the progress you've made, not just in how you look or feel, but in your mindset. The habits that once felt challenging will become second nature, and the benefits will extend far beyond your physical health.

A Life Well-Lived
At the heart of this entire journey is the simple yet powerful desire to live a life that is not only longer but fuller, richer, and more vibrant. It's not about deprivation, restriction, or guilt. It's about designing a life that feels good, every single day. Your personal Lifestyle Wellness Plan is a roadmap to that life, helping you make decisions

that enhance your well-being, happiness, and vitality at every age.

So as you embark on this next phase, take a moment to be proud of the work you've done so far. You've taken the time to educate yourself, to reflect on your habits, and to set goals that align with the life you want to live. That's no small feat.

Now, all that's left is to keep going. Embrace the process, celebrate the little victories, and remember that your healthspan is a gift you're giving to your future self—and to the people who love you. Because living a long, healthy life isn't just about you. It's about the joy, laughter, and memories you'll share with others along the way.

In the end, that's what it's all about: a life lived with vitality, purpose, and connection. And that's exactly what your Lifestyle Wellness Plan is here to help you achieve.

www.ingramcontent.com/pod-product-compliance
Lightning Source LLC
Chambersburg PA
CBHW071307110426
42743CB00042B/1201